Property

John L.

3666 Penn Ave.

D. Buque, Ia 52002

YOU'VE GOT TO HAVE BALLS TO MAKE IT IN THIS LEAGUE

My Life as an Umpire

Pam Postema and Gene Wojciechowski

SIMON & SCHUSTER

New York London Toronto Sydney Tokyo Singapore

SIMON & SCHUSTER
Simon & Schuster Building
Rockefeller Center
1230 Avenue of the Americas
New York, New York 10020

Designed by Irving Perkins Associates
Manufactured in the United States of America

10 9 8 7 6 5 4 3 2 1

Library of Congress Cataloging in Publication Data

Postema, Pam.
You've got to have balls to make it in this league : my life as an
umpire / Pam Postema and Gene Wojciechowski.
p.   cm.
1. Postema, Pam. 2. Baseball—United States—Umpires—Biography.
I. Wojciechowski, Gene.   II. Title.
GV865.P68A3   1992
796.357'092—dc20
[B]   91-45555
CIP

ISBN: 0-671-74772-X

*With love to my mom and dad, who are the greatest.
And to Peggy, Todd, and Rob.*

—P.P.

*To Alex, Ed, and Gene—three uncles who treated
a nephew like a son.*

—G.W.

Acknowledgments

I first wish to thank my lawyer and friend Renèe Wayne Golden, who made this book possible. My love and appreciation also goes to Gene Wojciechowski for his patience and hard work, to Jeanelle Smith, Trish Feldmann, Jeanette and Bill Nicely—friends through the years—and to Chris Carmean Silcox, Jack and Eileen Oujo, and Joe and Sherri Mickel. And a special thanks to Cindy Cordero, forever.

—Pam Postema

I wish to thank my wife, Dina, who never once complained when I disappeared into the Bat Cave for days at a time. I owe her more than she'll ever know. In addition, I would like to thank Rick Reilly and Bill Plaschke for their advice, their patience, and most importantly, their friendship. Also deserving of mention are literary agent Shari Wenk, editor Jeff Neuman of Simon and Schuster, and those umpires, minor league officials, and Postema family members whose cooperation helped make this book possible. A heartfelt thanks goes to Pam Postema herself, who taught at least one person that baseball is not only steeped in tradition, it is sometimes mired in it. May some enlightened commissioner one day have the courage to give a woman umpire an equal chance, nothing more. Postema's legacy deserves that much. And a final pat on the back to Elvis, man's best friend.

—Gene Wojciechowski

Contents

Preface

I drive a Federal Express truck now—not by choice, but out of necessity. Once a person whose daily life was ruled by a baseball schedule, I have now joined the nine-to-five crowd.

Before that, I was a professional umpire. For thirteen long, sometimes hellish seasons I made the climb from the lowest rung of the minor leagues to the very brink of the majors. That's when the people who control baseball decided enough was enough. In the fall of 1989, I received my unconditional release and was told that I was no longer a major league umpire prospect. I still can't believe it.

Since then, I haven't watched a single baseball game. I can't, it hurts too much. I can't think about former baseball commissioner Bart Giamatti without wondering what might have been. I can't think about National League supervisor of umpires Ed Vargo without feeling betrayed. And as far as I'm concerned, I can't think about Dick Butler, now a special assistant to American League president Dr. Bobby Brown, without remembering what a hypocrite he was and, I'm sure, still is.

I umpired more than two thousand games during my career. I was called every name in the book and then some. I was sworn at in two languages, blackballed by my own peers, ridiculed by fans, and abused by ballplayers and managers in five countries. The thing is, I didn't care. I didn't care because I wanted to be a major league umpire. If that's what it took, I was willing to put up with it.

Turns out I took more than anybody—just because I was woman, a she instead of a he. In professional baseball, there is no worse crime.

At first, I didn't want to write this book. After all, who wants to relive some of the worst times of his or her life? But then I started thinking: it wasn't all bad. In fact, there were moments that still make me laugh, that still, believe it or not, make me wish I were an umpire. If only major league baseball had given me the chance.

Open your sports section, turn to the box scores, and you will see name after name of big league ballplayers. Chances are I umpired games for them in the minor leagues or during major league spring training camps. Chances are I ejected some of them, too. Strawberry, Gwynn, Canseco, Mitchell, Clark, Hershiser, Bonds, Bonilla, Johnson . . . I saw them when they were scared and a little unsure of themselves. Just like me.

Keep on looking down those box scores, past the batting lineups and past the pitching linescores. There, right before the time of the game and the official attendance, are the last names of the umpire crew. Some names you might recognize, such as Kaiser, Wendelstedt, Harvey, Palermo, and Cooney. Others are not so familiar. I worked with most of these people, too. Some of them are good men and good umpires. Some of them are bigots and chauvinists and buffoons.

This book is about the players and umpires in those box scores. It is also a book about the game and the politics of baseball. The game, I could handle; the politics, I didn't have a chance.

Most of all, it is a story about someone who did something different, of one odd woman who wanted to be a major league umpire. Society loves conformists. I'm not a conformist. I'm a big believer in individuality, in freedom.

That's where the baseball establishment and I disagree. Baseball is built on repression. Baseball can't handle some-one going against the grain.

And don't give me that line "Baseball is America's game." To me, baseball is the exact opposite of what America stands for.

So now I make my living sitting behind the steering wheel of a delivery truck. Welcome to the real world, right? To be honest, though, I think I liked it better behind home plate.

CHAPTER 1

The W-Word . . . Why?

Other kids wanted to grow up to be doctors or lawyers or teachers or whatever. All I knew for sure is that I didn't want to grow up. I liked being a kid. I liked the freedom of being young and foolish, of making mistakes and blaming it on youth. Everyone gets so serious when they get older. They forget to have fun. That's why I always thought Peter Pan had the right idea.

Don't ask me why I wanted to become a professional umpire, because I'm not positive I know. I've probably been asked that question a thousand times and I can never provide an easy answer, maybe because there isn't one. I mean, why does anybody attempt the impossible? Why would the daughter of a vegetable farmer, a small-town girl from Willard, Ohio—population five thousand—try to squeeze her way into a profession that thinks a woman's place is behind the concessions stand, not behind home plate? Worse yet, why would anyone, especially a woman, think they could earn one of only sixty big league umpiring jobs? The odds are even worse when you consider that the turnover rate among major league umpires is about as low as for Supreme Court justices.

I wanted to be different; I always knew that much. If I had to grow up—and I fought it every inch of the way— then I was going to do something that went against the grain. Other girls played dolls or counted the moments until junior prom. I played football with the neighborhood boys or fast-pitch softball with a local team. Other girls wanted to go to college, join a sorority, major in liberal arts, and find a husband. I didn't care if I ever saw another classroom, and I certainly wasn't in a hurry to get married, have 2.3 kids, live in suburbia, and pretend to be happy. That wasn't the kind of life I wanted. Sure, it was safe and conventional. But it wasn't me.

My parents, bless their hearts, knew I wanted no part of the great American dream. I had my own dreams. My dad, Phillip, a farmer and World War II veteran, and my mom, Phyllis, quit loving each other when I was sixteen, but they never quit loving me or, I guess, my pursuit of a few of my crazy dreams.

Life growing up in Willard was about as fast-paced as watching paint dry. If you were a boy, you played sports. If you were a girl, you . . . well, I don't know what girls did because I was always outside playing sports. I was the youngest in the family. My sister, Peggy, was the oldest and didn't have an athletic bone in her body. To her, running to the mailbox was the same as running a marathon. She was a bookworm and proud of it. Needless to say, I didn't share her love of academia.

My brother, Todd, was much more my style. He used to let me pal around with his friends, and before long, I found myself having more fun with sports than I was with Suzy Homemaker ovens and whatnot. In fact, my dad still hasn't gotten around to replacing the screen door I broke one day while playing ball. And you don't even want to know how many windows we broke during our games.

I liked the feeling you got when you won something. I liked the competition. With sports, you knew where you stood. It didn't matter—at least, I didn't think it did at the time—if you were a girl or boy. The fastest person won the race. The quickest person eluded the tackle. The best batter hit the pitch.

There weren't many girls my age in the neighborhood,

which was one of the reasons I started hanging around my brother. I know it sounds stupid, but when I was about six years old, I decided I wanted my very own football uniform, complete with helmet. Willard is about sixty miles from Cleveland, so naturally, we were Browns fans and naturally I had to have a uniform that resembled the ones the Browns wore.

I begged for that silly uniform. As Christmas approached, I dropped every hint in the book. Dolls? Phooey. Coloring books? Bicycle? Dresses? Never. A Cleveland Browns kid uniform would do just fine, thank you.

My parents, who were probably beginning to wonder what sort of daughter they had on their hands, bought the uniform. Not long after that, I was playing in the backyard when another kid ripped part of the jersey. I must have cried for ten minutes before my mom came out, took me inside, and sewed the jersey back up. Another time, while making a tackle on some kid, I split the helmet right down the middle. That would probably explain a few brain-wave problems, eh?

By the time I was in fifth grade, I was hooked on sports. My sister had dried corsages and doily things pinned to her bulletin board. I had baseball and football pennants and photos of some of my favorite players. I must have had about a thousand football and baseball cards, and I kept them in an antique pot that belonged to my mom. She was cleaning it one day and said, "Pam, let's just throw these cards away."

I couldn't believe it. "No, Mom. I like these cards."

"But you have so many of them. You can always get more if you miss these."

"Well, okay."

What an idiot I was. I could probably have retired on the money I would have made from selling those cards today. How was I to know that card collecting would become a multimillion-dollar industry?

I swear, I think I knew more about sports and the different teams and players than my brother or dad. Every day the newspaper would come and every day my dad and I would fight over who got to read the sports section first. Since he paid for it, he won. I wouldn't even have thought of using "Ladies first."

I remember sitting on the porch one day, watching these two older girls across the street playing catch with a softball. I was too chicken to ask if I could play, so my mom went over there and asked for me. They were eighteen or nineteen years old and here I was, eleven. They must have thought they'd humor me for a few minutes and then send me back home. Well, a week later, I was the starting catcher for their fast-pitch team. I have to admit, I was pretty damn good for an eleven-year-old.

At one point, I thought about trying to play for one of the Willard Little League boys' teams. My dad even offered to sign me up, although I'm sure some of the stuffed shirts in town would have objected. In the end, I decided it wouldn't be worth the trouble. Looking back, I should have done it. The stuffed shirts would have never known what hit them.

High school was no great shakes. I made decent grades, but nothing like Peggy's. I didn't quite see the point in learning the Pythagorean theorem or memorizing the capitals of the Canadian provinces. I wasn't planning on becoming a mathematician or a travel agent. Of course, I wasn't planning on doing much of anything at the time. I was living with my dad and in typical tomboy tradition, lying about my whereabouts. On Sundays after church, I'd tell him I was going to visit my mom. Instead, I'd grab my baseball mitt and go play ball. My dad told me years later that he knew exactly where I was.

College was an option, but not much of one. I wanted to go to Kent State or maybe Cal-Berkeley. I didn't want to study as much as I wanted to become some sort of radical and demonstrate a lot. It seemed interesting and, as usual, different. Problem was, I didn't have much money. My dad would have tried to pay for it had I asked him, but what was the point of draining his bank account for something I wasn't sure I really wanted to do? So I didn't ask.

About the only career option I had available at the time was to become a professional softball player. Like I said, I was pretty damn good. I could catch, play first or third, and I wasn't a bad hitter, either. Our local team traveled to other towns for games, which allowed me to compare my talents to those of other players. In my humble opinion, I was better than most of them. Had someone done a scouting report on me it would have read: "Strong arm, don't run on her . . . Versatile . . . Hits mostly to right field . . . Decent power and speed."

Still, when one of the coaches made me the offer, I laughed in her face. I didn't think you could make a living playing softball. What people, in their right minds, would pay money to watch women play fast-pitch? I told her thanks, but no thanks. Shortly thereafter, I embarked on a working career that made fast-pitch-softball salaries look like a king's ransom at times.

Where to begin? Well, during the summers, dating back to my days in high school, I used to work in the muck, fields of very black and fertile dirt, and pull onions with the migrant workers who traveled north for the harvest. The bosses paid by the bushel picked, and I could pick as fast as anyone. I made $90, maybe $100, a week, which wasn't that bad, considering it was in 1969. Hard work never bothered me. I didn't care about getting dirt under my fingernails or calluses on my hands. In fact, I preferred the field work to being cooped up in an office. If I didn't work in the muck, I'd go to the sheds and help clean the celery that grew near the town of, you guessed it, Celery-ville.

From there it was on to the exciting world of full-time menial labor. There were three factories in Willard and I think I worked at each one of them. First was the Midwest factory, where I was stationed on the assembly line, given a screw gun, and told to fire away at the endless stream of lawn mowers that came winding down the track. That didn't last long; I was laid off.

Next came the Pioneer Rubber Company. For eight hours a day I printed balloons, which was about as thrilling as it sounds. Later, I was given a promotion of sorts, meaning I got to drive a truck around the factory, delivering assorted materials to the different departments. If you're wondering about my salary, it was minimum wage, with the emphasis on *minimum*. I made more pulling onions, but I was able to save about $1,200, which seemed like all the money in the world at the time.

Mobile homes were next. I took a job in a factory and installed doors and windows into the cheapest mobile homes you ever saw. We could build three of those things in one day and it looked like it, too. It was like working at a fast-food joint: once you see how they make the food, you never want to eat there again. Well, I knew I'd never want to live in a mobile home.

Simply put, I was going nowhere fast. If I wanted to remain a nobody, then all I had to do was stay in Ohio. So on a whim, I decided to move to Colorado and stay with my brother, who had a tiny apartment outside Denver. College could wait a little longer, I decided. I had an urge to go West.

What a mistake. Todd, his girlfriend, and I lived in that one-bedroom apartment and struggled to pay the rent. I took a job at Taco Bell and made $2 an hour. Then I took a second job, this one working at a Russell Stover chocolate factory, which isn't quite the sweet treat you might imagine. I was part of a crew that cleaned the massive chocolate machines. Willy Wonka's factory, it wasn't. One of the cleaning women walked around carrying a gun about the size of something Dirty Harry used. My shift was from midnight to four A.M., during which I spent about three hours cleaning and one hour stuffing my face with the rich chocolate. I gained weight, but who cared, right? I considered the chocolate scarfing a fringe benefit.

As for the Colorado experience, I considered the whole thing a disaster. I moved West in September. I was back in Willard by December, totally frustrated and confused. I was nineteen years old and didn't have a clue what I wanted to do with my life. I had done something different, all right, but poverty wasn't exactly what I had had in mind.

Another brainstorm arrived shortly after Christmas: I would go to Gainesville, Florida, and live with my sister, who was attending graduate school at the University of Florida. The plan was for me to become so enthralled with the idea of college that I'd eventually begin freshman classes myself. Fat chance.

For the next three years, I didn't become enthralled with anything, especially college. In the meantime, I was becoming pretty good at getting the worst jobs in America. For instance, Howard Johnson's hired me to be a short-order cook, which would have been fine had I known anything about cooking. I was a long-order cook, the slowest kitchen person in the history of Howard Johnson's. I had the midnight-to-seven-A.M. shift, thank goodness. I wouldn't have made it through a lunch or dinner rush.

If you must know, potato salad was my specialty. Too bad there wasn't much demand for potato salad at, say, three A.M. Breakfast orders were always interesting. If you gave me time—and I needed plenty of it—I could put together one hell of an omelet. Grilled cheese sandwiches I could do, too. Otherwise, you ordered at your own risk.

My longest stint was at the local Red Lobster, where I made a paltry $1.30 an hour, plus tips. I grew to hate that place, mostly because of my manager and the way you'd walk out of there every night smelling like grilled smelt. My manager, I'm convinced, hated to talk to women who were taller than him. This was a problem since my manager was about five four and I was five eight.

As careers go, this wasn't much of one, either. At least at the chocolate factory, I could eat stuff that I loved. Of course, there was always the danger of being wounded by an accidental gunshot. I was so desperate for a change, I even considered applying for a job driving a beer truck.

Call it destiny, fate—I don't know, call it whatever you like—but one day my mom called me from Ohio and said she had just finished reading a story about a woman named Christine Wren.

"Hey, Pam," she said, "here's something that would be good for you: umpiring. This woman tried it."

"Yeah, sure, Mom."

"Seriously, this is right up your alley."

"Jeez, Mom, I don't think so."

I didn't know it at the time, but Christine Wren was only the second woman ever to umpire a minor league game. The first was Bernice Gera, a Jackson Heights, New York, housewife who sued for the right to become a professional umpire. Gera went to umpire school in 1967, but was told by minor league officials that she didn't have the necessary physical requirements. According to the officials, Gera was too short (she was five two) to qualify for a position. She took her case to court, and in 1972, the New York State Human Rights Division Court ruled in her favor, forcing the minor leagues to finally offer her a contract. I'm sure the minor league bosses weren't pleased about letting some housewife into their league.

Poor Bernice. I read later that she received death threats from some crazy assholes who promised to blow her away if she stepped foot onto the field. Then, the night before she was supposed to make her debut, there was a disturbance outside the hotel room in which she was staying. Glass was broken in front of her door, and police had to be called to make arrests. The next day, after about a five-hour meeting with other umpires and various league officials, Gera said she could tell she'd never have a chance. She was right.

As it turned out, Gera left the field in tears. Her first and last game was in the New York–Penn League at Shuron Park in Geneva, New York, on June 24, 1972. The teams were the Auburn Phillies and the Geneva Senators. Gera, who was forty, worked the first part of a doubleheader, but after three disputed calls, one manager ejection, and no help from her umpiring partner, she resigned. Later, she worked in the public relations department of the New York Mets and eventually moved to Fort Lauderdale, Florida. In fact, she actually contacted me years later, although we never got together to talk. Bernice even wrote a letter to *Sports Illustrated* once, explaining exactly why she quit after calling just one game. She took exception to being known as the woman umpire who ended her very brief career with tears running down her face. I don't blame her. I would have been pissed, too. She deserved to be known as someone who fought baseball's bias and won— no matter if she lasted one game or not.

As for Wren, I only knew what my mom told me over the phone that day: Wren was a softball umpire who somehow caught the eye of a Los Angeles Dodgers official. After that, she was selected to call a game between the Dodgers and a local college team in a pre-spring-training exhibition at Dodger Stadium. Wren did so well that the Dodgers encouraged her to try umpire school, which she did in 1974, graduating tenth out of four hundred students at Bill Kinnamon's school in California. With the blessings of the powerful Dodgers organization, she got a job in the Northwest League, which is a summer rookie league. After spending two seasons there, Wren earned a job in the Class A Midwest League in 1976. Quite an accomplishment.

I was intrigued, but not convinced by the stories. After all, what sort of living is that, to get yelled at all the time?

Look what happened to Gera. And what might happen to Wren? I told my mom the whole thing was ridiculous, but thanked her for looking out for me.

I had just about forgotten about my mom's idea when I opened up my *Gainesville Sun* one Sunday. Inside the newspaper's magazine was a long story on something called the Al Somers Umpire School, which was located just up the road in Daytona Beach. The course only lasted six weeks, it was a lot less expensive than college, and better yet, I wouldn't have to worry about breaking any gender barriers. Gera and Wren had already done the dirty work for me.

All of a sudden this umpiring thing sounded okay. It was different, you had to say that much. And the more I thought about it, the more I thought it was, well, me. It wouldn't be another nine-to-five or graveyard shift in some fish restaurant. Best of all, it would be a challenge. I loved challenges. Always have. Always will.

Thus began my relationship with the legendary Al Somers, a nineteen-year veteran minor league umpire who was as conservative as a Brooks Brothers suit. Somers is the same guy, I learned later, who had once said, "There'll never be a woman student in my school. It's just not a job for a woman."

Of course, I didn't know how Somers felt when I sat down in September of 1976 and wrote him a letter requesting an application and information on his school. I thought I was real clever, too, because I purposely tried to make the first letter of my name seem illegible, so it looked more like Sam than Pam Postema. I figured ol' Al wouldn't notice a thing, and by the time he did, I'd already be calling my first out.

One problem: Somers never wrote back. It wasn't by accident, either. Somers didn't want a woman in his school, no matter if her name was Sam or Pam.

So I wrote another letter. This time he wrote back and

said that while he appreciated my interest, the school lacked the proper "facilities" for a woman. There were some more excuses, but that was basically it. It didn't matter: I had my challenge.

This time I wrote a third letter and dropped all sorts of hints about lawsuits and bad publicity. "There is something I can do if I don't get in," I half-threatened. I wasn't exactly sure what that would be or how I would pay for it, but at that point, I was desperate. I knew I would never sue. If he had written back and said, "See you in court," I would have dropped the whole thing and you wouldn't be reading a word about this. If he had called my bluff, I would have dropped the whole silly idea of becoming an umpire, and who knows, maybe I would have enrolled at Florida and made my dad happy.

In the same letter I told him I didn't need any special facilities. "I have strong kidneys," I wrote. "I don't need any special treatment."

Before he had a chance to respond to this unusual request, a few of my Red Lobster waitress friends and I hopped into a car and drove to Daytona to visit Mr. Somers. The only address on his stationery was a post office box. Ever the clever one, I looked in a Daytona phone book, found his home address, and off we went.

This was some group. There was Robin, who had bright red hair and would sleep with any guy who caught her fancy. And there were lots of them, too.

There was Lourdes, who wasn't the prettiest woman in the world, but she could sing. She was the sweetest person you'd ever want to meet.

And there was me, who liked to party. Countless nights we would leave work smelling like the catch of the day, retire to a local bar, and drink all night. We were frequent visitors to Daytona, too. We'd always try to find a bar with a live singer, where Lourdes could wrangle an invitation to sing a song or two onstage. She was so nice and such a good singer that soon the whole place would be clapping and cheering Lourdes. This was good for two reasons: first, it meant all sorts of people would buy us free drinks, which made me happy. Second, it meant all sorts of guys would stop by our table, which made Robin extremely happy. As for Lourdes, she was happy all the time.

Our Daytona itinerary was simple on this trip. First stop: the Somerses' residence. Second stop: the bars.

You should have seen Al's face when he answered the door and I introduced myself. He didn't know whether to call the cops or run inside. Instead, he stood at the doorstep with a frozen, sort of sad look on his face, as if he knew I would never go away.

"I'm sorry, young lady, but like I explained in my letter, we just don't have the proper facilities to handle a woman student," he said.

"Mr. Somers," I said, "I don't want or need any special treatment. I read about your school in the magazine and it said it was the best. Well, I want to go to your school because it's the best. I'm not here to create any problems, and I don't want to make any big scene. I just want to be an umpire."

I meant what I said and it must have worked. Sort of. Instead of saying no again, he said he'd think about it. And that was the end of our historic first conversation.

On to the bars, where I tried to drink to forget. I didn't know what Somers was going to do, but I didn't like my chances. The next morning, Lourdes, Robin, and I got in our car and returned to Gainesville and to the drudgery of nightly fish specials. I'm sorry, but you can only take so much seafood after a while. Also, my restaurant manager wasn't going to take much more of me. We didn't see eye to eye—literally, which bothered the hell out of the poor little guy. I wasn't exactly his most valued employee, and he wasn't my nominee for Boss of the Year honors. It probably didn't help my job security that I continually gave him shit for being so short.

I knew he wanted to fire me. He had tried about a dozen times before, but he could never find a semilegitimate reason to hand me a pink slip. At last he found an excuse. It wasn't much of one, but he got me.

My offense: not pinning my hair above my Red Lobster collar. To tell you the truth, I couldn't have been happier to get out of that place. It was time to move on. All I needed was that magical okay from my pal Al Somers.

Back in Ohio, feelings were mixed on my new career goal. My mom was happy because it was her idea in the first place. My dad didn't know exactly what to make of the whole thing. He knew college was out of the question. He knew I'd never become a farmer or return to the factories of Willard. Deep down, he knew I had to do something that satisfied me, not everyone else. I also think he was proud of me. Proud that I had gone off on my own and supported myself, although it wasn't easy. Proud that I had finally found something that truly interested me. Proud that I hadn't backed down when Al Somers didn't respond to my first letter.

When I was a kid, our family never went to a single Cleveland Indians baseball game. Not one. My dad thought the sixty-mile drive was like an overnight trip, like we were driving to Oregon or something. It seemed so far. And Cleveland was such a big city, a metropolis to us in Willard. Instead, we used to watch the games on TV. Me and my dad. Whenever Vic Davalillo would come up to the plate, we'd start yelling, "Chicken! Chicken!" Davalillo would always back away from any pitch that came within a yard of him. He was so afraid of getting hit. Second baseman Pedro Gonzalez was also on those sorry Indians teams. I'll never forget Pedro. And for some reason, I always liked shortstop Larry Brown and first baseman Fred Whitfield. They both stunk—the whole team did—but I didn't care.

There was one time, when we were watching the hapless Indians lose another game, that I turned to my dad and said, "Just once, Dad, wouldn't it be neat to go to the ballpark and catch a foul ball." Now, ten years later, I was trying to get into umpire school.

My friends, of course, didn't think too much of my scheme. They thought it was some kind of whim, which maybe it was. Then again, I didn't have many friends, mostly because the people I grew up with were content to stay in Willard, work the land or the assembly lines, raise families, and end up being buried there. I'm not saying there's anything wrong with staying in Willard; it just wasn't how I wanted to spend my life.

Before long, I began thinking that maybe Somers wasn't going to say yes, after all. Maybe I'd have to find another crummy waitress job, working in another crummy restaurant, making another crummy $1.30 an hour, plus tips. Maybe this time I'd return to the mobile home factory. The boss said I was his best worker. Or maybe I'd become a construction worker or even a carpenter. I was good with tools. I guess I was just mechanically inclined.

And then it happened. Somers, probably scared stiff of my supposed impending lawsuit, invited me to Daytona again. I was in. Or was I?

Somers wanted me to meet Harry Wendelstedt, the legendary National League umpire. I didn't know much about umpiring at the time, but I had heard of Wendelstedt. He was Al's chief instructor at the school. Al owned the place, but for all intents and purposes, Wendelstedt ran the day-to-day operations.

"Just so you know," Wendelstedt said, "we're not making any concession, not changing our program for you."

I told him I didn't need or want any concessions.

"You know, people think calling balls and strikes or safe and out is the big part of umpiring," he said. "Can you take the pressure when players and fans think you've missed a pitch? Can you do four hundred deep knee bends in a game behind the plate?"

I wanted to start laughing. Do four hundred deep knee

bends? Hell, he was talking to someone who had spent summers bent over in the muck, pulling onions with the hot Ohio sun overhead. Doing four hundred deep knee bends seemed like nothing.

The pressure of blowing a call? Who knew? I certainly didn't. I had never umpired a game in my life.

Not wanting to look like a smart ass, I simply said, "Yes, sir, I think I can handle those things."

Wendelstedt continued the mini-interrogation.

"Can you stand the pressure?" he asked again.

Again, I said I thought I could.

"Do you understand the problems a young, single, attractive girl will face being in class and on the field with some one hundred young men of different backgrounds and from thirty to thirty-five states?"

"Yes, I do," I said.

Wendelstedt seemed satisfied. So did Al. Not long after the interview, Somers approved my application. And while he was at it, he let another woman into the school, too.

In my case, I think Al realized that I wasn't out to prove a point. I didn't want to join his school so I could be the first anything. The only reason I had kept pestering him in the first place was because he had ignored my original letter and I hate being ignored. The truth is, I didn't have any grand illusions about setting the standard for women's rights everywhere. I had my own problems; I didn't have time for everyone else's. At least, that's what I thought way back then.

I went back to Al's house, this time at his invitation. When I got there, he introduced me to a sportswriter and photographer who were there to do a story on Somers's school and his surprising policy reversal on women students. It was my first brush with the media and I hated it. I was nervous and I didn't want anything to do with the reporter's questions, all of them stupid, as far as I was concerned. It wouldn't be the last time I would think that way about reporters.

For the first time in years, I was scared about leaving home. I was twenty-two years old and I was finally going away to school. Umpire school. God help me. God help Al Somers because he didn't know what he was getting himself into.

Of course, neither did I.

CHAPTER 2

The Class of '77

This was going to be my plan: I would keep a very low profile during my six weeks at Al's school, finish in the top fifteen—which is what I thought it would take for me to get offered a minor league job—and begin my umpiring career. Blend in, be cool, work hard . . . that was going to be my motto during my stay in Daytona Beach. All I wanted was a fair chance and to be treated just like any other student at the school.

I got one out of two.

There were 130 of us enrolled for the 1977 winter session of the Al Somers Umpire School. Only about 100 students would be there six weeks later. Some were sent home, while others would pack their belongings in the middle of the night and quietly slip away. Make no mistake about it: this was an umpire's version of boot camp—commanding officer, Al Somers; drill sergeant, Harry Wendelstedt.

Al was nicknamed The Whip. I'm still not sure why. To me, he was a sweetheart who pretended to be mean and gruff. He had never made it to the big leagues himself, but he knew what it took to get there. He had hired Wendelstedt to teach people what it took to stay there.

The Somers School had the reputation of being the most comprehensive in the country. And it didn't hurt business that at the time, Al's school churned out more than half of the umpires who made it to the majors. Also impressive were the number of graduates, an amazing seven thousand would-be umpires. And not one of them a woman. I was going to change all that.

But first I had to find a place to live. After paying my $554 registration fee (the last of my Red Lobster savings), I didn't have enough money to stay in the on-campus dormitory. To be honest, I didn't want to stay there anyway. I wanted a place away from everyone else, a place where I could study and practice and not look like a fool doing it. Problem was, the month of January is one of the busier months for tourism in Daytona. Winter rates were in effect, which meant most of the decent motels and apartments were already taken or were too expensive for my skimpy budget. So I compromised.

For $40 a week, I stayed at a place that gave the slums a good name. Basically, it was a rat trap with four walls and a floor. There was a small bathroom, a small kitchen, which was nothing more than a sink, a rickety old stove, and a tiny refrigerator, and an itsy-bitsy living area that served as my dining room, bedroom, and TV room. Of course, I didn't even own a TV. In short, this one-room hellhole was for people way below the poverty level.

The worst thing about my "apartment" (other than the fact that some slumlord actually charged $40 a week to live there) was the nightly visits from our neighborhood rats. The place was mine during the day, but the rats owned it after dark. Did they ever.

During my first night there, I made the mistake of leaving a loaf of bread atop the refrigerator. Bread and maybe a couple of beers were the only thing I could afford back then. Little did I know that I was paying for the rats' dinners, too. Wide-awake and scared stiff in the darkness, I heard the rats scurrying across the kitchen floor. Then I heard something running across the countertop and onto the refrigerator. I didn't know if I should scream or turn on the lights. Instead, I lay in my sofa bed and listened to my subtenants.

Somehow I fell asleep. I guess I was too exhausted to care anymore. When I awoke and ventured into the kitchen, I saw the damage. The rats—and they must have been big ones—had chewed right through the plastic surrounding the loaf of bread. You could see teeth marks on what was left of the bread. There were little rat droppings here and there, which was almost enough to make me immediately pack my things and look elsewhere. But what was I going to do? I had already paid a couple of weeks' worth of rent, and anyway, there weren't any vacancies I could afford. And hell, I told myself, look at the bright side: at least the rats hadn't been able to drink my precious beer. Of course, just to be on the safe side, I checked the refrigerator.

That morning I decided to go out for a run. I loved running. It was so relaxing to me and gave me time to think things through. When I returned about forty minutes later, I found that my apartment door was wide open. Standing outside was a somewhat frantic lady, who said she and her family lived next door. She looked as if she had seen a ghost.

"You're alive," she said. "We thought you tried to kill yourself. We thought you were dead."

I didn't know what in the hell she was talking about until I took one step into the apartment. There had been a gas leak, enough, if I was lucky, to kill a couple rats. The superintendent was called and the leak was fixed. But the lady was right: had I not woken up early and gone on my run, I would probably have been deader than a doorknob.

My life spared, I started umpire classes on January 2. That's the day I got my first look at my fellow students, or should I say, my competition. Most of us were after the same thing, a minor league job. Maybe twenty graduates would receive offers. And out of the twenty, Wendelstedt told us, maybe one umpire would make it to the big leagues. Maybe.

This was also the first day the other students could look at me. What they saw was a five-eight, 175-pound farm girl (hey, I was big boned) who was hell-bent on walking out of there six weeks later with one of those job offers. I wasn't scared of success as much as I was of failure.

Not every one of the 130 students at Al's school wanted to become a professional umpire. Some of them were high school and college umpires simply trying to sharpen their skills for the upcoming season. They weren't living any sort of dream. Other guys enrolled in the school just so they could play in the simulated baseball games we had each day. They were frustrated jocks, that's what they were. They had more fun pretending to be ballplayers than actually learning how to umpire. I didn't mind; that meant fewer threats to my goal. And then there were the diehard umpire nuts, people who spent their vacations at Al's school. *Their vacations.* Nothing made these kooks happier than rubbing elbows with the likes of Al and Wendelstedt. They seemed to have a grand time. All I can say is that they must not have been staying at my motel.

The other curiosity of the Class of '77 was a young woman named Julie, the bookend to Al's policy of finally allowing females into his school. It was because of Julie and me that Al told his instructors to curtail their use of swear words, which was almost as ridiculous as those people who were spending their vacation money on umpire school. I guess Al thought we might be offended by the foul language. I didn't know about Julie, but we learned how to cuss just fine in Ohio. We weren't Quakers or anything like that.

Still, Al insisted that the instructors be on their best behavior, which is exactly what I didn't want. I wanted to be treated like the other students. I didn't care if I got yelled at or cussed at. I was there to learn, not to be pampered like a newborn. Al wouldn't hear any of that.

Classes began early in the morning. At first, we assembled at one of the five baseball diamonds that Al used at, what was then, the Montreal Expos' minor league complex. We did some stretching exercises and then a few calisthenics. Anything more difficult and a couple of those guys would have keeled over from physical exhaustion. Then the instructors would split us up into groups, where we started with the fundamentals, such as the right way to call a strike. It sounds simple, but the good umpires have a certain flair, a certain style that gives them an air of authority. We didn't have any of that. When it was my turn, I made some sort of guttural noise that resembled the word "Strike," raised my right arm, and clenched my fist. It wasn't a bad first effort, but it wasn't good, either.

"No, no, no," said Somers, who roamed from field to field, checking on his students. "Use your voice. Scream it if you have to. And cock that right wrist."

The way Al yelled it, "Strike" wasn't a one-syllable word, it was four or five syllables long. We learned the proper way to make the "safe" call, which requires the arms to be held out just so, the knees bent at a precise angle, followed by another arm motion. We learned the "out" call, which meant that the right arm was raised high, the fist clenched and the thumb hidden. If you used your thumb, Al or one of the instructors would always say, "No thumb, no thumb." In fact, one night after classes a few of us students were driving to Edie's Bar, which was the big umpire-school hangout, when we noticed a hitchhiker. "Hey, buddy," said one of the students as we drove by, "no thumbs." Just a little bad umpire-school humor.

During those same morning sessions, we'd spend a lot of time going over the rules of baseball, of which there seemed to be too many to count. The last time I looked, the *Official Baseball Rules* book published by *The Sporting News* was 102 pages long. When I was in umpire school, it seemed as thick as the Bible. Worse yet, everything read like a law manual. For instance, there are eight ways the batter becomes a runner, including, reads the manual, "a fair ball, after having passed a fielder other than the pitcher, or after having been touched by a fielder, including the pitcher, shall touch an umpire or runner on fair territory."

What?

There were too many *shall*'s in the rule book. First of all, nobody in baseball ever says the word *shall*. Lawyers and priests say *shall*. Umpires say *shit* and *fuck* a lot. *Shall* isn't in their vocabulary.

And figure this one out: "Each runner, other than the batter, may without liability to be put out, advance one base when the batter's advance without liability to be put out forces the runner to vacate his base, or when the batter hits a fair ball that touches another runner or the umpire before such ball has been touched by, or has passed a fielder, if the runner is forced to advance . . ."

You see? At times I didn't know if I was studying to be an umpire or getting ready to take the California bar exam. Even the instructors would get confused. Dick Nelson, one of the best teachers at the school, would always attend the class on batting-out-of-order calls. He said he could never understand the damn rule. Now you know why.

We'd discuss the rules, and a lot of times we'd act out the situation on the field. Later on, we'd have a test. You could always count on a couple of tough rules questions. And it wasn't unusual to be asked about certain plays. For example, if there were two out, men on first and second, and a fly ball was hit to short right field, where would the first-base umpire go? Things like that. It wasn't rocket science, but it wasn't simple, either.

Lunch was always served on the field. Earlier in the morning, we'd place our orders with a school official, who would then drive to Burger King shortly before noon and ruin the day of at least one fast-food clerk. Imagine the poor clerk's surprise when someone ordered 200 hamburgers, 50 Whoppers, 120 fries . . . They dreaded the Al

Somers School at Burger King. And after a while, I dreaded the taste of another Burger King lunch.

No school is complete without a class dunce. Ours was a guy named Harry. Harry would ask a question about anything. He had a real deep voice and wasn't afraid to constantly use it. Harry thought that if you asked enough questions, eventually one of the answers would sink in. I swear, I think Harry asked how many balls you need to issue a walk. And Harry wasn't afraid to suck up to the instructors. With so much at stake and so few minor league jobs available, sucking up was a favorite umpire-school pastime.

The instructors at the school included Somers and Wendelstedt, of course, Dick Nelson, Dick Stello, Dan Morrison, Randy Marsh, Ed Hudson, Jim Waller, and Jack Lietz. Wendelstedt was the king, though. As corny as it sounds, I worshiped him. I thought the guy could walk on water. He seemed like an umpire's umpire, a guy who's always right, who always made the perfect call at the perfect time. We used to sit around and listen to Wendelstedt tell stories about his triumphs in the National League. We were spellbound.

Don't get me wrong: Wendelstedt was and is a great umpire. You don't last twenty-five years in the business without doing something right. The last time I looked, Wendelstedt had umpired three All-Star games, eight Championship Series, and four World Series. One time he let us look at his 1973 World Series ring. It was the size of a baby's clutched fist. I put it on my finger and thought about the thrill of calling a World Series game. Of course, Wendelstedt loved every minute of our adulation. I was so naive back then. I thought Wendelstedt was a fucking saint. But word was that when his lips started to quiver, he was lying—and Wendelstedt's lips were almost always quivering. I didn't believe the advice at the time. Now I know.

Stello was another National League umpire who worked

at the school during the off-season. It was easy money and what did Stello care? He was a jerk, especially to Julie and me. He didn't think we belonged in the school and he made sure we knew it. He was the ultimate chauvinist, and I can't say I shed buckets of tears when he died years later.

Nelson wasn't one of my favorite instructors, either. I know he was trying to be nice, but he was the exact opposite of Stello. Too many times he went out of his way to help Julie and me. I thought that was bullshit. Why treat us different? If we were good enough, fine. If we weren't, we failed. Why act as if we were fragile little princesses, unable to take care of ourselves? I didn't want the extra attention. In fact, I resented it.

Julie didn't. Julie didn't resent much of anything, actually. She seemed to be enjoying herself during school, and why not? Nelson was bending over backward to help her.

To top it off, I had to deal with a guy named Tom, who was one of the more eccentric students at the school. He was, well, in need of some psychiatric care, if you ask me. He used to hang around Julie, and once in a while I'd see him and say hello. Then one day he went up to Dick Nelson and made an announcement:

"I'm in love with Julie and Pam."

"You're kidding me," said Dick.

"No, I'm not. My problem is that they're both in love with me and I don't know who to pick."

I didn't find out any of this until years later. At the time, I thought everything was just rosy. Except for an occasional bedtime antic, I hadn't heard a single good rumor during school. I must have had my head in the sand.

After each day's classes, a few of us would grab a beer or two at Edie's. I always dreaded going home. Remember, the night belonged to the rats.

Sometimes I drove to the beach, and there in the darkness, I practiced my umpiring form. I pretended I was making strike calls and out calls and safe calls and balk calls.

I yelled, "STTTTTRRRRRIIIIIKKKKKEEEEE!" just the way Somers wanted us to. And I could always count on the pounding of the surf to drown out any mistakes.

This was also the final year for umpires to wear outside chest protectors. Perhaps you recall them? They looked like oversize pillows and they were the damnedest things to master. Being on the stubborn side, I dragged one of the chest protectors with me to the beach. Had you been able to squint through the darkness, you would have seen me wearing an umpire's mask and my protector. The trick was to take the mask off with one hand, drop your shoulder, which allowed the chest protector to slide down, squeeze the thing between your elbow and side, and pretend to run down to third. So what if I looked silly running up and down a beach sliding a chest protector under my arm? I couldn't have cared less.

Things were going well until someone handed me a copy of a *Sporting News* story on my admittance into Al's school. I wanted to run and hide.

"Ohio Gal Breaks Somers Ump Barrier," read the headline. Under the headline was a photograph of Al and me holding an umpire's mask. It looked as if I were some sort of stupid girl who didn't even know how to put the thing on my head. I had this silly grin on my face, which only made matters worse.

The story wasn't much better. I was referred to as "an attractive farm lass from Ohio" who had "an engaging smile and a direct gaze from hazel eyes." If you didn't know any better, you would have thought I was a Miss America contestant, not an umpire student. Later, word of two women students at Somers's school reached ABC, CBS, and NBC. Each network mentioned us in one of their newscasts.

My plan to keep a low profile was dead. I wanted zero publicity; I got almost a full-page story in *The Sporting News*. I wanted to blend in; I got singled out. I should have kept my mouth shut and said, "No comment." Instead, I blabbered happily away in the article, talking about how women had made the move to race car drivers, jockeys, horse trainers, harness drivers. "A couple of years ago that would have shaken up guys like A. J. Foyt and Cale Yarborough."

Yak, yak, yak. I had become, against my own wishes, a celebrity. And it was partly my own fault.

As the countdown to graduation became shorter, the tension grew thicker. We were past the days of students leaving in the middle of the night. Back then, we kept count of the defectors. "Three more gone," we'd say, proud that we had survived another day. But by Weeks No. 4 and No. 5, no one was going anywhere. Futures were being decided, which caused everyone to forget about daily body counts.

I also knew I had a chance to be a decent umpire. For whatever reason, I did well behind the plate. Calling balls and strikes came easily. During our games, I almost always felt comfortable back there. Maybe it was because I had great eyesight or because I had been a fast-pitch catcher for all those years. I was accustomed to seeing a ball whip across the plate. I also knew something about strike zones.

Where I had my problems was on the base paths. It took time to learn exactly where to position oneself for certain plays. Never having played baseball, it took me a little more time to understand how a situation might unfold. I hesitated at times, and if there's one thing you can't do as an umpire, it's hesitate. Remember, there's not much margin for error in umpiring. Someone figured it out once: a plate umpire makes an average of three hundred calls a game. If the umpire blows one or two calls, they say he had a bad game. But if a batter gets three hits out of ten, he's considered a star.

Somers had a working agreement with some of the local college teams: free umpires for free experience. The college coaches couldn't say yes fast enough. That's where we got our first taste of live umpiring. I wish I could say it was memorable, but it wasn't. All Al was trying to do was expose us to the elements. He constantly wanted to see how we reacted under pressure. After all, we were being evaluated not only on our ability to remember rules, but also on how we handled a bitchy manager or a close call at home. I'm proud to report that I did well. Most of the time.

By the end of the program, I knew Somers and Wendelstedt would have to give me a diploma. I knew the rules. I had shown a knack for calling balls and strikes. I handled most of their make-believe dilemmas. As for those "facility" problems that Al had fretted about, well, those never materialized. I had been a model student. So had Julie.

As usual, an awards banquet was held to honor the outstanding students in the school. I didn't figure to finish as valedictorian, but I was fairly confident of a top-fifteen spot. Instead, I came in at number seventeen. Not what I wanted, but probably good enough to earn me a minor league invitation.

Of course, that was before I almost ended my umpiring career before it even started. Midway through the banquet, one of the students, a guy named Pete, told me to report immediately to Wendelstedt.

"Why?" I said.

"Because he wants you and Julie to get your picture taken together," Pete said.

I thought Wendelstedt was the greatest thing since air-conditioning, but I didn't think much of this request. In fact, I was pissed. Again, all I wanted was to be treated as one of the guys and here's Wendelstedt trying to turn it into a dog and pony photography show. This is the same guy who said in that *Sporting News* article about me: "I believe she's sincere. I don't feel she's in it for the publicity as some women might be." So what does Wendelstedt do? He wants to get the two women in a picture so he can hang it on his wall and tell everyone what a liberal he is. I wouldn't have minded if Julie and I had finished in the top ten of the class, but we didn't. In fact, Julie finished behind me.

"Fuck that," I told a stunned Pete. "I'm not going to get my picture taken just because I'm a woman. I didn't do anything special. Let him take a picture of someone who did."

I was so idealistic, so naive. I was also stupid. Why? Because Pete went running back to Wendelstedt and told him that I had said: "Fuck, Harry." Wendelstedt went through the roof. A day or two later, when it came time to make recommendations to the minor leagues, Wendelstedt told Dick Nelson that there was no way in hell he was going to place my name on the list of available candidates. Now it was Nelson's turn to get pissed.

"Harry, you can't do that," he said.

Wendelstedt said he could . . . and would, too.

"If you don't recommend her for a job, then I'm quitting," Nelson said.

So Wendelstedt put me on the list, but only because Nelson, who was the best instructor in the school, threatened to quit. Funny thing was, Nelson didn't really know me. I had always kept my distance from him because I thought he catered too much to Julie. Now here he was putting his own job on the line for me. Imagine that.

All of this was hush-hush, of course. I didn't know about the power struggle going on between Wendelstedt and Nelson. When I didn't hear from anyone after the banquet, I figured that I hadn't been one of the lucky ones to get a minor league call. So desperate was I for money that I actually returned to Gainesville and worked at a seafood restaurant called The Yearling.

Since I usually worked at night, I figured why not put some of my vast umpiring skill to good use. So I drove to the University of Florida campus and met with the amused baseball coach.

"Here's the deal,' I said. "I went to this great umpire school and I'd like to umpire some of your games. You don't have to pay me a penny. I just want the practice."

"Great," he said. "When can you start?"

"How 'bout tomorrow?"

"Great."

Some negotiator, eh? I was dirt poor and I offered to umpire for free. But like I said, I was naive.

Florida always had a pretty good baseball team. But like everyone else, the players didn't know what to make of a woman umpire. During one of the games, one of the Florida pitchers kept calling me "Ma'am" and "Miss." Finally I said to him, "Just call me Blue, nothing more, nothing less!" Gawd, what a stupid thing to say.

Things were going well with the Gators. I had done about three games and had one left before they went on a road trip. As usual, I was behind the plate.

This was some game. Inning after inning passed without me missing a pitch. There wasn't one complaint from either bench, which was a little unusual since the players and coaches tended to jump on my case at the first sign of trouble. Had Wendelstedt seen me that day, he would have bumped me to the head of the class. I was fucking awesome . . . until the ninth inning.

I can't really explain what happened without feeling embarrassed. During the entire game, Florida got its ass kicked. But in the bottom of the ninth, the Gators staged a remarkable comeback. They hit every pitch. A single here. A triple to the wall. A home run. It was unbelievable. All of a sudden the score was getting tighter and tighter, as was the invisible collar around my neck. I started thinking, "When is this game going to end?" I'll admit it: the pressure was starting to get to me.

With two outs, bases loaded, and Florida behind by only one run, I decided I couldn't take it anymore. In stepped the batter, who worked the count to 3-2. What happened next is a perfect example of someone who was entirely intimidated by the moment.

In came the pitch, a fastball that had to be shoulder

high, maybe higher. The batter watched it pass—as he should have—and without a second's hesitation, I yelled, "SSSTTTRRRIIIKKKEEE!" Somers would have been proud of the yell, but not of the call. I knew it was a ball, but I had wanted a strike.

The Florida batter was furious, and rightly so. I had choked, pure and simple. As I walked off the field, he kept following me, which, for some strange reason, made me think of what Somers always preached to us: "The key to success is a good eye, an even temper, and being the boss of your game. You should also know where the nearest exit is. And remember to tell the scorekeeper where you want the body sent."

Believe me, I was looking for that exit when the Florida player rushed in front of me, stuck the nose of the bat in my face, and in my first-ever baseball confrontation, screamed, "You suck!" At first, I almost said something like, "Hey, two strikes . . . you've got to be up there swinging." But that probably wouldn't have been too smart. So I just kept walking. Needless to say, the Florida coach never invited me back.

My career—what there was of it—was finished. I worked at The Yearling, hit the bars until the wee hours, and sulked. Going back to Ohio was an option, but not much of one. The last thing I wanted to do was come crawling home in defeat. Of course, I was running out of choices fast.

March passed. So did April. May. Then, when I had just about given up hope of ever umpiring another game, I got The Phone Call. On the other end of the line was a gentleman by the name of George MacDonald, president of the Gulf Coast League and the Florida State League. Would I be interested, he asked, in an umpiring position in the Gulf Coast League?

How fast do you think it took me to say, "Hell, yes!"

CHAPTER **3**

The Debut

You'd think I could remember the names of both teams that played in my very first game as a professional umpire, but I can't. I think I was so nervous and so excited that I didn't pay attention to the surroundings. I should have saved the game program or the lineup cards, but those sort of things weren't on my mind that night. Survival was. So was getting through the evening without screwing up.

The game was at Payne Park, located in the heart of downtown Sarasota, Florida. The ballpark was demolished a few years ago, but back then, the place was the winter home of the Chicago White Sox and the summer home of the organization's rookie team, which featured mostly high school draft picks—teenagers, really. They were as nervous as I was.

I had the plate that night . . . thank goodness. It wasn't that I dreaded working the bases, it's just that I felt more secure calling balls and strikes. MacDonald, my new boss, was in the stands, which didn't help my nerves any. He was there, like most everyone else, to see the woman umpire sink or swim.

MacDonald was a good guy. He didn't have to take a chance on me, but he did. When Umpire Development, which is subsidized by the major league teams and basically determines how far an umpire goes in the minors, recommended me for a job, MacDonald didn't think twice.

MacDonald is the same league president who hired Eric Gregg to work in the Florida State League, a Single A league. Gregg is black and is a pretty damn good umpire. But when MacDonald bought his contract almost twenty years ago, not everyone was so thrilled with the move. MacDonald took some shit for that one (even though he shouldn't have), just as he took some shit for hiring me in 1977. Of course, Gregg's FSL contract was later purchased by the National League, and he remains one of only two black umpires (the other is Charlie Williams, also of the National League) working in the big leagues. So Mac-Donald knew what he was doing, especially when you consider that the National League purchased Gregg's contract even before he umpired in Double A and Triple A. I wasn't expecting the same sort of magic, but it made me feel good to know that MacDonald believed enough in me to offer me a job.   •

You may have heard of the MacDonald family. Mac-Donald senior was in baseball for forty-five years. He was a minor league umpire for eighteen seasons who went on to become a minor league general manager, scout, and then president of the Gulf Coast and Florida State leagues. In fact, when the New York–Penn League first turned down Bernice Gera's request to umpire, MacDonald senior wrote her and asked her to submit an application to his league. Gera decided she would make her stand with the NY-Penn League.

Now, years later, MacDonald junior was taking things a step further.

As I walked out onto the field, I knew people were skeptical. I could see it on the faces of those high school brats, what with their smirks and smiles and smart-ass remarks. The fans didn't seem to care. Or maybe they couldn't figure out who was who. My hair was cut short, so when I wore my cap, put on my mask, and crouched behind the catcher, it was hard to tell if I was a man or a woman. If this one guy in the stands would have quit screaming "Get back in the kitchen," I don't think anybody would have noticed me right away.

I had worked a grand total of eight college games before I yelled "Play!" that night in Sarasota. And when I yelled it, I purposely lowered my voice, so I'd sound more authoritative and more aggressive. I don't think anybody was very impressed.

What happened next was like a dream. I couldn't miss a pitch. It was as if the ball were the size of a melon and I could follow its flight from the moment it left the pitcher's hand to the time it popped into the catcher's mitt. Both pitchers were throwing strikes the whole game, which was supposed to be unusual for a rookie league. Only a few runs were scored, there were no close plays, no arguments, and the game was finished in a couple of hours. I thought, "This is easy." It was the perfect game.

Looking back on it, the odds of having that kind of game were phenomenal. So many things could have gone the other way, and I don't know how I would have reacted. My concentration level was unbelievable, but that was partly because the pitchers kept throwing strikes, which made it easy to make calls. But what would I have done had they been all over the place? I knew MacDonald was there. I knew there was pressure. I could have blown an obvious call. I could have had an argument with a player or manager, overreacted, and then dumped the guy. (That's what we call throwing someone out of the game.) I could have made a fool out of myself. But I didn't. I kicked ass. Even if it was just for one game—and an easy game at that—I made it. I survived.

The Gulf Coast League was a favorite of umpires because it didn't require much traveling. Only eight farm clubs were in the league, and all the games were played within fifteen miles of Sarasota. Because it was an entry-level league, the minor league instructors were generally more concerned about teaching their young players the fundamentals of the game rather than winning. That was okay with me; it meant less pressure. And better yet, the season lasted just fifty-five games.

MacDonald used to tell people that the Gulf Coast League was a perfect place for umpires to get their feet wet, to make some mistakes, to build some confidence. I needed to do all of those things. I also needed to show MacDonald that I was serious about doing this for a living. So in my first meeting with him, I asked that he not arrange any interviews for me with the press. I didn't want any distractions. I told him that I wasn't looking for any publicity, that I was there to learn how to become a better umpire. I think that impressed him.

After struggling through umpire school and then working for minimum wage and tips, I thought the Gulf Coast League was heaven. I made about $800 a month, which seemed like a lot after slaving away at Red Lobster. I even had my own apartment, and this one didn't have rats. In fact, all eight of the umpires in the league stayed at the same apartment building. Harry and Bob Black, two brothers who owned the building, gave us a break on the rent, which meant more money for beer.

Since the season was so short, we didn't have the same partners for the entire fifty-five-game schedule. Some games I'd have John Higgins as a crew member or Billy Hohn or one of the other five guys. For the most part, everybody got along pretty well.

The beauty of the Gulf Coast League was that most of the games were played during the day, leaving plenty of time for bar-hopping at night. We developed a routine: call a game in the afternoon, meet at the Beach Club in Sarasota in the evening. I thought that if I went drinking with the other guys, maybe they'd treat me less as a woman and more as a rookie umpire. I don't know if it worked, but I do know we got drunk as skunks just about every night. The next day I'd wake up with the worst hangover and swear I'd never drink so many beers again.

It got hotter than hell in Sarasota during the summer. And muggy, too. It seemed like every afternoon a storm would come through and make things even more sticky. That was always bad news for me because I sweated like a pig out there. I doubt many people, men or women, sweat more than me. I don't know why, but some games I would sweat so much the perspiration would soak through my pants and shirt and even through my ball bag. A pitcher would want a new ball and I'd have to throw him one that was almost a ready-made spitter. He'd throw it back because it was too wet, and I'd have to dig through the bag until I found a ball reasonably sweat free. It wasn't easy, either.

The Gulf Coast League is where I began to develop a consistent strike zone. I had to, because if I didn't, those players and managers would be all over my ass the second I made a questionable call. Higgins would blow a call and maybe somebody would yell, "Bear down!" If I made the same call, I'd hear, "You're brutal!" That's when I would dump the guy. I was so sensitive, so idealistic. I thought umpires were supposed to be like gods out there. That's the way we were taught at umpire school. We were told that a player couldn't say boo to you. If he did, he was gone. If there was even the tiniest possibility that the guy might be trying to show you up, he got dumped. I didn't know any better. If anybody argued with me for any length of time, I'd just throw him out. What I should have done was walk away and got the game going. But they didn't tell us that at umpire school. Come to think of it, maybe that's something they wanted us to learn on our own.

If it was, I didn't learn the lesson quickly. I had one of the quickest thumbs in the league that first season. No way was I going to let anyone intimidate me.

Of course, I could do nothing about my partners trying

an occasional power-play move. I'm sure each of them thought they were ten times the umpire I was. And to prove it, they used to go out of their way to overrule me when they thought I'd screwed up. For instance, Higgins was working the bases and I had the plate one day when a slow inside pitch hit the batter. Well, I hadn't been an umpire for very long, but I knew a faker when I saw one. The batter didn't attempt to move. Intead, he stood there like a statue and let the ball plunk him in the thigh. When he started running to first, figuring that I had awarded him the base, I stopped the game.

"Wait a minute," I said. "You stay at home. That's just a ball. You didn't try to get out of the way."

The player went nuts. So did the manager, who couldn't believe he didn't have a runner on first. Raw rookie umpire or not, I knew the rule. I also knew I was right.

That's when Higgins came down from first base.

"No, no, no, Pam," he said. "He gets first base."

"John, he didn't try to move out of the way of the ball. He just stood there."

"Pam, listen to me: he gets first base."

So I gave the guy first base. I didn't want to, but I let Higgins and the situation intimidate me. I should have stood my ground and told the player, the manager, and Higgins to go fuck themselves. Instead, I backed down. Dumb. Very dumb.

First base was also the site of my very first in-your-face, no-holds-barred fight with a manager—Joe Jones of the White Sox. I blew a call and Jones came rushing out of the dugout and stuck his nose about an inch away from mine. I wish I could have seen my face. I was shocked. I couldn't believe anybody could yell that loud and be, well, that rude. I had never seen anyone that mad before.

"The guy was safe!" he screamed. "The guy was safe!"

What was I supposed to say: "Yeah, you're right"? So I didn't say anything at all. I was too busy being surprised by his anger. I didn't even dump him, that's how amazed

I was by it all. But for the rest of that season, I couldn't stand looking at Jones. I hated him because of what he had done to me. I didn't understand that arguing was part of the game and that he was just trying to protect his player. Man, did I hold a grudge against him.

I also didn't realize that umpires had bad days, too. Once, after a miserable showing behind the plate, I had to write an ejection report for MacDonald. I described the incident and the reason for my dumping the guy. But I was so insecure that I also added, "Mr. MacDonald, I didn't have that great of a game, but I did look good cleaning the plate off." I'm sure he was impressed.

That was also the season I took my first foul ball to the knee. It was a real tough blow, and I dropped to the ground for three or four minutes. My knee hurt so bad I wanted to cry. I think the only reason I didn't was because Barney Deary was at the game.

I must have done something right that season because when the Gulf Coast schedule was finished, MacDonald switched me to the Florida State League, where the teams were finishing up their regular-season games. Once again, MacDonald took a chance on me when he didn't have to.

This was serious stuff. The second-half championship was at stake, and the players and managers were treating it as if it were a major league pennant race. My job was to work the final week of the FSL season and try not to embarrass myself or MacDonald's judgment.

At least one manager questioned MacDonald's decision—Lakeland Tigers manager Jim Leyland, who now manages the Pittsburgh Pirates. MacDonald and he were pretty close, which is why my boss probably didn't get too upset when Leyland asked, "How could you send the girl?" MacDonald told him that I had done a good job in the Gulf Coast League and that I could handle one week of FSL ball. But just in case, MacDonald said, I would only only work the bases, not the plate.

I did MacDonald proud that week with no screwups and

no complaints from angry managers. The only incident came before a game between Lakeland and the St. Petersburg Cardinals at St. Pete. Rich Humphrey and John Hirschbeck were my partners, but the idiot public address announcer decided to single me out.

"Pam, why don't you tip your hat to the crowd," he said during the introductions.

I stood there, seething. I know the guy meant well, but I didn't hear him ask Humphrey and Hirschbeck to tip their hats. Maybe I was being a jerk, but I wanted no special favors or attention, even if it meant just tipping my hat.

The next day, one of the local newspapers ran a story about me making my Florida State League debut and not tipping my cap to the crowd. The guy who wrote the article was the same guy who asked me if my promotion to the crew was a gimmick.

"Do I look like a gimmick?" I said. "I just want to look like an umpire."

The following season I returned to the Gulf Coast League, which was okay with me. I needed the experience; I just didn't need some of the trauma that went with it.

One of my partners was Steve Book. Book was semifamous among rookie-league umpires, players, and managers for his exploits with minor league manager Joe Klein.

According to the story, Book called a runner safe at home moments before the third out was made at second. Let me explain. We call these time plays. In this case, there was a runner on second with two outs. The batter hit a line drive and tried to stretch a single into a double. Just before he was tagged out at second, the runner came around and scored. At least, that's what Book saw that day. After the out, he turned to the press box, where the official scorer was, pointed to the plate, and yelled, "Run scores!"

Klein, usually a mild-mannered sort, didn't agree. In fact, he accused Book of not knowing what the hell he was doing out there.

This is where things took a turn for the worse. Instead

of simply yelling back at Klein, Book tried to reason with him, which is always a mistake with baseball people. Book reached into his back pocket, pulled out a rule book, and started thumbing through the pages looking for the exact sentence that would support his call. Every umpire in the Gulf Coast League carried a rule book on the field per orders of MacDonald. MacDonald never wanted a manager to protest a game because an umpire didn't know the rules. That's why he insisted we have one available at all times.

Of course, MacDonald never said anything about pulling a rule book out for a manager to see. And he never mentioned anything about what might happen if you did.

In this case, Klein couldn't control himself. Just as Book found the appropriate rule, Klein grabbed the thing from his hand and tore the pages into tiny pieces. Book stood there in disbelief.

Afterward, Book had to write a report to MacDonald explaining the entire situation. A few days later, MacDonald handed down his punishment: Klein would have to buy Book a brand-new rule book. Sweet revenge.

I got along okay with Book. In fact, it was Book who witnessed the absolute low point of my year and one of the low points of my career. It was the day I called MacDonald in tears.

"Mr. MacDonald," I said between sobs, "I was terrible today. If I could have changed every one of my calls, I would have had a perfect game. That's how bad I was. I can't do this. I think I want to quit."

MacDonald had probably heard this sort of thing before. He calmed me down, told me everything would be all right, and asked that I not make any rash decisions based on one game.

"What's wrong?" he said. "Is it because somebody called you a name?"

"No," I said. "After a while they were laughing, I was so bad. I don't like to do anything and not do a good job. If I'm this bad, then I don't think I should do this."

"Tell you what. Take it easy and think it over. You'll be okay. Give it a few more days and we'll talk."

I didn't need more time to think about it. I knew I'd stunk up the place that day. How bad was it? Well, I was working the bases when I called a guy out on a play when he was clearly safe. I don't know what happened. My mind said safe, but my hands said out. The player turned around, stunned by the call, and yelled, "You suck!"

"You're right," I said.

Thing was, I didn't even throw the guy out. I was so gawd-awful that day that I would probably have screwed up when I dumped him. I was so terrible that I didn't dare go near Book during the game. I didn't want him to get involved or catch any shit for being my partner. I decided to die alone and rightly so. I was the one who had blown every call, so why bring Book down with me?

It could have been worse. Luckily, the managers took pity on me. You know how hitters take the collar some days? Well, I was the umpiring equivalent of a hitter going 0-for-whatever. Thank goodness for a guy such as Klein, who would take me aside and offer a few pointers or suggestions. He genuinely cared, and I always respected him for finding time for a struggling young umpire.

But MacDonald was right. He almost always was. The next day I had another game and this time I did fine. And the day after that I had another good game. Before long, I had forgotten about the nightmare on the bases. I realized that if you screwed up, it was best to go on to the next game.

I improved. After that fiasco I couldn't help but get better. Once in a while I even showed up a manager or one of my own partners. For instance, one night I had the plate and noticed a batter step into the box who wasn't supposed to be there. He was batting out of order. Stupid rookies.

Just as I was getting ready to call the batter out for hitting out of order, I heard the scorekeeper yell down to her husband, who happened to be one of the managers.

"Woody, that's the wrong batter, honey," she said.

Too late. I called the guy out and quickly figured out who was supposed to be up next. Meanwhile, my partner, who didn't have a clue what the rule said, whispered, "Are you sure you're right?"

Hey, it was no big deal to me. I knew the rule. I called it. End of discussion.

As the season wound down, most everyone realized that I wasn't a human publicity stunt, that I was serious about the business. And by the end of that second year, the managers in the league gave me a little respect.

Well, almost all of them did.

The lone exception was Pedro Gonzales, who was manager of the Atlanta Braves rookie team. Gonzales was one of those damn Latin hotheads who thought he could scare me with his macho bullshit. Early on, he might have been able to. But after a while, I was ready for most of his tricks.

Then one day Gonzales did something I would never have expected. I was at first, and truth be known, I blew the call. It was a close play, but I probably missed it. Anyway, I looked up in time to see Gonzales sprint out of the dugout as if he were running the fifty-yard dash. The guy was fast. And mad. When he was about ten feet away, I could see his crazed face and also see that he wasn't trying to stop. A moment or two later, he barreled into me, almost knocking the wind out of my chest. I staggered backward, but somehow didn't fall. He hit me so hard that I thought my ribs were broken. After regaining my breath, I threw him out immediately, and MacDonald later fined and suspended him.

If Gonzales wanted me out of baseball, he was going to have to do a hell of a lot more than that. I wasn't going to budge an inch. Not for him. Not for anybody.

CHAPTER 4

The Promotion

Gonzales tried to knock me out of baseball, but Barney Deary, the executive director of Umpire Development, took a different approach in 1979. He tried to ease me out by killing me with kindness. Two different styles, but one purpose: make sure my career ended before it really had a chance to get started.

Deary showed up at MacDonald's annual preseason umpires meeting, which was held in Lakeland, headquarters for the Gulf Coast and Florida State leagues. This is where MacDonald, who loved to talk, would lecture us about league rules and policies and then assign us our partners for the upcoming season. We all sat at these big tables and wondered who would be paired with whom. Deary's presence just made everyone a little more nervous.

Deary was basically the king of minor league umpiring. He controlled the future of every umpire in that room. If he liked you or thought you had major league potential, you were golden with Deary. If not, you'd be out of baseball soon enough.

I didn't know Deary, but I had heard of him. I knew he was powerful and I knew he could make or break me. What I didn't know is that he thought I belonged anywhere but on a baseball diamond.

Luckily, MacDonald didn't agree. He had promoted me to the Florida State League, which was a Single A league known for its great ballparks and high quality of play. It was a strong league, one of the best at that level. After two years in the Gulf Coast and watching a lot of young, inept eighteen-year-old players go at it, I was ready for a move up. I wasn't the best umpire in the Gulf Coast, but I was as good as most of them. We all had our good games and we all had our dreadful ones. In fact, I think that's why MacDonald promoted me, because I had done no better or no worse than the rest of the umpires he had in the league. He could have fired me after the second season and said, "Well, I gave her a chance, but it just didn't work out," and nobody would have said a word. I don't even know if I would have disagreed with him.

But those two seasons in the Gulf Coast taught me a lot about umpiring and about myself. I was raw, but most days I could do the job. If nothing else, I was good enough to get another chance to fail. MacDonald thought the same thing.

The FSL used two-umpire crews. And unlike the Gulf Coast, FSL crews traveled up and down the state. For the first time, I'd have to deal with the driving, the motels, scanty per diems, a 144-game schedule, more interviews, and a full-time partner.

MacDonald was a little bit on the theatrical side sometimes. He used to like to keep everybody in suspense when it came to umpire pairings. One year we were sitting at the tables and he told everyone to turn to the right. We did, staring straight at the back of another umpire's head.

"Okay," said MacDonald, "that's your partner."

This time MacDonald was even more secretive. Near the end of the meeting he cleared his throat and said, "I need to ask the FSL umpires if any of you have any qualms about working with a woman."

So much for blending in. MacDonald, direct as always, was putting the issue up for discussion. Even though it made me feel uncomfortable, I guess I couldn't blame him for asking. After all, he had to make sure there wouldn't be any problems during the course of the season. If someone didn't think they could work with me, MacDonald wanted to know before the season started, not during it.

At first, no raised his hand. With me sitting right there, I can see why. They were probably scared. But then, a second-year FSL umpire named Tim Welke motioned to MacDonald. MacDonald immediately took Welke aside and they talked.

Turns out that Welke was worried about how his wife would react if MacDonald paired him with a woman umpire. Welke didn't have any problems with it, he said, but he wasn't so sure his wife would be as understanding.

"Well," said MacDonald, "why don't you call your wife and see how she feels. That way, just in case you and Pam ever have to work together, you'll know your wife's position on the matter."

So Welke called and his wife gave him the okay. He told MacDonald, who then told everyone to be seated.

"I'm now going to make your crew assignments," he said. "What I'd like you to do is look directly at the person sitting across the table from you. That person will be your partner."

I looked. It was Welke.

Welke and I talked for a few minutes and made plans for our first road trip. Meanwhile, I noticed Deary walking toward our table.

"Pam, could I talk with you a moment?" Deary said.

Welke took his cue and left, leaving me with the guy who could shape my career.

"Pam," he said, "I like you."

"Thank you, Mr. Deary."

"It's because I like you that I want you to know that if you want a job in baseball, you don't have to be an umpire. I can get you another job in baseball."

"I'm sorry, what did you say?"

"I can get you another job."

I stood there frozen, not knowing how to respond. All I could think of was, "Jeez, this guy must think I'm really bad. He's asking me not to umpire. He's telling me I don't have the ability to umpire."

I wasn't sure what sort of job he had in mind—secretary, probably—and I wasn't about to find out. I hadn't gone through umpire school and two seasons of shit in the Gulf Coast League to get sweet-talked by Deary. Job offer or no job offer, I decided to make a stand.

"Mr. Deary, I appreciate your asking, but no, I want to be an umpire. I think I can do it."

Deary didn't say much. He sort of nodded his head and rolled his eyes, as if he thought I had made a terrible mistake. Then he was gone.

I never regretted turning him down. A secretary? Me? No way. If I was going to bomb as an umpire, I wanted to do it on my terms, not his. If I stunk, let them fire me. But I wasn't going to give it up so I could sit behind a desk somewhere and wonder what if.

I had a few things going for me that season. First, there was MacDonald, who looked out for me. I wouldn't call it favoritism, but I think he appreciated what I was trying to do. He knew I worked hard and I think he was the kind of guy who liked to stick it to the baseball establishment once in a while. He had a little bit of power and he liked to use it. If that meant promoting me to the FSL, then he would do it. I guess he was like his old man in that regard.

MacDonald used to love giving advice. Some of the umpires hated the lectures, but I didn't mind. A lot of times, MacDonald made sense. For instance, he said we should always call the low ball a strike. That way the pitching coaches around the league would love you. Also, it was a good way to build a consistent strike zone.

He told us never to be afraid to tell a manager we blew a call. "If you admit you made a mistake," MacDonald said, "that manager can only say, 'Hey, then bear down out there.' If you don't admit the mistake, then you've usually got to eat a lot of crow."

And the one thing I'll never forget: no manager in the history of baseball has ever come on the field to congratulate an umpire on a call. He either comes out to exchange lineup cards, change pitchers, or argue a call. That's it.

The second thing I had in my favor was a better understanding of what the hell I was doing out there. I felt good behind the plate. The plate never moved, only the pitches did. Working the bases was a different story. Everything happened so fast. If you weren't in the right position and didn't have the correct angle, you were guessing on the call, simple as that. My problem was that I concentrated so hard on every play, I wasn't relaxed. Everything would sort of explode in front of me and I'd think, "Wow, what was that?" I had to learn to settle down, to quit being so tense.

The third thing was Welke. This was his second season in the league, so he knew where to stay, how to get there, which managers and players were red-asses and which ones would give you a break. He knew the ballparks and knew how to umpire, too. He saved me plenty of times that season.

Even then I knew Welke would eventually become a major league umpire. He was talented, and more importantly, he had been singled out as a phenom by Umpire Development. That's how it worked most of the time. You could have all the skill in the world, but if Umpire Development didn't give you its blessing, you could kiss your career good-bye. In Welke's case, the powers that be loved him and his work. And rightly so—the guy was damn good.

You could always tell when a guy had been given phenom status. The umpire supervisors would continually rave about him and keep bumping him up the minor league ladder. Then there were the borderline umpires, the ones who were jealous of the phenoms and were always kissing ass and buddying up to their league presidents or supervisors. Those guys were the worst. And finally there were the unphenoms: the guys whose careers started out fast and then fizzled out.

Kip Arnold became an unphenom. So did Steve Javie. One day they were hot umpire prospects, and then—poof—they were gone.

Arnold was a nice guy, but a little on the young side. Umpire Development loved him at first because he was a moose, a football-player type who had a real physical presence on the field. A few years later, he was released, and I'll never understand why. He was one of those umpires who you thought would zoom right to the top.

The same goes for Javie, who was easily the best young umpire I ever saw. This guy had everything: looks, style, talent, and attitude. He was a strong umpire who didn't take any shit from anybody. He was perfect, and I figured he would be in the big leagues within four years, maybe less. But just to show you what sort of politics are played behind the scenes, Javie never made it to the majors. In fact, it took him something like four years just to get out of Single A, which was a joke. Turns out that the bosses thought Javie was a little too perfect and suffered from an ego problem, which was completely untrue. They totally screwed this guy.

How good was Javie? Good enough that if my game was rained out in, say, West Palm Beach, that I'd make the drive down to Fort Lauderdale and watch Javie work a game. I liked the way he handled himself on the field, and I figured maybe I could learn something by studying his style. After all, I thought he was a cinch to be a big league umpire.

Unfortunately for Javie, Deary wasn't such a big fan. It also didn't help that things were a little bottled up in the minor league pecking order. So Javie waited for a break. And waited. And waited some more. Here was a great umpire, and Deary, for some petty reason, wouldn't bump him up. Javie quit baseball, but he didn't give up on the idea of staying in sports. Nowadays you can find Javie in the National Basketball Association. He's a referee and nothing gives me greater pleasure than seeing his name in those NBA box scores. Take that, baseball.

In the FSL, we got paid $300 a month in salary and received another $1,000 in expense money. That had to pay for everything: motels, food, gas, clubbies, clothes, and incidentals. Believe me, it didn't go far.

A new league meant new cities, which meant different newspapers, which meant the same old stories. I didn't want to be impolite, but I also didn't want to do many interviews. In fact, the fewer requests I got, the better I liked it. I was getting tired of reading headlines that said: "Female umpire will make history here tonight." I wasn't there to make history. I was there to call the game.

I'll say this for sportswriters: they're persistent. If I couldn't think of a decent enough reason to say no, I'd do the interview, but only if Welke was included in the story, too. Welke understood what I was trying to do. He knew I didn't enjoy the interviews or the attention. He also was honest, which I appreciated.

Out on the field, we were the only friends each other had. If I got in a jam, he was the only person who could bail me out. If he got challenged by a player or manager, then I had to make sure I was there to back him up if he needed me. That's the way it worked, especially with a two-umpire crew.

Welke wasn't above being a smart ass on occasion. We were in Fort Myers for a series and I was supposed to work the plate. Late that afternoon, one of those famous Florida thunderstorms came through and just about washed away the field. We waited to see if the grounds crew could do anything (they couldn't) and then postponed the game. We loved rainouts.

"Pam," said Welke afterward, "you didn't miss a pitch today."

"Yeah, I did have a perfect game, didn't I," I said, playing along. "Wish they were all like that."

Early on, Welke and I hardly heard a complaint from any of the managers or ballplayers. I think they were too consumed by this female umpire thing to notice if we were blowing any calls out there. And when they did watch, the postgame comments usually were favorable. The first time we worked a series in West Palm Beach, Expos manager Larry Bearnarth said that I was better than average. Bearnarth, who was nicknamed Bear, even took me aside after the game and gave me a quick critique.

"I thought you only missed one strike that might have made a difference in the game," he said.

"You know, you might be right," I said.

That probably shocked the hell out of him—an umpire admitting a mistake. Hey, I didn't do it just because I thought I might have missed the pitch. I did it because I remembered what MacDonald had said about eating crow. I also figured that if I was nice to him, maybe he'd leave Welke and me alone.

The plan worked for the rest of the series, but that was it. The next time we had the Expos, Bearnarth was all over us about a call. In fact, it seemed we always had a bunch of bangers (real close calls) with West Palm Beach. And each time, it seemed as if the calls always went against the Expos.

Bearnarth went ballistic on us during a July game with the Lakeland Tigers at West Palm Beach Municipal Stadium. The Expos were behind, 2–1, in the bottom of the seventh, but there was only one out in the inning and they had a runner, Steve Michael, on first. Bearnarth gave Michael the steal sign, so on the pitch Michael broke toward second. I moved into position, waited for the catch and the tag, and called him . . . out.

"I slid under the throw," Michael said as he jogged back to the dugout. "I beat the throw."

I ignored him. However, I couldn't ignore Bearnarth, who jumped all over my ass about the call. Bearnarth thought we had it in for his team and he said so. This wasn't exactly the same kind, undertanding manager I had met in April. This one was pissed.

His mood didn't improve when I dumped him. He didn't give me much of a choice. I didn't care if he questioned the call, but to accuse Welke and me of hating him and his team was ridiculous.

An inning later, Welke got into an argument with Expos starting pitcher Kevin Mendon. Mendon had given up three walks, as well as a hit an inning. So when the Expos pitching coach came out to pull him from the game, Mendon blamed it on Welke. Welke threw him out, which was kind of funny since Mendon was leaving anyway.

And then in the bottom of the inning, Expos shortstop Glen Franklin started ragging us about something. He got dumped, too. Two innings, three ejections.

Afterward, Bearnarth ripped us. We got to read about it in the newspaper the next day.

"Those are the two most vindictive umpires I have ever run across," he said. "I don't know what it is. They either don't like me or the team or something. But this happens every time we have them."

Then he got mean.

"They know this is as high as they are going to get in organized baseball. This is their last year and they know it. Next year they'll be doing something like collecting garbage."

If that wasn't enough, Bearnarth said there was "no possible way" that any crew could be as bad as Welke and me.

First of all, you could probably make more money as a

garbage worker than as an umpire, so that didn't hurt my feelings. Secondly, we didn't give a shit who won the game. As for that stuff about its being our final season in baseball, well, the last time I looked, Welke was a big league umpire and I should have been.

Bearnarth wasn't the only one who had his doubts about us. Some of the league's general managers, including Gene Lamont of the Fort Myers Royals, were worried that I couldn't take the traveling, the bad food, and the abuse for a 144-game season. "Everyone knows the male is stronger than the female," Lamont said.

Is that so? Sure, I got tired as the season went on. Everyone did. But damn if I was going to show it, not after hearing what Lamont said. In fact, the only two people who knew I was dragging a bit were Welke, who was dragging, too, and MacDonald. And the only reason MacDonald knew was because I was late filing an ejection report one time. We had worked a game in Miami and then driven all night to St. Petersburg. The last thing I wanted to do when I got there was write an ejection report. So I waited until the next day, which violated MacDonald's policy. Every ejection report had to be postmarked the day after the incident or you got fined. Sure enough, MacDonald fined me $5. Don't laugh. When you're making $300 a month in salary, $5 hurt. That was two less six-packs of beer.

A few weeks before the end of the season, I found myself in MacDonald's doghouse again. In fact, I almost got my ass fired.

We had just finished a series that included the worst-pitched game I'd ever seen, even worse than some of the Gulf Coast nightmares. Anyway, I had the plate for the final game, the night this one pitcher (I won't even mention his name, that's how awful he was) couldn't find the strike zone. He was all over the place, so I started balling him, calling every close pitch a ball. Every time I called a ball, he started rolling his eyes or stomping around on the mound. He was trying to show me up, which always pissed me off.

The more the pitcher showed me up, the more I started thinking back to umpire school. I remembered one of our instructors bragging to us about getting even with a batter who had complained about a call. He said he didn't dump the guy, but that he made life miserable for him every at bat. During one at bat, he called the guy out on a pitch that was six inches off the plate.

Well, I didn't want to dump this pitcher, but I had to do something. He was making me look bad. So on a 3-2 count, I balled the guy on a picture-perfect strike that split the plate. The pitcher almost jumped out of his skin, he was so mad. The catcher was furious, too.

"Pam, where was that pitch!" he snapped.

"I'll tell you where," I said. "Right down the cock!"

If I would have just kept my mouth shut, the guy would never have known. Those Single A players were so dumb, they thought an umpire could actually miss a pitch like that. If I could have just said, "It looked a little low," he would have bitched, but that would have been the end of it. Instead, the catcher complained to his manager, who complained to MacDonald.

A few days later, I got a message to come see MacDonald.

"I know what he wants," Welke said. "He wants you to work the playoffs."

Welke was just being nice. He knew I was in deep shit for my little stunt.

"Tim, I don't think so," I said.

MacDonald didn't waste much time when I got to his office. He told me to sit down and then started looking at a report, probably from an angry manager.

"Pam, on August tenth in Fort Lauderdale did you call a ball on an obvious strike?" he said. "I'm asking you this because I talked to the pitcher in question and he quoted you as saying, 'The pitch was right down the middle.' "

"No, Mr. MacDonald," I said. "What I told him was, 'It was right down the cock.' And it was. It was perfect. There was nothing wrong with the pitch and I called it a ball. But I was so mad at him for his arguing and fussing over every pitch, I didn't know what to do, Mr. MacDonald. I didn't want to eject him, but I was tired of watching him complain."

I had tears in my eyes by then. I thought MacDonald was going to fire me. He had a reputation for being a stickler for the rules.

"Well, Pam, you can't do that," he said. "Pam, I've got to have umpires with integrity." Then his voice softened. "You can't compromise your position like that."

He wasn't going to fire me. I was saved.

"You're right, Mr. MacDonald," I said. "I'll never do that again."

And I didn't, at least, not on purpose. The next time a pitcher showed me up, I dumped him.

Welke had a good season and mine wasn't bad. When 1980 rolled around, he moved up and I stayed put. Again, I wasn't upset about the assignment. I needed some more experience and figured there were worse leagues to be in than the FSL. MacDonald was doing me a favor by keeping me in Florida.

My new partner was Steve Temple. He was a real cowboy type, what with the boots and hat and country-western music. That's all the guy ever listened to. Still, we got along great, but his girlfriend, I later found out, was extremely jealous of the pairing. She couldn't stand the idea of Temple and me working together. Drove her up the wall, but hey, that was her problem. I was a professional and so was Temple. I wasn't out to break up any relationships. I was there to do what Welke had done: get promoted.

And that's what I did. MacDonald wanted to see improvement on the bases, so I worked on getting in better position for a call. MacDonald wanted a more consistent strike zone, so I gave him one. MacDonald wanted to see how I continued to handle situations, so I showed him.

To MacDonald, handling game situations was probably the most important part of the game. He always said that you could teach someone the strike zone, but you couldn't teach them common sense and grace under pressure. Umpires are always under pressure, but in my case, it seemed as if the demands on me were double that of any other umpire. In fact, MacDonald once said that if I ever expected to make it to the big leagues, I had to be 200 percent better than a male umpire. Those were the kind of expectations I had to put up with.

I handled all sorts of situations that season, the most difficult ones usually taking place in Miami. Remember how I said the FSL was known for its great ballparks? Well, that's true, except for one city: Miami. Without a doubt, Miami Stadium was the worst stop in the league. The place was about a hundred years old, or maybe it just seemed that way. Worse yet, it was located in a very nasty part of town.

One night we were working a game there and somebody got shot in the stands. According to the cops, a guy got pissed off at his "friend," pulled a gun, and blew a hole in his arm. That's the way it was in Miami Stadium. Fights were always breaking out in the stands, and it wasn't surprising to turn around between innings and see an arrest being made. I never felt safe at that place. I walked out one night and found that someone had broken into my MG convertible and stolen the *pennies* off my dashboard. Nothing else, just the pennies.

In late June we were back in Miami for more danger. Don't ask me how it happened in the middle of summer, but I had somehow caught a terrible cold. I felt miserable and my condition didn't improve when rain forced an hour delay and extra innings kept us there past midnight. By the time we took turns in the shower, got dressed, and headed to the parking lot, it was almost one A.M. We had a doubleheader in St. Petersburg, which meant we'd have to pull an all-night drive in Temple's pickup truck.

When we got out to his truck, someone had busted in and taken more than pennies. This time the thief took all of Temple's beloved country-western tapes. It made for an awfully quiet drive up north. To add to our misery, it rained again, which meant we had to pull over and throw a tarp over our luggage before it got soaked. Nothing like traveling in class, eh?

Four seasons earlier, MacDonald had said that he didn't know if I'd make it through the first week of the Gulf Coast League. Well, there I was, still standing after two years of rookie league and two years of Single A ball. The way I looked at it, I hadn't proved MacDonald wrong; I had proved myself right.

When the season ended, MacDonald recommended to Deary that I be bumped up to Double A. Good ol' MacDonald. And surprise—good ol' Deary, too. He approved the promotion.

CHAPTER 5

The Texas League

The month was December. The year was 1980. The news was this: I had been promoted to Double A, to the Texas League. I was one of only twenty-nine minor league umpires who got bumped up and one of only sixteen to make the jump from Single A to Double A. I suppose I should add that I became the first woman umpire ever to advance that far. It was a nice distinction, but I didn't go around patting myself on the back.

When I first went to Al Somers's school, I thought, "Okay, if I can just make it out of here, I'll be happy." Then I graduated from there and got the job in the Gulf Coast League. That's when I started saying, "This is great, but if I could just get a job in Single A, I'd be happy." So what happened? I got the position, but I found myself wanting more. "Okay, all I need now is a Double A spot and this time, I swear, I'll be happy," I said to myself.

And now I had it. By midseason, I'd want to give it back.

How do you begin a nightmare? I should probably start with the phone call I received from Barney Deary shortly after I got my big promotion. I was living in Las Vegas and working two jobs to help pay the bills. The first job was working for United Parcel Service. Basically I just walked in off the street and told the manager of the place that I wanted to work for him. I didn't know anything about the delivery business, but I knew how to drive a clutch—so how hard could it be, right?

The personnel manager didn't quite know what to think of me. But he needed drivers, so he hired me on the spot and gave me a crash course on the art of delivering packages. In a few days I was tooling around town in one of those U-Haul–sized brown monsters, grinding the gears and missing delivery time after delivery time. I had to be the single worst UPS employee of all time. I worked hard, but I was sooooo sloooow. That was partly because I did such things as throwing a package on a roof once. I didn't do it on purpose, of course. The box just sort of slipped out of my hand. I must have spent the next half hour figuring out a way to climb a nearby fence, get on top of the roof, and retrieve that stupid package.

I also had a slight problem with maps. The problem was, I couldn't read them. At least, not at first. However, on my last day of work there, I actually completed my route when I was supposed to.

"Pam," said my boss, "I can't believe it. Here it is your final day and you beat your time. Congratulations."

I didn't have the guts to ask him if he'd hire me the next off-season. It wouldn't have been good timing.

But it was the second job that caught the attention of Deary and caused him to call with an ultimatum: quit the job or quit baseball.

This horrible job? I was a change girl at Lady Luck Casino.

If you've ever been to Las Vegas, you've seen these people. Hell, they even work at the airport, where there are slot machines set up in the terminals. All a change girl does is walk around with one of those big metal machines strapped to her waist and trade coins for cash. Because I was honest and had half a brain, I was later moved to the cashier's cage, where most days I'd handle about $30,000. They loved me at that casino. I handled all that money, and at the end of my shift, the ledger would never be off by more than a penny or two.

Of course, this was about the same time that Commissioner Bowie Kuhn decided to crack down on any possible connections between baseball and gambling. You remember how he came down hard on Mickey Mantle and Willie Mays—banned them from baseball until they disassociated themselves with some casinos? Well, now they had worked their way down to the little people like me, who were struggling to get by on two measly salaries.

Hell, one of the reasons I moved to Las Vegas in the first place was because it was cheap. You could drive down to the strip and get a prime rib dinner for practically nothing. Everything was open all night. Rent was reasonable. I loved the city, especially after I learned not to walk through the casino after cashing my paycheck. Too many times I stopped at the blackjack tables and lost my grocery money.

The other interesting thing about Las Vegas was the people. The ones I worked with always seemed to be running from something. They all had these strange stories and dreams of striking it rich. I guess I wasn't much different. My story must have sounded odd, too: small-town Ohio woman goes to umpire school and hopes to make it to the major leagues. Of course, that dream was in jeopardy the minute I picked up the phone and heard Deary's voice on the other end.

"Pam," he said, "we might have a problem."

"What would that be, Mr. Deary?"

"Well, I understand that you're working for a casino."

"That's right, Mr. Deary. I make change."

"Well, you can't work there. If you do, you can't work in baseball."

It wouldn't have helped to argue. There was no way Deary was going to change his mind. In fact, I'm not even sure it was Deary's idea to call. Whomever's idea it was, it sucked. It wasn't as if I were gambling for a living. Or dealing blackjack. I was just working in the cage trying to survive. I was a lowly minor league umpire heading to Double A. Now I had to quit.

It was hard to get too mad at Deary, though. After all, he was the guy who had to get someone to take me in Double A. That couldn't have been too easy a task. Back then, there were only about three Double A leagues, including the Southern League, located smack-dab in the middle of the Bible Belt and probably not too keen about a woman umpire working there.

Deary eventually convinced Carl Sawatski, president of the Texas League, that I was worth the trouble. So Sawatski, after checking with MacDonald first, signed me and six other new umpires. When reporters asked him about the decision, Sawatski told them that I came highly recommended. And then he added: "I will help her in every possible manner, but once she crosses the lines, she's on her own."

Recommendations didn't do much for my earning power. My monthly salary and per diem totaled $1,100. We also got paid twenty cents a mile when we used our cars for road trips, which was only all the time. I never realized how big Texas was until I started driving to San Antonio, Midland, El Paso, and Amarillo. If that wasn't bad enough, the other cities were Shreveport, Louisiana; Jackson, Mississippi; Little Rock, Arkansas; and Tulsa, Oklahoma. It was a miracle that any car could last a season in that league. Come to think of it, it was a miracle that *I* lasted the 136-game season in that league.

Whether he knew it or not, Sawatski assigned me to the most eccentric and just plain weird partner I've ever had: the one, the only Larry Dagate. It was Dagate's first year in the Texas League, and like me, he was just trying to survive. That's all you ever did in Single A and Double A, just try to survive.

Dagate didn't fit the usual profile for an umpire. Then again, neither did I. But at least I had played sports as a kid. Dagate didn't have an athletic bone in his body. He did have a beer gut, though, developed over a long period of time by drinking countless Dixie beers. He loved Dixie beer, and I don't think I remember him drinking anything else but his beloved Louisiana brew. That's another thing: Dagate was from Louisiana. He had a Cajun accent and a lifestyle that bordered on the bizarre.

Let me ask you: What kind of person studies at the Massachusetts Institute of Technology, almost completes law school at Louisiana State University, and then decides to become an umpire? I bet his parents were ready to slit their wrists. But the guy loved umpiring. As best as I could tell, it was about the only thing he loved.

Dagate's goal in life was to make other people miserable. Only then could he be happy. On our first road trip, Dagate was driving his 1969 Toyota and I was trying to find a radio station to listen to. At last I came across a decent song that didn't feature Conway Twitty's gawd-awful voice.

"Good song, eh, Larry?" I said.

Dagate didn't say a word. He just leaned over and flicked off the switch.

"Larry, why'd you do that?"

Nothing. Not a word. I turned the radio on again, found another station, and started humming along to the song. Dagate looked at me, then flicked off the knob.

Dagate went out of his way to upset people, especially me. It made his day to really piss me off, which he did often. So I fought back. While living in Las Vegas, I had made friends with a weight lifter named Joe Louis. Louis got me interested in weight training, and before long, I went out and bought a small set of barbells. I worked out hard with those weights and I didn't want to stop once baseball season arrived. I lugged them down to Texas and then asked Dagate, whose car we used most of the time, if I could put "a couple" of weights in his trunk. He wasn't too pleased when he noticed he was getting about two miles to the gallon, thanks, in part, to the barbell set weighing down his car. He made me get rid of them about a month or two later.

Once we checked into our hotel rooms for a four-day series, Dagate would disappear behind his door until a few hours before game time. I asked once what he did all day. Turns out that he read calculus books and newspapers. How do you read a calculus book? Hell, I guess if you went to MIT, you can read anything.

If you walked into Dagate's room, you entered at your own risk. Newspapers were everywhere. So were Dixie beer cans. Dagate also had his own very personal method of laundry cleaning. At the beginning of a long road trip, Dagate would do his wash. Then, as the trip grew longer, he would start putting his dirty clothes in a pile. When he was all out of clean clothes, he would start picking clothes off the bottom of the dirty pile and wear them again. When that pile was finished, he started another pile of extradirty clothes. When the smell got too bad, Dagate would break down and haul his stuff to the laundromat. He was the biggest slob I had ever met. In fact, his record for disgusting habits is one that might never be broken. That's how bad he was.

Oddly enough, we got along okay. We weren't pals or anything, but beneath his goofy attitude and stinky clothes, Dagate was a decent guy. He didn't do much to help me that season, but I didn't exactly go out of my way to save his ass, either. He had his problems and I had mine.

As miserable a man as Dagate was, I went out of my way to try to make the season tolerable. I always figured it was my job to get along with my partner. I didn't want to be a thorn in anyone's side, and I certainly didn't want them to say, "Jeez, I had to work with the woman this year." So when it was time to buy beers after a game, I paid for more than my share. Or if Dagate wanted to do something other than read calculus books, which wasn't often, I made sure that I said yes.

Of course, we didn't go out on the town too often. That's because there wasn't much to the towns we visited. Ever try to have a good time in Amarillo? It's almost impossible. Also, we were too poor to afford a good meal. Dagate and I used to visit bars at happy hour so we could load up on the free hors d'oeuvres. We probably ate hundreds of those tiny hot dogs on toothpicks.

Despite being forced to quit my job at the casino and then getting paired with Dagate, I actually looked forward to the season. I was so excited that I even went to see an eye doctor just to make sure everything was fine. I didn't want to miss a play that year. If I had a great year—who knows?—maybe I'd get a Triple A assignment the next season.

For a while there, I thought they might bump me up before the All-Star break. I was getting all sorts of compliments—some embarrassing, some welcome—from unexpected sources. The embarrassing one came during an exhibition game between the Arkansas Travelers and their parent club, the St. Louis Cardinals. The Cardinals were taking the field in the bottom of the first inning when first baseman Keith Hernandez winked at me and said, "You're kind of cute."

I smiled back, but the whole time I was thinking, "What a stupid thing to say." What did he think I was there for: to umpire or to look for a date?

About a week later, we had a series with the El Paso Diablos, who were managed by Texas League rookie Tony Muser. Muser was so impressed with my work that he went out of his way to tell the local sportswriters. At last, I thought, an ally.

A few weeks later, the ally became my worst enemy. After I made a few calls against his team, Muser declared war on me. By the end of the season, I was booed regularly in El Paso. In fact, I think they still hate me in that town. Fuck 'em, that's what I say. They should have been booing Muser; he was the one who didn't know what he was doing out there.

I can't stand front-runners and Muser was the biggest front-runner of them all. He liked me at the beginning because I made a couple of calls in his favor. Then, when a couple calls went against him, he went nuts. Muser didn't realize that I didn't give a shit who won or lost. I wasn't out to screw his team. Problem was, he wasn't paying close enough attention to figure that out.

I was already on the edgy side by the end of May, which is when Dagate and I hooked up with Muser's El Paso team again. My mood didn't improve when Arkansas manager Gaylen Pitts and I got into an argument over a called third strike. With Muser watching from the other dugout, Pitts told me that as long as his players didn't cuss at me, they could say whatever they wanted. I told him to get back to the dugout. As he walked away, he said, "If you can't take the fucking heat, then get out of the kitchen."

"I can take the heat!" I yelled.

Pitts returned to the dugout, but he couldn't keep his mouth shut.

"Bear down out there!" he said.

"You're gone!" I said. I had heard enough. First the stuff about the kitchen and then the crap about bearing down. The last line was all it took to push me over the edge.

Pitts bolted out of the dugout. "That's the most horseshit thing I've ever seen, waiting until I got to the dugout to throw me out!"

"Hey, you waited to cheap-shot me when you got to the dugout and I'm not putting up with it."

Two nights later, things really started popping. In the top of the second inning, with Jackson runners on every base, no outs, and the count 3-2, Dagate, who had the plate, stopped the game to warn Muser to quit arguing balls and strikes. Meanwhile, El Paso pitcher Rich Kranitz started yelling at Dagate.

"You cocksucker, call the fucking pitches!" he said.

Dagate was too busy talking to Muser to hear Kranitz,

but I wasn't. I stepped in and immediately ejected the Diablos pitcher, which caused Muser to throw a fit for the ages. His nose was almost touching my cheek as he started to yell and spray my face, shirt, and arms with bits of tobacco and juice. I backed up, but he kept stepping on my foot, as if he were trying to keep me from moving away. The juice stung so bad that I finally shut my eyes and yelled back. I didn't have any choice.

"You're through, too, for getting tobacco all over me!" I said.

"Just tell me what my pitcher said! What did he say that got him dumped?" Muser said.

"Calm down and then I'll tell you. But first get all your players away from me. I'm not telling you a thing with all of them here."

Muser ordered them away. "Well?" he said.

"Your pitcher called my partner a cocksucker."

"Shit, you just can't throw out somebody every time they cuss. These guys cuss out here all the time. You're going to have to get out of the kitchen if you can't take the heat."

There it was, that fucking kitchen thing again.

"Listen," I said, "I don't care if they cuss out here and cuss at themselves. But when they cuss at me or my partner, I'm not putting up with it. And when they cuss my partner, they're cussing me, too."

The next day I bought a newspaper, and there on the front page of the sports section was a photograph of Muser and me. Sure enough, my eyes are closed, but I was still battling away. I did a lot of that in 1981. Too much. I wrote so many ejection reports to Sawatski that I almost got writer's cramp.

Reports No. 14 and 15 (I had reached double digits by mid-June) involved Steve Sax and San Antonio Dodgers manager Ducky LeJohn. I called Sax out on the tail end of a double play, and he whirled around and screamed, loud enough for anyone to hear in the stadium, "You're crazy! You're brutal!"

"Yeah," I said, "well, you're out of here!"

"You're an ass! You're crazy as an ass!"

Moments later, LeJohn was out there asking, "What did he say? Did he swear at you?"

"No, he said that I was crazy and brutal and that's why I threw him out."

"You can't throw him out for that."

"It was personal and I'm not putting up with it."

"You belong in the kitchen," LeJohn said. "You don't belong here. Go be a cook. You probably can't cook and that's why you're here."

That's when I dumped LeJohn.

"What did you throw me out for?" he said.

"For telling me to get in the kitchen and that I should go be a cook."

"That's it. I'm calling Carl tomorrow and I'm telling him exactly how terrible you are. And I mean terrible. And I'm going to read the ejection reports."

I just walked away. Later in the season, when LeJohn made the same threats about calling Sawatski, I was ready for him.

"You're gonna call Carl?" I said. "Here, let me give you a dime. And don't forget to spell my name right."

After the first LeJohn incident, I actually went four nights without dumping another player. But the lull didn't last long. A few evenings later, while I was working the plate in a game between El Paso and Midland, Stan Davis of the Diablos got pissed off at me after he took a called strike.

"That was outside," he said.

Davis swung at and missed the next pitch. Before he left, he said, "You suck. You fucking suck."

"You're fucking gone," I said.

Now he was really pissed. He tossed his helmet at me

and I had to dodge the throw. Then Muser came down from the third-base coaching box and drew a line in the dirt with his cleats. The line was about six inches outside the plate. He looked at me and then walked back to the coaching box. The asshole.

News of my ongoing battles with Muser reached Umpire Development. It also wasn't any big secret that I was on some sort of record pace for ejections. And when I wasn't dumping somebody, Dagate was. Hardly a game went by that we didn't have to defend ourselves.

I threw out El Paso's John Skorochocki, and Muser didn't do a thing. He stood there and let Skorochocki argue forever.

"You're fucking horseshit!" Skorochocki said. "You're going to fucking die in this league! You're no fucking good! You fucking are the worst! You fucking don't belong here!"

On and on it went until Skorochocki finally exhausted himself. As he headed toward the dugout steps, I glanced over to make sure Skorochocki kept walking to the clubhouse. That's when Muser, who was coaching third base, yelled, "Quit looking over there and get the game going."

"If you would've controlled your players and got him out of here, we wouldn't have to wait."

Muser turned his back on me.

I dumped just about everyone that year. Managers. Ballplayers. Coaches. I threw out Jackson Mets manager Davey Johnson when he said we blew a player interference call. Three innings later, I ejected one of his coaches, Junior Roman, for arguing too long about a failed steal attempt. Roman got so mad that he picked up third base and carried it back to the dugout.

Afterward, Johnson blasted Dagate and me, calling us "totally incompetent." He said I made so many bad calls that I was in a class by myself. He was just mad because Jackson had lost two one-run games in a row.

I even dumped a trainer that year. The guy's name was Charlie Strasser. He's with the Los Angeles Dodgers now, but back then, he was nothing but an ankle taper for San Antonio.

I had just walked to the Dodgers dugout to warn LeJohn about arguing pitches when Strasser said, "Get your head out of the dugout."

I said, "I'll put my head in the dugout anytime I want, and the next time I have to, you won't be in here."

You should have heard the howls of laughter. Strasser got pissed and yelled something back at me. I didn't hear what he said, but I dumped him anyway. When LeJohn asked what Strasser had said, I told him, "I don't have to tell you."

"Yeah, well, I'm calling Carl tomorrow morning, baby," he said.

Here we go again. LeJohn was always calling Carl. Let him call. I was so tired of the fucking arguing that I almost volunteered to pay for the phone calls.

My confidence was at a new low. So was my morale. Every game it was cowboys and Indians out there. The bitching usually started by the second or third pitch and didn't end until we walked into the dressing room two or three hours later. Sometimes it didn't end there. I dumped El Paso shortstop Willie Lozado, and after the game he was standing outside the dressing room.

"Hi, Pam," he said. "You're bad. You are terrible. You're no good."

Dagate and I couldn't catch a break. Things got so bad that even the stadium public address announcer in Tulsa thought it would be funny to hassle us. It happened when Dagate, who was our crew chief of sorts, made a call against the home team one night. The next thing we heard was some stupid recording of Howard Cosell saying, "A pure and simple disgrace."

I looked at Dagate in time to see him walking off the field. He motioned for me to join him.

"Uh, Larry, where are you going?" I said. "We're in the middle of an inning."

"Unless they promise not to play that recording ever again, we're going to the dressing room," Dagate said. "I'm not going to listen to that shit."

Dagate was steamed. He contacted the announcer up in the press box and threatened to leave unless the Cosell tape was put away. The announcer didn't like it, but he quit playing the tape. After that, I had a little more respect for Dagate. I still didn't think he was a great umpire, but I admired him for taking a stand and not backing down.

Another time we were in San Antonio and some asshole in the crowd started yelling, "Kiss the umpire! Kiss the umpire!" Soon the whole crowd was yelling it. The fans were so loud that you couldn't even hear the stadium announcer. I was so pissed I wanted to punch the fan in the mouth. That was the same night someone threw a beer can at us from the stands.

Alarmed by the number of ejections I was sending in, Umpire Development sent Dick Nelson, one of their supervisors and an instructor at Somers's school, to check on me. What he found was an umpire about ready to quit and move back to Ohio. That's how depressed I was.

One time Dagate and I walked out to home plate for the exchange of the lineup cards. Sitting on the plate was a frying pan with a note attached.

"You know what to do with it. Signed, Billy Martin Fan Club."

What I wanted to do with it was smash the face of whoever put the fucking thing there in the first place. Since that was out of the question, I had the pan removed by one of the batboys.

In the bottom of the eighth inning, with El Paso (who else?) trailing, 9–4, I called Stan Davis out at first base on a banger. That's when someone yelled from the dugout: "You guys have been sticking it up our ass all year! You've

been shoving it up our ass so bad that we need Preparation
H!"

"I've heard enough!" I said. "I don't want to hear anymore!"

Muser stood up. "Shut up!" he said. "Shut up, leave those
guys alone, and get your head out of the dugout!"

As usual, I had to dump him, which only made things
worse.

"You're no fucking good!" he said. "You just run people
all the time and you've got no reason to! You've been
sticking it to us all season!"

Dagate tried to calm Muser down. Fat chance.

"She can't throw me out!" he said.

"Well, she just did," Dagate said.

Muser started kicking dirt on my shoes. He did it three
times, once kicking my foot in the process. Meanwhile,
some of the players threw towels, gloves, baseballs, and
even the frying pan out onto the field. It was, quite simply,
a disaster.

That's when I decided to quit. I woke up one morning,
sat up in bed, and thought, "There's no way they're going
to let me umpire. There's no way I'll make it to the major
leagues because they won't let me do my job. This is the
day of reckoning."

I couldn't take it anymore. Muser and the rest of those
assholes had broken me. At that point, I didn't know if I
was a good umpire or a horseshit umpire. You listen to
the Musers of the world long enough and you start believing them a little. Or in my case, a lot.

I sure as hell knew I wasn't a rich umpire. In the August
edition of *Inside Sports* magazine, the salaries of seventy-
two sports figures and sports-related employees were
listed. I made $6,500, which was less than what the chauf-
feur for Los Angeles Lakers owner Dr. Jerry Buss made.
It was less per game than a Minnesota Twins batboy, and
a lot less than Millie's Special, a greyhound racing dog.

I was serious about quitting and Nelson knew it. He even called one of my friends and had her try to talk me out of it. When that didn't work, Nelson tried building up my ego. He told me I had the tools to make it to the big leagues and that there were always going to be assholes like Muser in every league. He said to use the bad experiences to my advantage, to learn from them.

I wasn't convinced until I did a game a few nights later. Wouldn't you know it—El Paso was one of the teams. I was on the bases and the Diablos were on defense. With a runner on second, a line drive was hit near the shortstop, who made a diving catch, turned, and quickly threw to second to double up the runner. I was in perfect position when the throw came in. The play was close, but the runner got back in the nick of time. I would have staked an entire paycheck on the safe call.

Muser disagreed. Muser disagreed with anything I did. As he yelled at me, I got this kind of peaceful feeling. That's when I realized that it didn't really matter what Muser thought. Whether I made the right call or not, none of those assholes was going to let me umpire without a fight. I had made the correct calls, so fuck 'em. I decided I didn't care if they yelled at me for the rest of my career. I only knew that I wasn't going to give them the satisfaction of forcing me to quit.

From that point on, I realized I only had to satisfy myself. Not Muser. Not LeJohn. Not Sawatski. Not Deary or any- one else. I wasn't the one with the problem—I could um- pire—it was Muser and the rest of them who couldn't stand seeing me on the field. If I couldn't take it, then I should get out. But, dammit, I *could* take it.

Before it was over, I think I finished the season with twenty-eight ejections, and I don't apologize for one of them. I should have thrown out more of the assholes.

Sawatski didn't seem too upset by the ejections, either. The same went for Umpire Development, which assigned me some winter-league ball games in Phoenix during the off-season. Since I couldn't work at the casino anymore, I packed my things and moved to Arizona. I would make a new start.

So what happened? Well, before I umpired my first winter-league game, Nelson called. He told me to be on the lookout for a winter-ball manager named Ed Nottle. According to Nelson, Nottle planned to introduce himself to me at home plate with two baseballs stuffed under his jersey. Nottle didn't think any woman should be an umpire, so that was going to be his way of getting the point across.

"Nottle is going to be a handful," Nelson warned. "When he comes to home plate, wait until he gives you the lineup card and then say, 'Your humor underwhelms me.' And then eject him."

I was all set to follow Nelson's advice, except that Nottle never followed through with his plan. When he handed me the lineup card, he didn't say much at all. I had the plate that night, and as usual, I hustled my ass off. Nottle must have been impressed because after that game, he was one of my biggest fans. He said I did a great job. I think he respected me because I worked hard out there. After that, he just let me umpire. That was my whole philosophy. If people just gave me a chance to do my job, they usually saw that I was as good or better than the other umpires. The trick was getting that chance.

Compared to the previous season, 1982 was a breeze. My partner was Gary Darling, a decent guy and a pretty good umpire, who, thank goodness, didn't read calculus books for fun. The most interesting thing about Darling was a childhood accident that almost cost him the use of one of his arms. When he was a kid, he and a few friends climbed a power pole and got a severe shock. The shock caused his arm to bend a certain way, which, when you think about it, wasn't so bad. After all, said Darling, he was lucky to still be alive.

Of course, we did have a few tense moments that season. On our first road trip, Darling asked if I wanted to drive for a little while. It was late and he needed some sleep. So did I, but I didn't tell him that as I got behind the steering wheel of his green, foreign pickup truck.

About an hour later, I could barely keep my eyes open. I didn't want to wake up Darling, so I kept driving. It was useless. My eyelids slowly came down until the next thing I knew, we were headed off the road and into the high grass.

I snapped awake and steered us to the side of the highway.

"Jesus," Darling said, "did you fall asleep?"

"Yeah, but don't worry. I always wake up in time," I said, smiling.

Darling never let me drive his truck again. It didn't matter if we went from El Paso to San Antonio, which is a 570-mile trip—my driving days were over as far as he was concerned.

"Gary, pleeease let me drive," I'd say on those long road trips.

"No, no," he'd say politely. "I don't mind."

I must have done something right that season. My ejections went down and my ratings went up. In fact, I don't think there was a better umpire behind the plate in that league in 1982. I wasn't the only one who thought so. Arkansas general manager Bill Valentine, a former American League umpire, said I was the best they had. Of course, I still had my bad days, everyone did. But I also had a lot more good days.

Without a doubt, the best day came not long after the season ended. That's when Bill Cutler, president of the Pacific Coast League . . . a Triple A league, rescued me from Texas. From redneck fans. From happy-hour dinners and ten-hour drives.

PCL, here I come.

CHAPTER 6

The Political Coast League

The list of believers grew by one in 1983, my first season in the Pacific Coast League. Guess who it was. None other than Al Somers, my gruff, old umpire-school teacher.

Somers sent me a newspaper clipping and attached a note to it.

> Congratulations to you for your success in reaching Triple AAA ball. I hope that you will reach your goal to the Major Leagues soon. Work hard, study your rule book daily, and try to improve your umpiring daily. Hustle all the time and be an aggressive umpire. You are now preparing yourself for the Major Leagues and I am in your corner all the time. Drop me a line now and then and let me know how you are doing.
>
> Sincerest wishes to you.
> Al Somers

I was so happy with my promotion to the PCL that I didn't need to write Somers; I could have shouted the news back to Daytona Beach. In six seasons' time I had made the most crucial jump in the minor leagues and had landed exactly where I wanted—in umpire paradise.

The PCL was considered a plum assignment for lots of reasons, beginning with the travel schedule, which included stops in Honolulu, Las Vegas, Phoenix, Vancouver, Portland, Tacoma, Edmonton, Salt Lake City, Albuquerque, and Tucson. Ten cities and not a bad stop in the bunch. Also, my salary zoomed, from $1,400 during my final year in the miserable Texas League to about $1,900 a month in the PCL. Better yet, Bill Cutler, the president of the league, had somehow cut a deal with the various team hotels that would save me loads of money. In Triple A, you had three-person crews as opposed to the two-person crews of Single A and Double A. Rather than have to pay for three rooms out of your own pockets, Cutler convinced the team hotels to provide two complimentary rooms. The cost of the third room would be split by the three umpires. That left more money for shopping, food, and drinks.

The PCL was known as the country club of the minors. It had the best cities, the best perks, the most opportunities for fun. But there was a downside. For all of its advantages, the PCL was considered the worst place to try to earn a big league job. That was because very few umpire supervisors liked to travel that far west to evaluate candidates. The supervisors mostly preferred the East Coast, the South, the Midwest. The PCL was considered almost a distant land.

I didn't care. I wasn't planning on a big league invitation until, say, 1985. After all, I still had to learn the intricacies of a three-person crew, get used to a higher quality of play, and endure a whole new set of asshole players, managers, and sometimes, umpires. This was going to be my get-acquainted year, the year I started to establish myself. The big leagues could wait. For the moment.

It turned out to be my survival season, and for a while I didn't think I was going to make it. Somehow, word of my ejection record in the Texas League spread like wildfire in the PCL. Cutler knew about it, of course. He had to; he was the one who had purchased my contract from the Texas League. During one of our first meetings, I asked him if I could get a few umpire report forms. He brought back a stack that must have been an inch thick. "Here, take these," he said. I guess he figured I'd be doing a lot of ejection notices my rookie season. He was right.

Despite its reputation as the laid-back league, the PCL had plenty of great players, all of them in the same situation as me: a heartbeat away from the big leagues. Tension ran high. So did the talent. The fastballs were faster. The curves curved more. The sliders dove for cover when they got near the plate. The hitters were better, too. Most of them were more selective, which put more pressure on the plate umpire to make the right call. And if you didn't, you heard about it.

As you might expect, the umpiring was a cut above the usual Texas League stuff. If you didn't have big league potential, you never saw the light of Triple A ball. In the PCL, every umpire did something well. I had a good eye behind the plate, but some guys were great on the bases while others were perfect on the rules or handling situations or controlling a game.

My season began in Portland, and after the first few games, I wasn't sure if I belonged anywhere near the PCL. I'm sure my partners, Dana DeMuth and John Higgins, were thinking the same thing. I was brutal.

I knew I was in trouble from the very beginning of my first plate job. The Portland pitcher kept making these bastard pitches that were always an inch or two inside. He was making me look terrible back there. The next thing I knew, the catcher started getting on my ass. "Where the hell was that one?" he'd snipe after another close pitch went against his guy. Then I started hearing shit from the dugout. From where they were sitting, each of those pitches looked like cockshots down the middle. And it wasn't as if you could turn around and explain that their pitcher was missing by an inch or so. If this had happened in the Texas League, the catcher would have told his manager that, yes, the pitches were close, but that I was being consistent with my calls. But that day in Portland, the catcher didn't do a thing. I didn't expect him to. He didn't know me or trust me. Anyway, when you're a rookie, you expect no favors.

By the end of the game, my confidence was shot. I had been tested on every pitch and had failed miserably. One plate job into the season and I was already doubting myself.

About the only thing in my favor was that I knew DeMuth and Higgins from way back when. Higgins, of course, had been a partner of mine in the Gulf Coast League. And DeMuth I knew from Somers's umpire school. They were good guys, but they didn't go out of their way to help me, which would explain why I later heard that they blasted me to other umpires. It never hurt my feelings if a partner didn't try to make me a better umpire. We were in competition for the same big league jobs, so I didn't expect any preferential treatment. I didn't want any, either. All I asked was that they work with me, not against me. DeMuth and Higgins always did that, at least.

Boy, could they party. I never knew how much a person could drink until I met those guys. I partied with them, figuring that if I acted like one of the boys, maybe they'd cut me a break on the field. It worked, but I just about ruined my liver that season.

I also tried to involve them in the never-ending requests for interviews. When the people from ABC called, asking if I'd appear on "Good Morning America," I told them I'd do the show only if they took care of my partners, too. True to their word, the ABC people arranged for a limousine to take us from Tacoma, where our series concluded, to nearby Seattle for the studio appearance. They paid for our rooms at some ritzy downtown hotel, then flew us out the next day to our next series. I was impressed and I think DeMuth and Higgins were, too.

DeMuth was a good umpire. He had style. Higgins wasn't

as talented, but he had his moments. So did I, but none of them very satisfying during those first few weeks. The change from a two-person to three-person crew was more confusing than I'd expected. The whole system was like learning a playbook. You had to know where to station yourself in certain situations. For instance, if there were runners on first and third and the ball was lofted toward the left-field line, well, that meant the third-base umpire had to go out on the ball. Okay, now let's say the ball landed fair and the runner on third scored and the runner on first rounded second base and headed toward third. The home-plate umpire had to move toward third, too, in case there was a play there. Meanwhile, the first-base umpire had to sprint to home plate, to cover the possibility of a scoring play. If one umpire botched his assignment, then it was cowboys and Indians.

It also didn't take long for me to make my share of enemies. Early on, Salt Lake City slugger Ken Phelps, who has since bounced around the majors, decided he didn't like my style of calling balls and strikes. The feud started when I called him on three inside pitches that just nipped the corner. I loved calling that pitch, but Phelps was so pissed he wanted to break the bat over my skull. He stormed back to the dugout and started yelling, but I couldn't quite understand what he was saying. To me, it sounded like some sort of guttural sound.

During his next at bat, Phelps glared at me and then settled into the box. The pitcher tried working the same inside corner, but this time his control wasn't as precise. Four pitches later, Phelps was standing on first base with a walk. Afterward, someone told me that Phelps was gloating about the base on balls.

"Oh, yeah? Why would he do that?" I said.

"Because after he called you a cunt from the dugout, you gave him a walk the next time up."

"He called me what!"

Nothing pissed me off more than being called the C-word. In fact, that will be the only time you see that word in this book. So that was the guttural sound I'd heard, eh? If I had known, I would have dumped Phelps without thinking twice. Instead, the son of a bitch thought he had intimidated me. Worse yet, DeMuth and Higgins had heard him yell it and yet didn't tell me. Hey, you've got to protect your partner in those circumstances, and they didn't lift a finger. In fact, word got back to Cutler that Phelps had said what he said and that I didn't do anything about it. I wonder how that news got out?

My hearing got much better after the Phelps incident. One time, when I called a high pitch a strike, I heard someone yell from the Vancouver dugout, "That was boob high!" Another time, someone popped off with a riddle. Went the joke: What's another name for a female umpire? A call girl.

In no time at all, I was branded a red-ass. I was the umpire you couldn't talk to much or argue with. Back then, I probably took things a little too personally. But the truth is, a lot of times that year, ballplayers and managers tried to see how far they could push me. In response, I pushed back.

I wasn't the only person who had received a Triple A promotion in 1983. Tony Muser had been named manager of the Milwaukee Brewers' Vancouver affiliate, and one could only wonder what would happen when we met again. But much to my surprise, Muser was all business during our first series. I mean, he didn't invite me out to dinner afterward, but at least I didn't have to worry about any tobacco-juice showers. Maybe we both had become a little smarter.

The highlight of the season was my first-ever trip to Hawaii. The PCL umpires loved Honolulu because they never had to worry about any supervisors watching their every move. The way the schedule worked, you were there either eight or sixteen days at a time. It was like a paid vacation, and I quickly settled into a comfortable routine. After doing a game, we'd visit the bars, which stayed open until five A.M. in Honolulu. At noon, I'd drag myself out of bed and onto the beach to dry out. At three, I'd head back to the hotel, get changed, and head for the ballpark. I didn't party that hard every night, but you get the general idea.

Whenever a new crew arrived on the island, the members would always make friends with a guy named Wada. Wada was this huge native Hawaiian who owned a place on the beach that rented chairs, catamarans, surf-boards . . . whatever. In exchange for baseballs and our complimentary game tickets, Wada would let us use the rental stuff for free. In fact, I've still got a photograph of me surfing on a Wada-supplied board at Waikiki. I think it was Wada who also told us about Earl.

Earl owned a local bar and was a favorite of umpires everywhere because he only charged us half price for drinks. Charge an umpire half price for anything and he's your friend for life.

Earl was no exception. One time, Larry Poncino's crew came into town and was presented with T-shirts that had the name of Earl's bar silk-screened on the front. Poncino, who could be on the headstrong side at times, decided his crew would do Earl a favor and wear the shirts during their next game. In Hawaii, Cutler allowed us to keep our usual dress blues on the hangers and instead, wear those bright Hawaiian shirts with the floral patterns. It was a fun touch and we loved it.

But this time, Poncino's crew left their flowered shirts back at the hotel and simply wore the T-shirts given to them by Earl. Everything was fine until late in the game. Poncino, I think, had a tough play and ended up ruling against the Hawaiian team. Sure enough, one of their officials, pissed off about the call, later contacted Cutler and asked him what the hell kind of shirts his crews were wearing these days.

"What do you mean?" said Cutler.

"Jesus, Bill, they've got T-shirts with a bar name on them," said the Hawaii Islander official.

Cutler reportedly went nuts and almost fired Poncino for the stunt. But it didn't end there.

Bill Hohn's crew, so the story went, once let Earl actually umpire third base during an entire game. Earl was another huge Hawaiian guy, so none of the players or managers, who didn't know any better, were about to give him any shit.

Then . . . disaster. Late in the game, with the score close, an Islander player ripped a laser shot down the third-base line. Earl didn't have a choice: he had to make a call.

"Foul!" he said.

The Islanders ended up losing the game and word got back to Cutler that the guy who made the call was a Honolulu bartender. I'm still not sure how Hohn and his crew survived that one.

Earl was great, though. He gave guided tours of the island and told us the best local spots. And even the Islanders were fun to deal with. They didn't lose too often, mainly because the visiting team was usually suffering from jet lag or sunburn or from too many mai tais the night before. Tommy Sandt was the Islander manager. He had one of those mean-looking Fu Manchu mustaches, but he didn't cause much trouble. Every once in a while he'd throw a fit just so people would know he was still alive.

Near the end of the season, Cutler mentioned something about the possibility of me working the plate for the Triple A World Series. I had been doing much better, and apparently the reports had made their way back to his desk. But then news leaked out that I was being considered for the game, and Cutler caught all sorts of shit from people who said there were more experienced umpires who deserved the honor. They accused him of using me as a publicity stunt. I was a little embarrassed by it all. In truth, I probably wasn't the best umpire for the job. I mean, I would have done it had Cutler asked, but the critics were right—there were more deserving umpires than me that season.

Once you got to Triple A your career is basically at the mercy of the National League and American League directors of umpire supervision. In my case, that was Blake Cullen and Dick Butler, respectively. A few years later, Ed Vargo would replace Cullen, and Marty Springstead would assume Butler's job. But until then, Cullen and Butler were the main decision makers. If you got on their shit list somehow, you were dead.

That first year in the PCL I didn't give anyone a reason to put me on any sort of list, good or bad. I struggled early, recovered by midseason, and finished decently. I didn't knock anybody's socks off that season, but I survived, which was half the battle. I filled out my share of ejection notices, but didn't have to deal with too much out of the ordinary.

In an effort to get me more experience, the Office for Umpire Development strongly suggested that I accept their invitation to work in winter ball. When Umpire Development "suggests" something, you had better do it. If you turned down winter ball, I was told, your career was finished.

I had no intention of declining their offer. Even when they told me I was going to Colombia, South America, I didn't care. As far as I was concerned, this was an honor. It meant that the higher-ups at Umpire Development thought I had some serious big league potential. This was their way of fine-tuning it.

I had heard stories (none of them good) about Colombian baseball. There were supposed to be brawls and near-riots every night—and that was just in the packed stands.

On the field, Latin players were known to show little respect for umpires. With their macho attitudes, it was going to be interesting to see how they treated a woman *árbitro,* as they called umpires.

For the most part, the players and fans loved me, and I'm still not sure why. Maybe it was the novelty of a woman umpire, I don't know. In fact, I was told later that Colombian baseball officials had specifically asked that I be sent to their league. From what I heard, they thought my presence might boost attendance and interest. Well, it boosted interest, all right—the wrong kind. I got plenty of weird propositions, including one from Carmelo Martinez, who was playing down there during my stay. Martinez used to spend half of his time in the batter's box trying to sweet-talk me.

"I love you, honey," he'd say.

I'd ignore him.

"Mi amour," he'd try again.

I'd start to laugh and say, "Okay, honey."

I mean, why fight an entire Latin culture. Anyway, Martinez was harmless. He used to ask me to marry him, and I'd tell him, "Not until you get to the big leagues and make a million dollars." You know, the last time I looked, I think he had done both.

Of course, not everyone was so pleased with my arrival. I had one manager who was so upset with one of my calls that he ran out and spat in my face. Came right up to me, collected the stuff in his mouth, and spat. He got suspended.

And then there was the night we were doing a game and it must have been about ninety-five degrees with 90 percent humidity. It was like working a game in the heart of the jungle. I had the plate and had just called one of the local players out on a close pitch, which caused the manager to start bitching at me again. The guy had been muttering the whole game from the dugout, but this time he made a little scene, which got the crowd involved. I should have dumped him, but the game was almost over, so why bother?

After the inning ended, I took a few steps toward the stands and then looked out onto the field. That's when I got slugged in the back. Well, that's what I thought had happened.

As soon as I got hit, I clutched my back and turned around to face the idiot who had punched me. There was nobody there. There was, however, the pulpy remains of a huge orange that had been hurled from the stands. The orange was the size of a softball and about as heavy, too. I picked it up and wanted to throw it at someone. Jesus, was I furious. And Jesus, did my back hurt. Finally, I tossed the orange to the ground and resumed the game. Later, someone told me I was lucky it was an orange.

"Lucky?" I said. "Why do you say that?"

"Usually they throw rocks."

"Oh."

You expected shit like that to happen in Colombia. In fact, that's partly the reason why Umpire Development liked sending people down there: to see how they responded to bizarre situations. And believe me, there were plenty of them to go around.

As an umpire, all you wanted to do was get out of the stadium alive. And I mean that literally, too. It wasn't by accident that we never left the field without a police or army escort. It also wasn't by accident that each of those guys carried machine guns. That's how crazy it got in Colombia.

Of course, I didn't know exactly how serious they took their baseball in that country until midseason, when a Colombian baseball official requested that I leave the game. In the fifth inning.

"Are you nuts?" I said. "The game isn't over, so I'm not going anywhere."

"But we have dinner all prepared for you. You do not want to spoil the dinner, do you?"

"I don't know what the hell is going on, but I'm not leaving the game so I can go eat dinner."

Two innings later, the official ordered me to leave the field. And he didn't say anything about dinner being ready, either. What someone did say is that that someone had threatened to kill me. Hey, they should have said so in the first place.

Nobody called me Pam in Colombia. They wouldn't or couldn't say the word. Intead, they called me Pamela, but it came out "Pa-may-la." I wasn't much better with their language. At times, I felt so stupid, so uneducated. Here I was in a foreign country and I could barely say *gracias* or *por favor*. Reporters would approach me for interviews, start asking questions, and I would stand there with an embarrassed smile on my face. Finally I'd say, "Uh, I don't speak Spanish, guys." I hated that feeling of total helplessness.

Here's how bad it got. On my very first shopping trip to the local food market, I left the store almost in tears after realizing I couldn't buy anything. I had plenty of money, but I couldn't read the packaging or tell one item from the next. And I certainly didn't know how to ask anyone for help. So I ran out of the store totally frustrated. I thought I wouldn't last the week, much less the whole four-month season. I was hungry. I couldn't communicate in Spanish. And I was the Yankee female umpire.

Not making things any easier was one of my partners from the States, Phil Jansen. Jansen was the Ugly American, the guy who complained about everything. Every morning he'd get up and say, "I hate this place. Give me America." Jansen thought every corner should have a McDonald's or Pizza Hut on it. He couldn't understand why no one spoke much English or why the water tasted strange. His idea of compromising was not whining as long.

I'll admit, Colombia was a zoo. But it was an interesting zoo, at least. I ended up loving the culture, although I could have done without some of the local food dishes. For instance, meat on a stick was big down there. It wasn't until later that one of the other umpires told me the meat was usually burro or dog. And then there was the time when a Cartagena baseball official and his family invited me to their home for dinner. Their place was wonderful and the aroma from the kitchen was even better. I couldn't wait.

"What's cooking in there?" I said.

"Chicken," my host said.

And then they brought out the main course. It was chicken, but not much of one. In fact, the whole dinner platter was full of, well, chicken claws. Not chicken legs . . . chicken claws. I sat there with my mouth open, and not because I couldn't wait to dig in, either. Soon, one of the other guests picked up a claw and started nibbling away as if it were filet mignon or something. To this day I have no idea what she was chewing on. There wasn't any meat on the claws. There wasn't anything. In fact, at that point, burro on a stick sounded pretty good.

"Here, why don't you try one," said my host.

"Uh, nah," I said.

That incident aside, I did try to adapt to the country's customs. I knew in its own way, the whole experience would make me a better umpire. It had to. If you could survive Colombia, you could survive anything, I figured.

Things didn't work out so well for Jansen. He contracted some sort of virus and became so sick that the Cartagena doctor who examined him thought Jansen was dying. So did we.

"Are his cheeks always so sunken in?" the doctor said.

That's when we knew Jansen, who was as gaunt as a skeleton, wouldn't be staying in Colombia a whole lot longer.

No one knew for sure how he had caught the disease, but the doctor guessed—and this is no lie—that it could have been the food he ate at a local Moroccan restaurant. Whatever the cause, Jansen was shipped home, where he eventually recovered.

Poor Jansen. Nothing went right for him. To begin with, he got hammered in the newspapers for his umpiring. He couldn't read or speak Spanish, so Ed Schemel, a Colombian umpire who was sometimes assigned to our crew, translated for him. Jansen bitched even more after he heard the rips.

As a veteran of countless newspaper articles—some good, some bad—I told him to forget about it. "Phil," I said, "it's in Spanish. Who cares? You can't even read it." But Jansen was too miserable to forget about anything. He hated everything about the country, and that was before he stepped off the plane. He just wanted out of Colombia. In the end, he got his way.

Of course, I was a little on the shaky side myself until Schemel offered to help out us American umpires. Schemel was the Colombian version of Earl, my Hawaiian buddy—and about as good an umpire, too. And just like Earl, he had a soap opera life. He explained it to me one time, and there were so many twists and turns in his love life that I'm not sure I can remember them all. Some of the umpires down there had mistresses, and almost all the ballplayers did. More Latin macho crap.

Schemel was the best Colombian umpire in the league. His temperament was similar to that of an umpire from the States, and he also didn't take any shit from anybody. Most of the Colombian umpires were so bad that their American partners rarely let them work the plate. Not so with Schemel. He took his turn behind the plate just like we did.

The Colombians meant well, but they couldn't handle the pressure and were easily intimidated by the managers and players. At first, I didn't understand why they were such chicken shits. But then Schemel told me about the inner workings of the Colombian baseball system. It was a bigger mess than Schemel's love life.

For starters, a lot of the Colombian umpires were homers. Unlike American umpires, they actually cared who won the games. We didn't give a shit. And we didn't take any shit, either, which was another thing that separated us from our Colombian counterparts. Those guys practically got the shakes when they had to make a tough call.

It wasn't unusual to have one Colombian umpire call a player safe while another Colombian crew member called the same player out. Then I'd have to run out there from behind the plate and make the final decision, which always pissed off at least one of the managers. And it wasn't uncommon for the Colombian umpires to make a call, change it, and then run up to me and say, "What do you got?" Then I'd have to fix another mess. Sometimes no one would make a call at all. There would be, say, a steal attempt, and the guy working second base would stand there and do nothing. He'd choke. So from the plate, which is 127 feet away from second base, I'd have to make the best guess I could. You could imagine how well the players and managers reacted to the call. Fuck 'em, right?

Things weren't so simple for the Colombian umpires. If a manager or owner of a team didn't like the job they did, he could pretty much make sure that guy didn't work anymore. Because of that, a lot of umpires were careful not to piss off the Colombian bosses. That's partly why there were so many conflicting calls and why they always depended on the American umpires to put their asses on the line when the game was really close. About the only Colombian I saw who didn't pass the buck was Schemel. At least he tried to stay impartial.

And then there was the gambling. Colombians gambled on anything, especially baseball. The fans gambled on the final score, on who got hits and who didn't, on whether a player would fly out or hit a ground ball. They also gambled on balls and strikes, walks and strikeouts, and steal attempts. That's where the umpires came in.

I can't swear to it, but some of the calls I saw in that league looked as if the Colombian umpires had a stake in the outcome. I don't know if they were bought or if they had some action on the side, but something was fishy about cockshots being called ball four or ankle-high pitches passing for strikes. I know I made some horseshit calls in my life—every umpire misses some obvious ones—but these guys blew the easiest plays when it mattered most.

About every two weeks, we switched cities. Two weeks in Cartagena, which is sort of a resort town. Two weeks in Barranquilla, which isn't. Barranquilla is an industrial city with about a half million people. Compared to Cartagena, it was a dirty place, but I still enjoyed my stays there. That's because I had friends in the city, including Schemel, who showed me around town. In Cartagena, I was desperately lonely. I even spent Christmas by myself.

The umpires traveled by public bus when making those trips. Greyhound, it wasn't. The buses were rickety old things with balding tires and rusty bodies, usually crammed with people. Needless to say, there were no on-board bathrooms. One time I turned around and saw some guy snorting cocaine. After a few moments, he stopped, unzipped his pants, and started peeing out the window of the moving bus.

Sometimes I made the trip alone, which was sort of nerve-racking. Back then, the drug wars and terrorist acts were heating up, and it wasn't considered safe for people, especially Americans, to be traveling the countryside by themselves. So I enlisted help. On one trip from Barranquilla to Cartagena, I got another American umpire, Don Nachtrab, to ride with me. It wasn't that I was scared of traveling by myself, it's just that I figured the more friends, the better.

Halfway through the ride, our bus lurched to a stop. A police roadblock had been set up.

The police came on board and started yelling at all the men to get off the bus. Nachtrab did as he was told and soon found himself getting frisked. Then the police started going through the baggage. They found Nachtrab's big black equipment case and started asking the driver what it was. The driver didn't now. Finally, they lost interest in the locked case and put it back in the bus.

Why they didn't frisk the women or search our luggage, I'll never know. I could have been carrying a machine gun and a kilo of cocaine and they would never have known. The whole thing was funny and scary at the same time.

Of course, Nachtrab didn't think it was so hilarious at first. Then again, he was the same guy who was so afraid of getting infected by some Colombian bacteria that he wouldn't eat the food or drink the water. Instead, about every two days, he would have a cup or two of yogurt. In place of water, he drank beer. No wonder Nachtrab lost about forty pounds that season.

I left Colombia with mixed feelings. I thought it was a wonderful country, but things were getting dangerous. In fact, Umpire Development suspended the use of American crews in that country the next season. Too much threat of terrorism, I guess.

And as much as I loved the culture, I didn't miss squabbling over paychecks with the Colombian officials. They preferred lying to your face rather than simply telling you your money wasn't there. To them, it was like a game. To me, I needed to eat.

Before I left, one of the owners of a local team presented me with sixty pounds of fresh coffee. The guy owned a coffee plantation, and this was his way of saying thanks for my work. So I crammed the bags in a suitcase, got on the plane, connected in Miami, and then flew to Bermuda, where I was going to spend a few hard-earned vacation days.

Everything was fine until I landed in Bermuda. After collecting my bags, I gave the customs officer my passport and waited for him to wave me through after a few questions. No such luck. The officer looked at my papers and then looked at the bulging coffee suitcase. He wanted to know why an American would travel from Colombia to Miami to Bermuda. And what were in the bags?

I told him my story, but he wasn't convinced. Before long, he was poking holes in the coffee bags, looking for drugs. Some other customs people wandered over to his station. They thought they had discovered some sort of drug courier. All they had really done was get coffee all over the airport floor.

Did I care? Not a bit. I had survived fruit throwers, wild bus trips, inept Colombian umpires, death threats, language barriers, and burro on a stick. A little search at customs never hurt anybody.

CHAPTER 7

The Wonder Years

Some things never change. I did a minor league spring training game in 1984 and San Francisco Giants pitching coach Herm Starrette was there. Starrette didn't like some of my calls, so he told me to get a job "with a needle and thread." Starrette wasn't around to see the end of the game.

Then I heard that Cutler got a call from Jocko Conlan, a Hall of Fame umpire. Conlan was pissed that Cutler had hired me. Cutler later told me that Conlan was yelling at him over the phone.

"When are you going to get rid of that broad!" Conlan said. "Women have no place in our game! You ought to know that!"

And then, I took a foul ball off the top of my foot and broke a bone. It was my own damn fault. I had home plate in a spring training game and decided it was too hot to wear my big, bulky steel-plated shoes. Instead, I wore a lighter pair with cardboard padding sewn under the leather. Yes, well, foul balls don't give a shit about cardboard. The broken foot caused me to miss the last two weeks of spring training and the first two weeks of the regular season.

By the time I reported to my crew, I had to contend with another brushfire. That's because some chicken-shit PCL umpire, who didn't have the guts to use his name, told a sports reporter that the only reason I was in the league was as a publicity stunt. Hell, for all I know, it could have been one of my partners, Craig Brittain or Randy Knuths, who popped off that season. Actually, that wouldn't have been Brittain's style. He looked out for me. In fact, Brittain looked out for every one of his partners. He was the ultimate mother-hen type, always worrying about a hundred different things, always trying to take care of everybody else's problems. Not surprisingly, we called him Mother. It wasn't very original, but it fit perfectly. He was a prince.

As for Knuths, who knows? Knuths worried about himself, which was okay. But I knew right away that he didn't care too much for me. It wasn't that he was a total jerk. It's just that he didn't think women belonged in umpiring. He didn't come right out and say it, but he was one of those guys who thought women were meant to do certain things. I always got the feeling that Knuths thought most of those things involved wearing an apron. Anyway, Knuths never talked to me much. He had his own style, I had mine.

According to Cutler, I had finished the 1983 season rated in the middle of the pack. Considering the shit I took, the change to the three-umpire crew, the difference in leagues, and my unfamiliarity with the managers and players, I thought that was pretty damn good. Now that I was a little more established, I figured a jump into the top three or four of PCL umpires (there were fifteen altogether) wasn't out of the question.

That was before we made our first road trip to Portland. That was before I wrecked a brand-new rental car and later became a legend in the PCL for dumping, well, I'll tell you about it in a moment.

First, the car. It was a shiny new Ford Thunderbird, an absolutely beautiful automobile. I loved driving the thing. I loved driving it so much that I decided one rainy morning in Portland to go to the bank and cash my PCL paycheck. So far, so good.

I got to the bank and that's when one of the tellers told me they wouldn't take the check.

"But it's a paycheck from the Pacific Coast League," I pleaded. "It's not a personal check. I do this all the time and I never have had a problem."

"I'm sorry, but we can't authorize payment on that check."

I was pissed and let her know it. I then stormed to my brand-new Thunderbird, started the car, stuck it in reverse, and proceeded to broadside some poor guy's car with the rear of the Ford. The guy never knew what hit him.

I didn't have insurance. Can you believe it? Since I rarely drove my car during the season, I let the insurance run out on my regular policy. And since the rental car companies charged an arm and a leg for their insurance, we always decided to take our chances. Well, I took mine and lost. Big time.

They towed the cars away and Avis billed me for $2,000 worth of damage. I only made $1,950 a month, and I didn't have a dime in my savings account. In fact, I didn't have a savings account. How in the hell was I going to come up wiith $2,000?

Once again, my dad came through for me. Somehow he convinced his insurance company, State Farm, to stick me on his policy. I don't know how he did it, but State Farm agreed to pay for the damage. I was saved . . . until that night's ball game.

What a fucking game. Eighteen innings, each one worse than the last. First of all, Portland manager Lee Elia hated Knuths. Couldn't stand him. I think the feeling was mutual, too. Elia always bitched at Knuths, from the first pitch to the last. In a way, it was kind of nice. Mind you, I wasn't crazy about seeing my partner get ragged by a manager, but it was a pleasant change to see somebody else besides me get bitched at.

Knuths had the plate, Brittain had third base, and I had first. In the twelfth inning, with two outs and the score tied, 7–7, Portland outfielder John Russell started arguing balls and strikes. You never do that, especially not in the twelfth inning, when everybody is dog-ass tired and wants to get the hell out of there. Tempers are short.

Knuths, who wasn't in any mood to listen to Russell, dumped him. Elia went crazy. He ran from the third-base coaching box to home plate and started calling Knuths every name in the book. Knuths threw him out faster than he threw out Russell.

The crowd, what was left of it, got all over Knuths. And Elia, maybe sensing that he ought to put on a real show, went to the dugout, grabbed a metal folding chair, walked back out onto the grass, and heaved the thing into short right field. It was a hell of a toss.

Portland's dugout was on the first-base side of the field, my side. Well, I knew I wasn't going to go out there and pick up the folding chair. And Knuths sure as hell wasn't going to go out there. The same went for Elia, who had, by then, left the field and stormed to the clubhouse. That's when I noticed the batboy standing nearby. Like everyone else, except Knuths, Brittain, and me, the kid was enjoying himself. Elia had really stirred things up. The crowd was booing and the Portland players were cheap-shotting us from the dugout. It was a real shit-house situation.

"Hey, you," I said, pointing at the surprised batboy, "Go out there and pick up that chair and take it back to the dugout, will you?"

The batboy nodded his head and started to jog toward right field. As he did, one of the players noticed and stopped the kid dead in his tracks.

"You work for us," the player said. "You don't do what she says. You do what we say. Don't go out there. Let her pick up the chair herself."

The poor batboy didn't know what to do. He knew I was ordering him to get the chair, but he also knew that he made money from the players. So he dropped the chair and started to return to the dugout. Without thinking twice, I said, "All right, if you're not going to do what I say, then you're outta here!"

The kid's eyes got real wide, as if he couldn't believe what he had just heard. The players, the fans, even my partners, looked at me as if I were crazy. After all, I had just dumped a fourteen-year-old batboy.

Eventually I got the other batboy to go pick up the stupid chair and we resumed play. Just as things were settling down, I heard someone popping off from the Portland bullpen. It was Mike Diaz, who was still pissed at me for calling him out on strikes the last time I had the plate. Those ballplayers, they never forget a single at bat.

"What's the matter, Pam?" he said, trying to be real cute. "What's happening? Having fun?"

"Diaz, just keep your mouth shut," I said.

That set him off.

"I don't have to!" he yelled. "If you don't like it, go ahead and kick me out!"

So I kicked him out. He was looking to get dumped anyway.

Diaz, who was a few cans short of a six-pack to begin with, turned into a wild man. Muser was bad in the Texas League, but compared to Diaz's performance, Muser was an angel.

As Diaz ran toward me, I could see that his dip was halfway out of his mouth. That way he could spit at me better. When he was about a yard or two away, I stuck out my arm so he couldn't get nose to nose with me. That pissed him off even more. Frustrated by my arm, he decided to spit the whole wad of dip at me. That done, he started yelling again.

"You fucking c———!" he said again and again. "You're a fucking dyke and you're horseshit!"

Then he grabbed his crotch in front of me. Brittain came over from third base and pulled Diaz away, but not before Diaz nailed him with some leftover dip. Brittain had the stuff on his shirt and I had it all over my face and shirt. Finally, we got Diaz out of there, but it wasn't easy.

Six long innings later, the game was finished. Of course, my troubles were just beginning.

The newspapers treated the ejection as if I had committed child abuse or something. Then the wire services picked up the story and before long, the batboy and I were famous. Just what I needed: publicity, and negative publicity at that. All of a sudden I was Pam Postema, the woman umpire who got so flustered that she threw out a poor, innocent batboy. Jesus, what a mess.

According to the stories, the batboy's name was Sam Morris. After I dumped him, the kid shuffled into the clubhouse, all scared and nervous, and told Elia what had taken place. Elia supposedly said something like, "Kid, it happens to everybody in baseball sooner or later."

Of course, when the sportswriters asked Elia about the incident, he wasn't too supportive. I shouldn't have expected anything less.

"I've seen fans removed and radio announcers removed by umpires, but never a batboy," he said. "I thought I'd seen everything in my twenty-six years in baseball until that poor kid came into the locker room and said, 'Skip, I've been tossed out, too.' "

My phone rang every five minutes that next day. Reporters from every damn magazine and newspaper were asking me to comment. What was there to say? As an umpire, I had the right to remove the kid from the game if he didn't do as he was told. I suppose I could have handled the situation a little more diplomatically, but it was cowboys and Indians out there. The twelfth inning. Everybody is going nuts. We're tired. The last thing we needed was some kid not picking up a chair. By then, I didn't know what the hell to do, so I threw him out. Big deal. We didn't need him in the game anyway, right?

And what everybody forgets about that whole thing is that the batboy loved it. He said later that every kid at his junior high school knew his name after that. He was big man on campus. People should have been thanking me rather than ripping me.

As expected, Cutler called, too. He wasn't mad, just curious.

"What happened, Pam?"

So I told him. I even added that I probably overreacted a tiny bit.

The next day I picked up the sports section and read where Cutler said that I shouldn't have thrown the batboy out of the game. He also said the kid wouldn't get fined the customary $25 that comes with an ejection.

Cutler wasn't trying to bury me, but his comments made me look bad. He should have backed me up on this one. Instead, he tried to appease everyone. Cutler was a good guy and a good league president, but he had this habit of working both sides of the fence. Maybe that's what good presidents do. All I know is that I looked like horseshit because he second-guessed me in the newspapers. I wouldn't have minded it so much had he called me back and said, "Pam, I know why you did what you did, but here's what I've got to say to calm everybody down." Then I would have understood. Or if he had chosen to question my judgment in private, fine. But to stick it to me in the newspapers, accidentally or not, was horseshit. I was just doing my job. Like I said, I'm not trying to rip Cutler, but in this case, I shouldn't have had to take any heat for what I did.

Brittain and Knuths didn't really say much about the whole thing. They probably thought it was amusing. I know Tony Kubek of NBC did: he mentioned the incident on that weekend's Game of the Week. I cringed when I heard about it.

There was, however, one person who stuck up for me. Barney Deary called, and unlike Cutler, he agreed 100 percent with my decision. It was the first time anyone in Umpire Development had ever told me they agreed with my ruling.

"You were exactly right," he said. "You can throw out batboys, ball boys, anybody."

That's what I needed to hear. I needed to know that somebody believed in me. Hell, I even got a few letters from baseball fans who said they thought I had done the right thing. Of course, I don't remember any of those letters being from the Portland area.

Incredibly enough, the incident never died. When we returned to Portland later that season, you wouldn't believe what the Beavers general manager, a guy named Jon Richardson, wanted me to do. It was almost Mother's Day, so he thought he would make me part of one of their holiday promotions:

"Pam, we thought it would be a nice gesture if you came out to home plate before the game and let Sam, the batboy you threw out, present you with a dozen roses."

"No fucking way."

"No, really. It would be like Sam forgives you and you forgive him for what happened in that one game."

"Get real."

Was he nuts? The last thing I needed was another sexist display, with me as the main attraction. Knuths and Elia started the whole thing. Let *them* meet me at home plate and exchange roses. Can you imagine the photos from that kid giving me a bouquet of flowers? I bet that would have gone over real big with Umpire Development. And wouldn't the major league directors of umpire supervision have been real impressed, too. No, I wasn't going to take part in any of that stuff. If Richardson wanted to sell tickets, he was going to have to find some other gimmick.

• • •

Slowly but surely, the three-umpire system had become second nature to me. I was moving better and not thinking about where I was supposed to be on certain plays. I reacted, instead of pausing first and then finding my spot. It was like anything: the more you did it, the more familiar and easier it became.

I also noticed that fewer managers and ballplayers were challenging me. It was as if I had survived their initiation rites the previous season, and now some of them were giving me a little room to operate. Of course, everybody's patience lasted about as long as it took for me to make a disputed call.

For instance, Bob Cluck was the manager of the Las Vegas Stars that season. He was a good guy and generally gave me the benefit of the doubt. But one time he couldn't help himself. Looking back, I can't say that I blame him.

I was working the bases. There were Las Vegas runners on first and second and the batter bunted. Rather than throw to first for the sure out, the catcher turned and threw to third. My job was to get my ass from second base, where I had started the play, to third, where I would supposedly be in a better position to make the call. Well, this time I hesitated a moment too long and made the call on the run. I called the Vegas runner out, even though as soon as I raised my arm, I knew the guy was safe. What can I say? I screwed up. It happened more than once during my career.

Cluck was furious. He wanted to know how I could make such a call. The only thing he didn't do was go out and buy me a pair of glasses. I didn't really have my heart in it when I dumped him, but he didn't leave me much choice. Yes, I made the wrong call, but there was nothing I could do about it. In the scorebook, it read, 1–5. And no, even though I botched the call, I couldn't let Cluck show me up.

Cluck didn't leave without a final bit of theatrics. He

started kicking dirt on my pants and shoes. I don't know why they do that, but they do. All it meant was that I'd have to use more space on the ejection report. It also meant that the chances were good that Cutler would fine and suspend him, which is exactly what happened. To this day, I feel sort of bad about Cluck's suspension. But not a whole lot. He shouldn't have kicked the dirt.

As usual, I kept getting pestered by reporters. I never knew what to tell them. I was so bored with their questions that after a while, they all sounded the same.

"How did you get involved in umpiring?"

"Do you have a favorite team to umpire for?"

"How do you take showers?"

"Do you work the plate?"

One woman reporter asked me, "Do you wear makeup on the field?"

I told her that if I thought it would make me see better, I'd wear a lot of it.

The people from the "Good Morning America" show called again. How would I feel about making a second appearance on the program? Since I couldn't come up with a decent excuse, I told them I'd give it another try.

We were in Alburquerque, which meant, with the time difference, I had to get up at four-thirty A.M. or something ridiculous like that to get ready and meet the television crew at the ballpark. I wasn't much of a morning person. I was even less of a TV person.

The regular host, David Hartman, wasn't on the show because of a broken leg. So a guy named Steve Bell was supposed to handle the interview. Standing there on the baseball field, the lights shining in my face, the camera just a few feet away, I got a sudden case of stage fright. It was overpowering.

The interview started and I was terrible. I could go nose to nose with a manager in front of a packed house, but for some reason I couldn't utter a word that morning to a national television audience. I died.

Bell lobbed all these easy questions at me, and I couldn't think of a thing to say. I hemmed and hawed and must have sounded like a complete dunce. The earpiece was bothering me and I could barely hear the questions sometimes. After a few minutes of this, Bell graciously put me out of my (and the viewers') misery and said, "Well, we have to move on. Thank you, Pam."

When we were off the air, I thanked him for cutting the interview short.

"Steve, I'd rather have a three-two pitch, bottom of the ninth, bases loaded, than do this again," I said. "I'm terrible at this."

"No, you did a good job," he said.

What a liar. But I appreciated his trying to cushion the embarrassment. The whole interview couldn't have lasted more than a few minutes. But when the words won't come out of your mouth, it seems like hours.

Later that day, Brittain, Knuths, and I stopped to say hello to the Albuquerque general manager, Pat McKernan. McKernan carried a lot of weight in the league and the word was, his opinion could help make you or break you. So it wasn't unusual for crews to visit with him. He liked it when you stopped by. I guess it made him feel important.

McKernan had seen the program that morning and couldn't quit talking about it. I wanted to slug him.

"Jeez, what happened in that interview?" he said.

"Was it bad?" I said.

"Oh, it was brutal."

The asshole. Couldn't give me a break, could he?

Albuquerque is also where I had some, uh, equipment problems. The two clubbies, who were brothers, were also cousins of Doug Flutie's, the former quarterback for Boston College who went on to a career in the USFL, the NFL, and the CFL. The brothers were also a little absentminded.

Every night after the game, the clubbies were supposed to take our clothes and wash and press them and also shine our shoes. We'd tip them according to how good of a job they did. One day I walked in the dressing room to get ready for the game and I couldn't find my bra. It was gone. Vanished. The rest of my uniform was there—but no bra.

"Hey, guys," I said to the clubbies. "Do you know where my bra is?"

They looked at each other and suddenly one of them said, "That was your bra? I thought it was my girlfriend's."

So I had to do the game wearing two T-shirts and no bra. I didn't have a lot to hold down, but still it felt weird to call a game without my bra on.

I did okay that season. I finished in the middle of the ratings again, but I did read a story where a PCL manager, who wished to remain anonymous, said that I was good enough to be in the big leagues if only I had "outdoor plumbing." Some compliment.

However, I did receive a letter from Ben McLure, who was the eastern scouting supervisor for the Toronto Blue Jays. McLure, who first saw me work when I was in the Florida State League, wrote that he had recently been scouting a game in the Triple A International League and had run into Ed Vargo. Vargo was a longtime National League umpire who had retired in 1983. Apparently he was doing some consulting work for the league.

"For what it's worth," wrote McLure, "he told me that he felt that it was only a matter of time . . . [before] you would be in the major leagues. He says that there are no major league prospect umpires in the International League and that you and another PCL umpire were the best bets to move up in the future."

McLure's letter made my day, maybe my year.

For the second off-season in a row, Umpire Development sent me to winter ball. This time my destination was Puerto Rico. Paradise, right?

Wrong. Puerto Rico was great—it was a hell of a lot safer

than Colombia—but the league officials, managers, ball-players, and local umpires were awful. They lied more often than the Colombian officials, which was pretty hard to do.

Especially frustrating was the attitude of league management. We would throw out a player or manager and the league president, Alcides Oquendo, would hardly do a thing about it. His idea of a stiff fine was $60. Suspensions were practically unheard of.

Oquendo was gutless. And don't think the ballplayers and managers didn't notice. When they saw that Oquendo didn't have the nerve to back up the umpires, they started challenging us on everything. I did a game one night and the equipment manager of the Ponce team started making gestures to the other team from the dugout. He kept pointing at his rear end and yelling something. This guy was always trying to incite miniriots, so I dumped him. Oquendo must not have done a thing about it, because the next time I saw the same equipment manager, he was mouthing off again.

The scariest incident involved John Higgins and a manager named Victor Pellot, who, when he played in the United States, was known as Vic Power. Higgins and Power got into an argument during a game and Power punched him. Power was a huge guy and he could have killed Higgins with the blow. Umpires are ready for just about anything, but they aren't ready for a punch like that.

Power would receive a substantial fine and get suspended, no doubt. Then came the news that Oquendo had decided to do what he did best: nothing. We were outraged. If Power could get away with something like that, what was next? It was like giving a murderer his gun back.

We called Barney Deary as soon as we heard and told him we weren't working another game until Power was suspended. He asked us to wait a day, to let him see what he could do.

Wouldn't you know it that I was scheduled to work a

game the day after the Power incident. It was a terrible feeling walking onto the field and knowing that your winter-league president was as spineless as Jell-O. Nor was it much comfort to work with the local Puerto Rican umpires. Most of them were worse umpires than the Colombians. They were nearly as gutless as Oquendo. The players and managers walked all over them as if they were sidewalk.

Despite Deary's best efforts and our threat of a boycott, Oquendo refused to change his mind. He didn't see what was so bad about a manager striking an umpire.

We did, so we did some striking of our own. We told him we weren't doing any more games until Power was reprimanded, was forced to apologize for his actions, and was suspended. Until then, we spent our days on the beach, getting deep, dark tans and bitching about Oquendo. In a way, it was fun.

Deary kept in touch. He wrote letters that began. "To the hostages in Puerto Rico . . ." We were stuck. We couldn't leave because there was a slim chance Oquendo would change his mind. Also, the league refused to pay us until we started working again.

As you might expect, Oquendo forced the Puerto Rican umpires back to work. They went almost without a struggle. The rest of us weren't going anywhere. We knew they needed us more than we needed them.

About two weeks after the umpire boycott began, Oquendo and Power gave up. Power issued a statement, which was then distributed by Oquendo's office to the local media and to all the American umpires:

I have repeatedly stated to the news media in Puerto Rico how sorry I am for the events which occurred on January 5, 1985, at the Caguas baseball park. I have learned a great lesson and wish to present my excuses to all Puerto Rico baseball fans and especially to Mr. John Higgins. I promise the people of Puerto Rico and their great baseball fans that a similar event will never happen again, as far as I am concerned.

I urge all baseball players in Puerto Rico, as well as all club managers, to respect the umpires, since they are the maximum authority at the baseball field. And this should be taught, as I will certainly do, at all baseball clinics, that sports professionals should respect the umpire's authority.

I believe that the umpires perform a great work which should be praised.

What a politician this guy was. Of course, everybody forgave him, except Higgins and the rest of the American umpires. You can't forget somebody who throws a punch like that. Nobody was in a big hurry to forgive and forget when it came to Oquendo, either. Still, he did force Power to make the public apology, and he finally came through with our paychecks, too.

Despite the gestures, I wasn't very sorry to leave Puerto Rico. There were few highlights, unless you count the time I decided I couldn't wait any longer for my Puerto Rican umpire partners to take their showers one day. So while they took their time to hop in the shower, I stripped, grabbed a towel, and dashed under the water. You should have seen their faces. That was the first and last time I ever did anything like that in the dressing room. But I wanted to get the hell out of the ballpark. If it meant they saw me naked for a few seconds, big deal.

By going to Puerto Rico, I had fulfilled my obligation to Umpire Development—I had done the required two seasons of winter ball—and now I was ready to concentrate on moving up the PCL ladder.

Some of my friends and supporters had other ideas. One friend bought me a personalized T-shirt that said, "Major Leagues in '85." Sounded good to me. In fact, it almost sounded possible, especially when I was told I would be doing some American League spring training games in 1985. Not many, mind you, but enough for American

League supervisor of umpires Dick Butler to see me work.

I wasn't holding my breath for any miracles that spring. I wanted to do a good job and then hope for the best. I didn't spend much time trying to guess what people such as Butler would do. If he liked me, he liked me. If he didn't, I'd be back in the PCL.

Of the handful of games I did, I can honestly say I did well, but not well enough to deserve a big league offer. I knew how to call a game, how to interpret the rules . . . that sort of stuff. But I didn't know how to handle situations as well as the big league umpires did. As much as I hated to admit it, I could see the differences in the way a big league umpire controlled the flow of a game compared to the way I did. I could dump everybody in sight if I had to, but that's not handling a situation, is it? I could tell you had to be more diplomatic in the major leagues. Fans paid their money to see big-name ballplayers play, not to watch the umpires monopolize the game.

If Butler would have offered me a job, I wouldn't have hesitated to say yes. But the truth is, I wasn't ready. They would have eaten me alive up there. I might have survived if an established and respected umpire would have taken me under his wing and helped me out. That would have been my only chance. Of course, I can think of very few, if any, American League umpires who might have done that for me.

Rookie umpires need help, no matter if it's the big leagues or minor leagues. I guarantee you that nine times out of ten, the ballplayers and managers will go after the rookie umpire harder than the veteran. They figure the rookie can be intimidated, or maybe his partners won't be so quick to rush to his aid. That's why a first-year umpire needs a protector, someone who will back him up when things get tough, someone who won't let him get buried if all hell breaks loose.

I know one guy I'd never want to depend on for help:

Mark Johnson. He hated my guts so much that if I were drowning, he'd wave good-bye to me with a life vest in his hands.

Johnson started working for the American League in 1984 as a roving umpire. Because there weren't any full-time openings in the league, he spent part of his season in Triple A. He got a big league salary, but he had to work in the minors until one of the American League regulars got sick or went on vacation. That's when Johnson would fill in.

Triple A crews usually loved it when a fourth umpire was assigned to them. Our crew—Brittain, Bob Duncan, and me—was no exception. When Cutler put Johnson with us early in the season, we were thrilled. One person had the plate, while the other three umpires would take a base. You still had to worry about making the correct rotations on a play, but for the most part, a four-umpire crew was a luxury that was usually limited to the big leagues.

Believe me, Johnson made sure we knew he was special goods. He acted as if he were doing us a favor, as if he were God's gift to umpiring. The guy was so pompous.

Still, I figured that I could work with him. That didn't mean he had to like me or I had to like him, but at least we could coexist. Not this time, we couldn't. Johnson wanted no part of me. He thought I should be working in the concession stands selling hot dogs or something. He wanted me anywhere but on the baseball field wearing an umpire's uniform.

When we were in the dressing room before the game, Johnson would ignore me, but talk to Duncan and Brittain. He wasn't even subtle about it. And when we stepped on the field, he was even worse.

We had a game where I was stationed behind second base and he had third. I didn't see it happen, but apparently the pitcher was standing on the rubber and raised his fingers to his mouth. That's against the rule, and with no runners on base, you're supposed to call an automatic ball.

Like I said, I must have glanced down the exact moment that it happened, because I never saw the guy go to his mouth. But Johnson had seen it and he started yelling at me from third base.

"Why didn't you call that!" he said. "Why didn't you fucking call that!"

American League umpire or not, I wasn't going to let Johnson make me look bad. He didn't think I belonged out there anyway, so what did I have to lose by jumping down his throat?

"Listen, you fucking asshole," I said, "don't ever talk to me again. Don't look at me. And don't you ever fucking do that to me again."

I didn't care how much you disliked another partner, you never showed him up in front of the teams and fans. To me, it was one of the worst things you could do. It made us seem as if we didn't know what we were doing out there. In fact, I can still remember the look on Phoenix Giants manager Jim Lefebvre's face as he watched Johnson and me go at it. Lefebvre was in the third-base coach's box, which meant he had a front-row seat to this awful confrontation. His expression was a mixture of digust, amusement, and disbelief. We must have looked like idiots out there.

Cutler found out about the shouting match and immediately pulled Johnson from our crew and put him with someone else. That made me happy, but Brittain and Duncan were probably pissed because we went back to the three-umpire rotation. More work.

They could blame me. I didn't care. I was glad to see the asshole leave. I mean, here was Johnson, who was a big league umpire and making big league money, and he was worried whether I saw a pitcher go to his mouth? The guy hadn't acknowledged my existence since he joined our crew, but yet, he expected me to sit there and take his bullshit on the field? Talk about screwed up. I never saw the son of a bitch the rest of the season. Can't say that I missed him, either.

This was my second tour of duty with Brittain, so we got along just fine. Duncan was okay, too—at first.

You could say the same thing about my career. It was doing okay, but nobody was in a hurry to bump me up to the majors. The closest thing I had to a promotion is when Cutler asked if I'd be interested in ordering the PCL uniforms from JCPenney. I didn't mind. After all, I liked shopping and it was kind of fun to watch the lady's face when I ordered thirty-two short-sleeve, light blue cotton shirts with neck sizes that reached into the high teens. One umpire liked his shirts really big, so he had me order a size 22 neck.

Otherwise, things plodded along as usual in 1985. Once in a while, I'd sit back and try to pick the future big league stars. I saw plenty of phenoms in the minors, so it was always a challenge to choose the guys who might move up.

One guy who I thought would do great was Sammy Khalifa, a shortstop in the Pittsburgh Pirates organization. I had Khalifa in the PCL that year, and I would have bet money that he was destined for stardom. When the Pirates called him up after two months of the season, he was hitting about .280 and 20 of his 61 hits were for extra bases. Khalifa was a pretty good defensive player, too, so I was almost positive he would stick with the big club.

He struggled. Every time I looked at a box score it seemed as if he had taken the collar. The next time I saw him, which was on some Game of the Week telecast, Khalifa looked like a beaten man. He kind of dragged himself to the plate, as if he didn't care anymore. The pressures of playing in the big leagues had worn him down. They can do that to you in the majors. Either you're strong-willed, such as a Jose Canseco, or you collapse, as Khalifa did. Maybe he was brought up too soon. Whatever the case, he never made it big.

Of course, I had my own problems. Even though it was my third year in the league, I still had to listen to a few sexist remarks. I was used to it, but that didn't mean I had to like it. Luckily, there were some light moments, too.

One night we were doing a game in Vancouver and Brittain was behind the plate. I had first base. Late in the game, one of the Edmonton players kept popping off from the dugout, complaining about Brittain's calls. I was closest to the dugout, so I told the guy to knock it off. He didn't, so I ejected him.

Afterward, I had a little fun with Brittain.

"He called you horseshit, Craig," I said. "He said you've been horseshit for years. He was right, but I still had to run him."

"Thanks for sticking up for me, Pam," said Brittain half-jokingly. "If I had heard him, I'd have done it myself."

Opinion was mixed about my prospects for moving up. Tom Trebelhorn, who was the manager of the Vancouver Canadians that year, told a *Los Angeles Times* reporter that he thought I had two chances: slim and none.

"No matter how good she is, I don't think she'll be the one," said Trebelhorn, who's a decent guy, by the way. "As an umpire, I think she might be able to handle it. But I just think our sport's not ready for her."

I didn't know how to respond to that one. How could the sport not be ready for an umpire who might be able to do the job? Why was baseball so concerned about having a female umpire? I could never figure that out.

In that same *Los Angeles Times* article there was a quote from my crew member Bob Duncan, who said that a woman "is at a disadvantage. Unless they grow up with [baseball], like little boys do, they don't have those baseball instincts."

Duncan wasn't a fan of mine. He had ripped me earlier

in the season and then backed off. Whenever a reporter asked him to talk about my work, he'd say, "No comment." Translation: I think she's horseshit, but I'm not about to say it in print.

Cutler was still rooting for me. Rumor was that I'd be back in the PCL in 1986, but that I'd also get another shot at some American League spring training games. That was encouraging, but nothing more. I decided I had to do something a little out of the ordinary. So I did.

I burned the T-shirt, the one that read, "Major Leagues in '85."

CHAPTER 8

Mr. Despicable

We were called The Mod Squad in honor of the 1960s TV show. I was Julie. Chuck Meriwether, who is black, was Linc. And Jerry Layne, as white as they come, was Pete. That was my crew in 1986, the season I met the most miserable man in baseball, Larry Bowa.

Bowa had spent sixteen years in the majors as a shortstop. He was known for his competitive nature and his temper. When I heard he was coming to the PCL, I thought, "Great, just what I need: a rookie manager with an attitude."

Even before the season started, I thought the guy might have a screw loose. Since when do you turn down a $250,000 offer to be a utility player for the New York Mets and instead, accept a job as a Triple A manager? I would have taken the money in a minute. Of course, I was making $2,150 a month at the time.

But Bowa wanted to manage. I read one story where Greg Luzinski, Bowa's former teammate on the Philadelphia Phillies, said he couldn't wait for his buddy to get a taste of the minor league life.

"I think I'd be willing to pay the price of admission," Luzinski said. "I'll tell you what's going to happen. An umpire is going to make a call against him and Bowa's going to blow up. Then the umpire is going to squeeze his neck off. It should be fun."

I was the umpire. And no, it wasn't fun.

Before facing Bowa, I first had to take care of some preseason business. For starters, I was assigned to work some minor league spring training games for the Oakland Athletics. The A's are one of the best organizations in baseball and do everything first class, right down to the way they treat umpires in spring training. What you have to remember is that the A's were completely responsible for my hotel costs, meal money, and miscellaneous expenses. Of course, since I was living in Phoenix at the time, which was just down the street from where Oakland's training facilities were located, the A's could easily have declined to pay for the hotel part of the deal. But they didn't. Instead, they went ahead and paid for both, which allowed me to pocket some much needed money.

One of my favorite members of the A's organization was Karl Kuehl, Oakland's director of player development. He was part guardian angel and part teacher.

"Pam," he said, following a game, "we want you to do good. You know that, don't you?"

"Sure I do, Karl."

"Well, we've been watching you and we think we know why you've been having some problems out there."

Here was a change of pace—someone trying to help me. I told Karl to go on.

"Well, we think you're too tense out there on the bases."

"Too tense?"

"Way too tense," Karl said. "When the play happens, we've noticed that you're holding your breath. We've found that you have to be breathing normally during pressure situations. You're concentrating too hard out there and thus, missing the call. When you breathe normally, you can see the play happen."

With that, Karl launched into all these technical reasons why breathing normally is so important. He said that they had done some sort of study on hitters who held their breaths during their swings and found that they couldn't see the pitch as well as those who had regular breathing patterns. At least, that's what I thought he said.

A few days later, while working the bases, I tried to do as Karl had suggested. Rather than tense up on every play, I kept telling myself to relax. I mean, it wasn't as if I had never umpired a game before. You know what? It helped. I actually felt as if I could see the plays better. And people wonder why the A's have done so well. To begin with, they treat players, coaches, and even umpires, as people. Secondly, they don't miss a trick. They realize the difference between winning and losing might be something as basic and simple as the way you breathe. As for Karl, I'll never forget his kindness. Team officials, especially those of Karl's stature, usually never make it a point to help out a struggling umpire. But Karl and the A's were different. They just wanted the best for me. They wanted me to make it to the big leagues.

Shortly before the beginning of every season, Cutler would have a meeting of PCL officials. In '86, I heard that part of the meeting was spent figuring out the odds on who would dump Bowa first and when it would happen. And in spring training camp the San Diego Padres, the parent club of the Las Vegas Stars, started a pool to see when Bowa would get thrown out—winner take all.

Apparently, I was the early favorite to do the dumping. That figured. Those guys thought that since I was a woman and Bowa was supposedly such a red-ass, I'd be the one throwing him out. They were wrong. Someone else dumped him first. But nobody else dumped him as many times—three—as I did.

Of course, I didn't have any special vendettas against Bowa when the season began. I had more important things to worry about, such as how to impress Dick Butler. His people were still scouting me, so I knew I'd have to continue to improve.

In early April, Jerome Holtzman, a baseball writer for the *Chicago Tribune*, talked to me after I did a Seattle Mariners–Cleveland Indians exhibition game in Tempe. Holtzman is in the Baseball Hall of Fame, so when he writes something about you, it pays to read it.

Well, according to his article, National League president Chub Feeney wasn't interested in me as an umpire. That meant the American League was my only chance. There were a couple of other surprises, such as Phil Seghi, the former general manager of the Indians, saying that I was good enough to get a chance at the majors. And Mel Didier, a Los Angeles Dodgers scout who had seen me for about five seasons, said that I was much improved, could stand my ground, and was tough. Didier would know: I threw out his son, Bob, once when he argued about a call on the bases.

Holtzman also talked to Butler, who was now a special assistant to American League president Dr. Bobby Brown, but Butler wasn't saying much. I wished Holtzman would have asked him about the quote in 1984, when Butler said he thought there would be a woman umpire in the American League by the end of the 1986 season.

On occasion, Butler would take me out to dinner during spring training. During one of those dinners he mentioned the possibility of me joining "his league," as he referred to the American League. I didn't know how serious he was. I did know, however, that I was willing and available for a promotion.

Of course, a new person was involved in the equation: Marty Springstead, Butler's replacement as American League supervisor of umpires. Springstead was a great umpire, a twenty-year veteran of the league. He'd worked three World Series, five Championship Series, and three All-Star Games. The guy knew his stuff, or at least, I hoped so: part of my career was in his hands.

As part of my new strategy, I decided that maybe I'd

become a better umpire if I wrote down my mistakes and studied them. So I started to keep a diary. I went to Woolworth's and found one of those hardbound composition books that kids use in elementary school. That book had about 125 blank pages and I was determined to fill every one of them with a daily record of my life that season.

I lasted about a month and a half.

Still, it was a busy forty-five days. You'll see.

Monday, April 14

This is a diary and already I'm three days late on it. Hopefully what I write here will be a reminder for me about past game situations, plays, mistakes. I'll remember them better if I write about them.

Tonight with Meriwether behind the plate, we had a 1–0, two-hour ball game, with Las Vegas beating Portland. Love those quick games.

Nothing much happened. Talked to Layne after the game and he gave me some good advice on a couple of things, including how to look more comfortable out there. Just what I've been trying to do—look more relaxed and less tense. I swear I'm not nervous or tense out there. I just look that way. I try to look strong and assertive, but it makes me look too tight and tense. I firmly believe my so-called "bad on the bases" tag is because of this. I don't want that nonchalant or cocky look, either.

Anyway, the U.S. attacked Libya tonight and Reagan's speech was great. I thought he was pretty much a figurehead, but he's got me on his side forever now. And I'm worried about a game? Pretty much puts things in perspective. I didn't do anything today except work out my legs. I didn't gamble (hooray). That's about it.

Tuesday, April 15

Had the plate tonight. Won't say I had an excellent game, but better than average. Just one of those games that make you look bad. The pitchers were missing outside and then they'd put one on the black. I called a high curveball and Bowa had to yell from third. He chirps too much so I'm going to have to do something about it soon. He's got to learn.

I was always in control tonight. I did have a situation when the batter fell down on an inside pitch that he hit. Bowa, who wanted me to give him the base, comes running down and says, "It hit him in the foot!" At the same time, the batter said, "It hit me in the hand." Nice try. Then Bowa complains that I'm squeezing his pitcher, which was his way of saying that I was calling every pitch tight. I warned him about arguing balls and strikes, so he went back to the other conversation.

Anyway, I think I'm so lonely, I might as well lose some money here tonight.

Wednesday, April 16

Well, I can't wait to write this shit down tonight. Have a close steal play at second, and Bowa comes out and argues. Jesus, Meriwether has a banger go against him and Bowa doesn't say a word. I'm in the fucking wrong line of work. I don't need this shit. I love these rookie managers.

But that's not all. I have a rundown play and they throw the ball at the runner and it hits him. Tacoma wants interference because the runner stuck his arm out. The guy was running away from the throw, has no idea where the ball's going, and they think he's smart enough to think about throwing his right arm out? I said to Keith Lieppman, the Tacoma manager: "Well, why didn't he throw his left elbow out?" I tell you, I don't need this shit.

Dick Nelson's in town. I'm a little tired of him, too. I guess I just feel rotten because I didn't blast Bowa. I just let him say his stupid little lines. He'll say, "I just want you to put a little effort out here." Or, "How come I can't get a call from you?"

I was always taught just to let people talk and ignore them, unless, of course, they curse or personally degrade you. But this obviously doesn't work for me because now I'll see Bowa come out on the field on anything close. Human fucking nature. Men really suck.

Thursday, April 17

It only gets worse before it gets better. Tonight I looked like a rookie umpire, not even a Single A umpire. Where do I start?

I didn't take a pivot on one play, so I overran the runner to second and he stayed at first. Meriwether came up to first, though, and covered me.

Then the topper. I've probably changed three calls in my career. Well, make it four.

There was a runner on third and the batter hit a bastard ball to right center field. I had first, so I go out on the ball. I see the guy make a diving lunge for the ball and it looks like he's caught it. But he gets up right away and throws the ball toward the infield. Now I'm thinking, "He must not have caught it because he got up and threw it in so fast." The thing is, I forgot there was a runner on third, tagging up. I just plain forgot. The reason the outfielder was throwing the ball in so fast was that he was trying to get the runner at home. I mean, I know he caught the ball—my eyes tell me this—but you're not supposed to entirely trust your eyes. So I didn't and said, "No catch, no catch." I was going by the action of the fielder.

Then I look up and see the runner on third. "Oh, shit," I said. "He caught the ball and there was a runner on third. Oh, shit."

Lieppman, the Tacoma manager, is one of the nicest guys in baseball. He wouldn't say shit if he had a mouthful. He didn't know the rules, though, so he'd practically never come out and argue. You could fuck up a double play and he wouldn't come out. You'd say to yourself, "I can't believe

I got away with that." But this time Lieppman comes out. "Pam, Pam, I thought he caught the ball, didn't he?" I said, "I called no catch."

Then I go over to Meriwether and Layne and say, "Jeez, you guys, I thought he caught the ball, but the way he threw it in . . . He caught the ball, didn't he?"

They say, "Yeah, yeah. He caught it."

I said, "Okay, I'm going to change my decision."

So I make it a catch. The only reason I did it is because Lieppman is such a nice guy and I wanted to get the play right. But I guess I shouldn't have done it. I should have died with the call. But in a way, the fact that it was against Bowa, well, I was kind of happy.

Bowa comes running out and he's livid. He rushes up to me, gets in my face, and starts hitting me with the bill of his cap. Bowa isn't that tall. In fact, I think I'm taller than him, which also makes me happy. Anyway, he's spitting all over my face and yelling, "You're a fucking liar! You're fucking horseshit!" He says that shit four or five times before I dump him. Now he's furious because I've changed the call and because I've dumped him. Well, changing a call is pretty horseshit. Usually, if it's a horseshit manager, you die with the call. But Lieppman is a good guy, so I wanted to get it right.

Gawd, I can't believe I'm this bad. I make myself sick. I really think I wasn't concentrating the whole game. I don't know why, either.

Still, I had to dump Bowa for pecking me with his cap. I screwed up, but he still doesn't have the right to step on me.

Friday, April 18

Just got done packing. Ugh! I have way too much stuff.

Well, long game tonight. I had the plate for a 3½-hour game. Vegas won, 7–5. I had a real good plate job (I think). Thought I was pretty consistent. Had two time plays, which is rare. No problems anywhere tonight. Just a long, boring game. It's late (1:20 A.M.), but I have to write the Bowa ejection so I can mail it to Cutler before I go to Canada. Jeez, I'm tired.

Saturday, April 19

We're in Calgary now. We had a 5:05 game and everything went smooth, no problems. I made a good call at third when the Albuquerque runner tried to stretch a double into a triple. I told the third baseman later, "I don't know how you held on to the ball." I don't usually talk to players, but it was one hell of a play.

Anyway, watched the Holmes-Spinks fight and ate pizza with the guys and Dave, our clubbie. Layne gives him a hard time, the poor kid.

Bed is going to feel good tonight. I need to make up for all the sleep I lost in Vegas.

Sunday, April 20

Day game, 2:05 start. Everything went smooth. I made a couple of good calls. Bought a bucket of chicken and we all watched the Oilers-Flames playoff game. Layne fell asleep and Meriwether left to go watch a Friday the 13th movie. So I went back to my room where I did a few exercises, nothing much. I'm bored. I should run, but I probably won't.

Tuesday, April 22

I have to write twice today because I forgot to yesterday. I had a 2-hour-and-25-minute plate job last night. I called a lot of strikes, but they were throwing them. I'm trying for consistency back there, although I may have called a few high pitches. But all in all, I think I had a very good game.

It's going to be miserable today. It's cold and rainy. After the game last night, had some beers with Layne and Meriwether. Then we ordered an extralarge pizza.

Now, on to the next day . . .

It had rained all night, but we still played. The field was in good condition, but the first couple of plays I had were sloppy. On a force play at second, the shortstop never touched the base, but he was in the vicinity. Then, on another play, the shortstop for the other team never tagged the runner on a steal. The ball beat the guy by about five seconds, but still it made me look bad when the shortstop missed the tag. I called him out anyway.

Geezus, it is really getting cold. Hopefully we'll get rain in Portland.

Saturday, April 26

I haven't written in a while. A doubleheader was rained out tonight, and last night I had the plate. I still don't feel great about this year. I'm having a hard time concentrating. I don't enjoy it much this year. I don't know why. I mean, I work with two great guys this season. Hell, maybe I'm not used to that part of it, eh?

Promise that I'll start writing again on regular basis beginning manana. I have a 5 A.M. wake-up call tomorrow.

Tuesday, April 29

So I lied. Now I have to get back into writing this diary. So far we've had three games here in Albuquerque. The game was 16 innings. The second game—and I had the plate—lasted 10 innings. But I had a nice comment from Ed Farmer, pitcher for the Hawaii Islanders. He said I did the best job he's seen in seven years or so. He said I called both the outside and inside pitch for him. That was nice of him to say. He wasn't joking around, either. He said he meant it.

Anyway, I've had a good series here, but then again, I haven't had anything real tough. I'm more relaxed out there this year and I think everyone can tell. But I just don't have the desire this year to try to make it.

I was talking to a friend last night—we had a couple of drinks after the game—and I said that I was around people who are just the exact opposite of me. They're all so conventional, traditional, sexist, macho, etc. Some nights I think I will go nuts.

Tonight I told Meriwether and Layne that the female bartender (we were at Bennigan's) would not like to be called "dear." I'm always telling them that. So we asked her what she would prefer to be called: "Excuse me, dear?" or "Excuse me, miss?" or "Excuse me, ma'am?" So she picked "Excuse me, ma'am."

Later, I tried to explain to the guys that women don't really like to be called that. But why try? It's too tough. They really think women like being called that. These two are too far gone. Anyway, the point of all this is that five minutes later, the female bartender comes up to me and says, "Would you like another, hon?"

The irony of it all. Well, at least I can take it better if a female says that, than a male.

Sunday, May 4

How do you like this? Very first batter of the first inning of the first game of a doubleheader and Dion James of Vancouver argues a good called third strike. He yells directly in my face, "The fucking pitch was fucking outside!"

I told him, "No, it wasn't."

This time he yells, "The fucking pitch was low! You don't know shit!"

I ejected him, he left, and the game resumed.

Tuesday, May 6

I've been very lax about writing. I am so tired of this bullshit lately. Layne is a fucking pain in the ass. What a con. A politician couldn't do any better. Too bad, because

I thought at first he might be a good guy. Turns out that he's on the phone all day constantly calling his buddies in the major leagues. He's always trying to figure out what's going on up there. I swear, the guy must have $250-a-month phone bills. Meriwether and I call him The Lonely Guy. He can't stand being by himself. If he's not knocking on my door wanting to do something, he's knocking on Meriwether's door. And when he's not doing that, he's on the phone with another umpire. Anyway, I don't really trust him.

I just keep thinking, "Why am I in this game when I don't like or believe or live like any of these macho asshole people I meet or work with?" I sit back and see all the inequities we women have to put up with: it's totally different from being a male. If you don't assume their needs and desires, if you don't put those needs and desires above your own, well, they can't accept that. I don't know if I can live like this for a whole career. It's not the umpiring anymore—I have never umpired better. It's the day-to-day bullshit that I can hardly stand.

For example, I still cannot miss a pitch or a play before someone goes nutso. As much as I hate to say it, I can't see them letting me umpire in the major leagues. I can't see them letting me alone after I make a close call on a pitch or a play.

Anyway, I think I'm happier when I'm alone. I'd rather be alone than be around people I don't like. That makes a lot of sense, eh? I guess I still have a hard time describing my feelings. But I'm really going to try to start writing in this every day . . . hopefully.

Wednesday, May 7

Don't feel like writing, but here goes:

I hurt my knee real bad last night while working the plate. I had three flawless innings, got hit with a pitch, and then everything went downhill. For starters, I dumped

Portland manager Bill Dancy for arguing balls and strikes. It was the top of the fifth inning, a runner on second, no outs, and the score, 3–3. Dancy kept arguing on a pitch after I warned him, "I've heard enough."

He said, "No, you haven't. The ball isn't low."

I ejected him. He came out of the dugout and yelled for a while and then left the game.

Then, in the bottom of the 11th inning, with Tucson leading, 5–4, a runner on first, two outs, and the count 3–2, I called Portland shortstop Ken Dowell out on a half-swing. It was clearly a swing. Anyway, Dowell threw his bat toward the stands.

I said, "That's $25 for throwing your bat."

"You're fucking horseshit!" he yelled as he left the field.

Dowell is a jerk and he's always arguing on pitches and plays.

I just felt miserable today. I didn't do anything but sit around the hotel. I ate at Kentucky Fried Chicken and then went out and bought a leather jacket, hoping it might cheer me up. It didn't.

I'm pissed because my knee was killing me during the game. I couldn't bend it and probably missed a few pitches because of it. But I'll tell you what, I never got a break. On the first close pitch Dancy was on my ass. It's incredible.

Today I just thought about what an asshole world we live in. I need to work out to keep my sanity. Of course, with my knee hurt, I probably can't work out for at least five days. I didn't think I got hit that hard at first, but now my knee is huge and purple.

In tonight's game I had third base, but it was quiet. I didn't really have a play, which is good since I wasn't in a good state of mind. Anyway, Meriwether's wife is here in Portland. She's nice.

Friday, May 9

It poured all day. I didn't do a thing, except call Domino's for pizza and watch a movie called *City Heat.* I slept and ate—that's it.

It was raining hard at 4 o'clock, so I thought for sure we would be rained out. All of the sudden, the rain stopped, the sun came out, and we started the game at 7:30.

I had a good game. If nothing else, I was consistent and called a lot of strikes. I also jumped around on a lot of bad pitches. I guess I was a little nervous about getting hit again. I don't want to get hurt, and anyway, my knee is still sore from the last time I got nailed.

Ate pancakes after the game tonight. Geezus, what a lot of junk I've been eating. I need to get a tan, diet, and work out.

Thursday, May 22

I know, I know . . . I haven't written. Now I have too much to write. That's because I had another run-in with Bowa.

I had the plate tonight. Edmonton at Las Vegas. It was the top of the 8th inning and Edmonton was leading, 7–4, with one out and a runner on first. A high inside pitch came in and hit the bat. So I called it a foul ball—a strike.

All of the sudden, the batter, Jack Howell, turned around and said, "Pam, Pam, it hit me on the elbow."

"Hey, it sounded like all wood to me," I said. "Let me see where it hit you."

I'll be damned if he didn't show me his elbow, and sure enough, I could see the marks from the baseball seams on his skin. I could see both rows of the seams, that's how hard it hit him. So now I had to change another call. And again, it was against Bowa's team. Can you believe it?

I awarded Howell first base, and a few moments later, Bowa ran out of the dugout and started ranting and raving.

"That's the second time you've changed your decision on me!" he yelled.

In fact, he kept yelling the same thing over and over. "That's the second time you've done that! The second time!"

"Hey," I said, "don't be bringing up past games, Larry."

The guy wouldn't even give me a chance to explain. Finally, I had to scream right back.

"Now wait a minute! There's fucking baseball seams on his arm. I can't do anything but give him first base."

"All I know is that you've changed your decision on me twice."

I had warned him about bringing up past games. As usual, Bowa didn't listen. So I dumped him.

Then he really went nuts.

"You can't throw me out!" Bowa yelled. "I didn't cuss you!"

That's when he said he wasn't going to leave the field. He went on some wild rampage. First, he started to go after me again, but Meriwether and Layne restrained him.

"You can't touch me!" he screamed at them.

Then he started kicking dirt all over the plate. When Bowa finished there, he walked up the first-base line, where Meriwether and Layne tried again to get him to leave. He wouldn't listen. Instead, he walked to the plate two more times and kicked some more dirt. While he was there, he started screaming at me again.

"You cocksucker!" he said. "You're horseshit!"

Before he left, he kicked up another bunch of dirt and lime from the baselines. Layne was standing the closest to Bowa, and the stuff went all over his shirt and pants. Some of it also went in his right eye. It was so bad that Layne couldn't work the rest of the game. He had to go to the emergency room to get medical treatment.

Meriwether and I finished the game and Edmonton won, 14–6.

What an asshole that Bowa is. He has no style at all. He's ugly to look at, which is another reason I don't like him. I can't stand arguing with ugly ballplayers or managers, especially ugly rookie managers. He totally repulses me. He looks like a little weasel out there.

Tuesday, May 27

No Bowa for two whole days. Cutler fined and suspended him for kicking dirt in Layne's eye. Cutler also sent Dana DeMuth to join our crew while Layne's infection gets better.

Things had been pretty quiet until today. You know what that means: Bowa's back.

I had the plate and didn't know what to expect from Bowa. Maybe Cutler's suspension taught him a lesson. Maybe it didn't.

It didn't. By the third inning, I had to warn Bowa about arguing balls and strikes. A couple of pitches later, he walked out to the mound to talk to his pitcher, glaring at me the whole time. He was trying to stare me down, trying to look real arrogant. How childish and how stupid can you get? I just let him make a fool of himself in front of everybody.

After ample time to talk to his pitcher (no one was warming up in the bullpen), I went out there to tell them to get going. As I got to the mound, Ed Wojna, the Vegas pitcher, said to me, "Pam, those are good pitches."

"Don't talk about pitches, Ed," I said.

That's when Bowa had to stick his nose into it.

"Don't talk to my pitcher," he said.

I just looked at him and didn't say a word. That wasn't good enough for him. This time he screamed it at me.

"Don't talk to my pitcher!"

I could tell he just wanted to get into an argument, but

I wasn't going to give him the satisfaction. I just said, "Let's go!"

Just to try to piss me off, Bowa took his time leaving the mound. I could have dumped him then, but I didn't.

As the game continued, I could hear him every so often yelling, "Brutal!" or "Ooh" and "Aah" on some close pitches. What an asshole. The truth is, I wasn't giving Bowa's pitcher anything . . . nothing, not even the inside corner, which is my favorite pitch. I did it because of Bowa.

In the ninth inning, with Phoenix leading, 7–4, a runner on first and two outs, I called a strike on Vegas' Ed Rodriguez for a count of 1-1. That's when Bowa yelled, "You stink!"

I turned around and yelled back, "You're gone!"

Bowa ran down and threw another fit.

"What did I say! What did I say!"

I told him, "You said, 'You stink.' "

"How did you know I was talking to you? I didn't say your name! You can't throw me out! I wasn't talking to you! You're a fucking c–––!"

He repeated the last sentence about a dozen times. While he was doing that, he was hitting me with the bill of his cap and spraying me with spit. Then he started yelling again.

"You keep writing your fucking reports because you're going to die in this league! I'll make sure of that! You're horseshit!"

I guess I kind of snapped:

"I'll keep writing reports because you're just a fucking jerk, and I'll keep dumping you because I'm tired of your bullshit!"

You should have seen his face. I think he finally realized who the boss was.

It took about four minutes to get Bowa off the field. Meriwether and DeMuth got him to leave, and Phoenix ended up winning the game, 7–4.

● ● ●

That was about it for my diary. I got bored with it. Mostly I was too tired after games to stay up and write. And anyway, sometimes it made me pissed off all over again to think about the games. So I quit writing.

The way our schedule worked out, we never had Bowa and Las Vegas again for the rest of the season. It was just as well. I was tired of dealing with the asshole.

Also, I learned that Cutler disliked Bowa almost as much as I did. I learned this a few days after I filed my ejection report. Cutler called me up and said, "Pam, did you really call Larry a 'fucking jerk'?"

I didn't know what to say. I couldn't tell if Cutler was going to fine me for my conduct or if he was just amused by the whole thing. So I stalled for time.

"Uh, well, Mr. Cutler, let me see . . ."

"Pam, that's okay. I don't care. I think he is, too."

Cutler backed me up on the Bowa ejections. He blasted him in the press.

"He baited her the whole game," Cutler said of Bowa. "I'd have dumped him in the third inning. I can't let this get out of hand. If my mother did the same thing, I'd fine and suspend her.

"He wasn't an angel in the major leagues. I just didn't think he'd be this bad."

I guess Bowa even asked him for a hearing, but Cutler told him it wouldn't do any good; he'd lose anyway.

There was some other Bowa-related developments. For instance, I know this is going to sound bad, but I think Layne milked that eye infection for all it was worth. I'm sure dirt and chalk to the eye is serious, but Layne sure had a lot of days off because of it. I just don't think he was in a hurry to get back to work. He'd cry about his eye every day, saying how his eyesight might be affected. Meanwhile, I didn't miss a game when my knee was the size of a football and as purple as a grape.

As I look back on it, Bowa had the same problem that a lot of rookie managers have: they don't know how or when to argue. Bowa never knew when to stop, shut his big mouth, and return to the dugout. He thought he could stay out there forever, that we'd let him bitch and bitch and bitch. He thought that if we missed a call, he had the right to come out there and argue as long as he wanted and hit the umpire with the bill of his cap. I mean, you can come out and argue a call and you might be upset at first. But you've got to know when to calm down. Bowa couldn't get that through his thick skull. He didn't realize that when you kick dirt on an umpire, you're going to get thrown out.

He also didn't know how to control his players. He never had any control of them and you can't do that in baseball. Of course, in my opinion, he didn't know how to manage, either. Hell, his own players hated him. He used to scream at them in the dugout, in front of everybody. Vegas players would come up to me and say, "I wish you would have gotten rid of him five innings earlier."

Bowa was a miserable man that season. I don't know how he is now, but back then he was terrible. If I were on a desert island with him, I'd swim for another island—I don't care how far it was. I didn't like him and he didn't like me.

After the Bowa stuff settled down, a sportswriter asked me about the profanity on the field, if it bothered me.

"Oh, shit, who cares?" I said.

Was this guy kidding, or what? I told him some of the things Bowa said out there. I didn't care about the cussing. Some sportswriters would say that the game would be better if there weren't so much cussing. That's a joke. Most of the players and managers out there don't understand anything except profanity. And anyway, why was this guy asking me about cuss words? Why didn't he go ask the religious players, the born-again Christians, about what they thought of the profanity. After all, what's so hard about living with a little "Fuck you"? I heard it all the time. They're just words, right? I mean, I'd rather get sworn at than hit.

So then the reporter said, "Well, it will be a better game if everybody just toned it down."

I had to laugh. It will never be a better game as long as you have fucking little assholes like Larry Bowa in it. He doesn't understand anything *but* swearing, and even then, I'm not sure he understands.

I was hoping things would grow calmer once Bowa and Vegas were off our crew's schedule. It was calm all right— for three days. Then we had a Hawaii-Vancouver day game that featured one hellacious brawl.

I loved those fights, mostly because as an umpire all I did was stand to the side and take down the names and numbers of the players and managers involved. Our policy was this: if we could stop the fight before it really got started, we would. If we couldn't, we'd move away and let the players beat the hell out of each other. After a while, we'd get together and start comparing those names and numbers. By then, the managers had usually restored calm.

This one happened May 31 at Vancouver, the bottom of the third inning, one out. Glenn Braggs, a big, muscular outfielder for the Canadians, was up. By the way, I was behind the plate.

The first pitch from Hawaii's Bob Patterson, a left-hander, comes way inside, moving Braggs off the plate. The next pitch hits Braggs in the head. I can still hear the sound of the ball smacking against Bragg's batting helmet.

Braggs fell to the ground and didn't move an inch. I looked over to the Vancouver dugout to see if the trainer was coming. As I did, Braggs suddenly jumped off the ground and rushed out toward the mound. Before anybody could catch him, Braggs karate-kicked Patterson in the groin and then wrestled him to the ground. Before I knew it, both benches had emptied and we had a full-fledged brawl.

Luckily, Mike Paul, a Vancouver coach, helped make the fight a short one. He got out there and pulled his players off the field and back into the dugout.

I had to dump Braggs because he was the one who started the fight and caused the miniriot. I know what you're thinking: I should have dumped Patterson, too. Problem was, I didn't know if he was intentionally throwing at Braggs. I didn't think so, which is why I let him stay in the game. Sure, the pitch was suspect, but I couldn't say absolutely that he was trying to hit Braggs.

Poor Patterson. We had to delay the game while he went back to the dugout and put on another pair of game pants. The pair he had on had a huge tear from where Braggs had kicked him. Patterson's face was bruised, scraped, and swollen, but he came back and pitched. But before he did, I warned both pitchers and managers that I'd dump any-one who tried to retaliate. For a change, they listened.

A couple of weeks later, I had to listen to Winston Llenas, the manager of Edmonton. He started bitching at me dur-ing the tenth inning of a game between the Trappers and Vancouver.

At the time, the score was tied, 3–3, there was a Van-couver runner on first, two outs, and the count was 3-2. On the pitch, the Vancouver batter started to swing and then held up. Still, I wasn't absolutely sure, so I went to Meriwether on the appeal. Meriwether said the batter didn't go on the swing.

That's when Llenas started yelling at me from the dug-out. I couldn't hear him at first, but then he marched toward the mound to talk to his pitcher. As he did, he turned to me and yelled, "Have some guts out here!"

I said, "I've got guts and you're done!"

He ran up to me, got in my face, and started sticking his chest against mine. He tried to walk me back a step, but I wouldn't budge. Then I tried walking him back a step. It probably looked funny to the crowd and the players.

The whole time we're semibumping each other, Llenas is yelling at me. He wasn't saying anything obscene—in fact, we sounded like a couple of Little Leaguers arguing—but he kept spraying me the whole time. I still didn't know how to spray him back, so I had to stand there and let the spit nail me in the face.

Llenas was mad because he thought I took too long to go to Meriwether for the appeal. He was also mad that I had asked Meriwether for help, even though his own catcher hadn't asked for an appeal. Figure that one out. And then he decided he was upset because he thought I didn't pay enough attention on the field.

"Well, you're done," I said, not particularly caring what he thought of my concentration level. And that was that.

Before long, the same could be said of my slim prospects for an American League job. In late July, while our crew was in Phoenix, Marty Springstead paid a surprise visit to watch us work. He naturally chose the one night I was sick as a dog. I didn't see a doctor, but I swear I had pneumonia or the worst cold in the history of all colds. I was dizzy and nauseous and looked absolutely terrible.

Still, I didn't have any choice but to go out there that night. I wanted to show Springstead that I was tough, that I could umpire even when I was ill. He had never seen me work before, so I wanted to make a good impression.

About an hour before the game started, I took some cold and flu pills that I had bought at the drugstore. By the first pitch, I was a zombie out there. Whatever they put in those pills almost knocked me out. My nose was stuffed up, I could barely breathe, my joints ached, and I could hardly move. What a space cadet I was. The whole time I was on the field, I was thinking, "Jesus Christ, I've got pneumonia and Springstead's going to think I'm a terrible umpire."

Gawd, was I awful that night. A ball was hit to right field and I quit running on the play much too early. The ball could have gone under a fence or something and where would I have been? About fifty yards away, wheezing and coughing. As it was, I'm sure I looked as if I were just wandering out there.

I didn't belong on the field that game. I couldn't focus on the plays, I sure as hell couldn't run without wanting to puke, and the pills had made me drowsy enough to want to take a nap on the infield grass. All I wanted was to get the hell out of there, go back to the hotel, and get some sleep.

One problem: Springstead wanted to go get a couple of beers after the game. Well, I couldn't turn down the American League supervisor of umpires, so I went. Later, during a lull in the conversation, Springstead turned to me and said, "You know, you should have gone all the way out on that line drive to right." Springstead was an ex-umpire; he knew when someone had made a horseshit play.

I can't be positive, but I think my chances for a job in the American League ended that night. Springstead wasn't a jerk about my mistake, but in his mind he probably thought I wasn't a hard worker, a hustler. The next day he was gone, as were most of my American League hopes.

It only got worse. The Bowa incidents had reminded every sportswriter in the country that I was still around. Every season it was something. In the Texas League it had been the frying pan on home plate. In the PCL it was the batboy and then Bowa. Jesus, when would it stop?

The *Wall Street Journal* sent somebody first. Why anyone who subscribes to the *Wall Street Journal* would want to read anything about me, I do not know. What did I have to do with business?

USA Today also sent a reporter. It always did. It seemed as if *USA Today* did more stories on me than any other paper. When I got a copy of their latest article, I couldn't help but read the part about Butler and Barney Deary. I was always interested in what they had to say.

Said Butler: "Her greatest strength is her ability to call balls and strikes."

And Deary said: "I've gone to the [umpire] schools each year. So far, the women didn't show the ability Pam has. Pam has raised the standard."

For what, women? I didn't care about that. I wasn't competing with the women in the umpiring schools. I was competing with guys such as Layne and DeMuth and Meriwether.

Butler's and Deary's comments didn't make me feel too good about my chances of moving up. And it didn't help when Cutler said I was still rated in the middle of the pack. I thought I did better than average that season.

Whatever the case, my PCL career was finished. The American Association, another Triple A league, had picked up my contract. I was headed to the Midwest.

As fate would have it, Cutler was in Las Vegas addressing a group of local baseball officials and fans. When he told them I was leaving the PCL for the American Association, they started applauding. The jerks.

In a way, I was glad to get out of there. I needed a fresh start. Four seasons in one league was long enough.

You know, Cutler always said that I was a step away from the majors. I just didn't realize how big a step it was.

Of course, not everyone had such a difficult time making the jump from minors to majors. Two months after the season ended, the San Diego Padres hired Larry Bowa as their manager. I didn't know whether to laugh or cry.

CHAPTER 9

A Step Closer

I'm not sure how to break this to all those people who think Elvis Presley is still alive, but he isn't. He's deader than a doorknob. Trust me on this.

My source is Dr. Charles Harlan, who is the medical examiner for the State of Tennessee, as well as for the city of Nashville, and one of the biggest fans of umpires I've ever met. He and his wife, Dr. Gretel Harlan, who is the Davidson County assistant medical examiner, took me and my 1987 crew—Gary Cederstrom, Jack Oujo, and Zach Bevington—under their wing and treated us like royalty. In fact, Doc and Gretel were always doing nice things for the crews that came through Nashville.

Nashville is the home of the Sounds, the Triple A farm club of the Cincinnati Reds. We opened our season with a series between the Sounds and the visiting Omaha Royals. After the game, somebody introduced us to Doc and Gretel, and in no time at all a friendship was born.

Doc and Gretel loved to talk about umpiring. They were softball umpires in their spare time, and I swear they would have given up their regular careers for a chance to umpire professionally. They were addicted to it.

The Harlans first started befriending umpires in the late 1970s, when Doc was the Shelby County assistant medical examiner in Memphis and Gretel was a pathologist at St. Joseph's Hospital. After reading a story in the local newspaper about the shortage of softball umpires for city-park games, Doc volunteered to help out, no pay required. The next season, Gretel joined him. They were hooked.

At the same time, they would go see the Memphis Chicks, who were a Double A affiliate back then. The Harlans started talking to the umpires at the games, found out how desperately poor the umpires were, and invited them to their modest house for a home-cooked meal. Word spread among the umpires, and soon the Harlans were known throughout the league for their generosity.

In 1983, they moved to Nashville, bought a bigger house, this one with a guest room, and started feeding umpires two or three times a week. Then one night a crew asked if it could crash in the guest room, thus saving the umpires hotel money. Doc and Gretel said yes, and the Harlan Hilton, as it became known, was established.

The Harlan Hilton was going strong when I joined the American Association. Back then, it could be as late as eleven P.M. or so and Doc and Gretel would still invite us to their huge house and then treat us to some of the best meals I've ever had. One night there would be lobster. The next night steak would be served. The night after that pork chops would be waiting on the dinner table. It was crazy. Hell, they were crazy.

The Harlans were rich, but not stuffy rich. They had this mansion of sorts, but it had a real lived-in look. It was as if they didn't want to show off their success. Instead, all they really wanted to do was sit around the table and shoot the bull about umpiring.

The Harlans were local celebrities. When one of the singers for the Oak Ridge Boys organized a four-day fantasy baseball camp, which featured former major league greats Brooks Robinson, Johnny Bench, and Gates Brown, Doc and Gretel umpired one of the games. In fact, Doc got Brown on a called third strike.

The Harlans also went to just about every Sounds game

they could. If there was a close play, you could bet Doc or Gretel would ask you about it later. Of course, we didn't have the heart to tell them that umpires hate to be second-guessed, especially by people who call softball games for fun. I used to love to visit Doc and Gretel, but after a while, you wanted to talk about something other than the infield-fly rule.

One time, as we were finishing up another late-night dinner feast, I made the mistake of asking Doc and Gretel what it was like to be a medical examiner. There are some things you don't discuss after a meal, and this was one of them.

The Harlans immediately started describing, in detail, a half dozen of the most disgusting and vile death scenes that you could imagine. Electrocutions in bathtubs. Sex murders. Various suicides, complete with descriptions of what happens to the brain when a bullet blasts through the skull. It made my stomach turn.

Naturally, it didn't bother the Harlans a bit. They would sit there and nibble on a piece of lobster while telling us one gross story after another. They were used to the goriness.

Then, out of the blue, Doc mentioned Elvis's name.

"What about him?" I said.

That's when Doc told us that he had served as a consultant on the medical team in charge of determining exactly what killed Elvis. According to Doc, the official cause of Elvis's death wasn't just drug related. Drugs were in Elvis's system when he died, but Doc and the other examiners said the drug combination wasn't lethal. They said his death had more to do with a weak heart than anything else.

Then Doc explained, in medical terms, what might have triggered the heart problem. I can't remember the exact name, but basically, Doc said Elvis died on a toilet seat at Graceland. I guess he was straining too hard while he was going to the bathroom.

So now every time I read about another Elvis-lives theory, I have to laugh. After all, I have the real inside information on what killed The King.

Aside from the Harlans and their hospitality, there were other differences between the American Association and the PCL. The PCL, even with Bowa in the league, was more laid-back, more calm. I noticed that right away. In the PCL, if the score was 7–0 in the eighth inning, the losing team had usually packed it in and didn't care what happened. But in the American Association, the score could be 25–0 in the ninth and both teams would still be battling as if it were the seventh game of the World Series. These guys were hard on themselves, and they were also hard on the umpires. They wanted you to work as hard as they worked, which seemed fair enough.

My crew was semi-interesting that season. Cederstrom was the crew chief. I knew he didn't care for me, but we never had any problems. He did his job and I did mine.

Oujo was a nice guy. He had won some sort of award in 1985 as the top minor league umpire prospect, so I figured he must be pretty good. He was. We played racquetball together (I usually beat him) and hit the bars on occasion. Oujo also knew how to needle me just so. You see, I used to have all this nervous energy before the game. I'd pace in the dressing room and worry about the stupidest things. Naturally, Oujo couldn't help himself:

"Pam, I don't know how to say this, but I've got a real bad feeling about tonight's game."

I knew he was kidding, but I couldn't help myself: I'd get more nervous.

Sometimes the tables would get turned on Oujo, like the night he was working the plate but lost count of how many outs were left in the inning. His wife, whom he hadn't seen in weeks, was flying into town later that evening, so naturally Oujo's mind was elsewhere. After punching out a guy on a called third strike, Oujo, thinking the inning was finished, started walking off the field. I had third base and as tactfully as possible, yelled, "Uh, Jack? Jack, there's only two outs."

Startled and embarrassed by the mistake, Oujo said, "Oh, okay," and hurried back to home plate to complete the inning.

Another time, Oujo was working home plate in Nashville and he had to call a balk on the Sounds pitcher. It was a close call, but a good one. Up in the radio booth, the announcers started ripping Oujo for what they thought was a horrible call. Listening to the broadcast were the Harlans, who told Oujo about the announcers' comments when the half-inning was finished. Oujo promptly wrote a note ripping the announcers, attached a rule book to it, and had the Harlans deliver the message. That was Oujo for you.

But Zach Bevington was my favorite. Bevington was different from almost all of the other umpires I had met. He wasn't one of those macho assholes who thought that the only way you could be a good umpire was by putting on a tough-guy act. He drank only distilled water, fasted on Sundays, worked out, and was very independent, which made some of his partners nervous. Not me. I admired Bevington for daring to be different. In fact, Bevington was the only partner I ever had whom I would have thought about dating. You know my rule, but Bevington would have been worth an exception. Of course, he never asked, which is just as well.

Bevington was also on the hardheaded side. For example, the Harlans warned him about drinking too much distilled water. They said it could hurt his kidneys, or something like that. Sure enough, about a year later Bevington was in an airport and he got sick—kidney stones. The cause: all that distilled water.

By 1987, Bart Giamatti had officially become the National League president, succeeding Chub Feeney, who had been there for seventeen years. Ed Vargo, a former National League umpire who had worked four World Series, four League Championships, and four All-Star

Games, was the new director of umpire supervision. His consultants were Al Barlick and Augie Donatelli. These people, along with Barney Deary, controlled my hopes of making it to the big leagues.

The American League, as best as I could tell, was out of the picture. Butler said he liked me as an umpire, but I think he was only jerking me around. I liked the old man, but I knew deep down that he didn't really want or think a woman umpire belonged in baseball. I hope I'm wrong, but I don't think I am. Already Butler was telling people that I had to be better than a male umpire to get a big league job.

"She's got to be better because of the fact that she's a girl," he said. "I'm not saying it's fair. It's just the situation. I don't think it's fair, but it exists and she's not going to change it."

Also, it hadn't helped that I'd botched up things when Marty Springstead came to see my crew a season earlier. I'm glad I didn't have to read that report. It probably said I was lazy, unfocused, and slow to move. I'd also bet that it didn't say anything about me umpiring while I was sick.

None of the eight stops on the 140-game American Association schedule could compare with Honolulu, Vancouver, Las Vegas, or just about anywhere else in the PCL. Instead, there were Oklahoma City, Omaha, Des Moines, Denver, Nashville, Louisville, Indianapolis, and Buffalo. Also, we had no sweet hotel deals like the ones in the PCL. Here, we had to pay for our own rooms. There were no freebies in the American Association.

So we adapted. We used to take baseballs and hand them out as if they were breath mints. You'd be surprised at the power of a single baseball. We would give one to a hotel clerk and get bumped to a nicer room. Bartenders would buy you a round or two if you tossed them a couple of baseballs. Airline ticket agents also melted at the sight of a couple of official American Association baseballs.

Oujo was the master of the bribe. We checked into the

Des Moines Marriott during our first trip into town, and before we knew it, Oujo convinced the hotel manager to give us suites, including the presidential suite. We paid $35 a night for the huge rooms. Unbelievable.

Oujo was amazing. He could walk up to an airline ticket agent, flash a couple of baseballs, and in no time at all we'd be in first class. I think we had twenty-eight flights that season and Oujo got us bumped up to first class twenty-six times.

Once, he convinced me to try my luck with the baseballs. He had asked me before, but I had always begged off. I was chicken, and anyway, why should I ruin a good thing? But this time I felt I could do it. So I made my way to the airline ticket counter, baseballs and coach boarding passes in hand, and started schmoozing.

"Uh, hi," I said to the ticket agent.

"Hi, what can I do for you?"

"Well, we're professional baseball umpires in the American Association, and we were hoping you might have some room up in first class for us. By the way, I think I've got a couple of baseballs I'd like to give you for looking."

"Thank you," said the agent as he took the balls and started checking his computer. "No, I'm sorry . . . nothing up front today. But thanks for the baseballs."

Oujo got a laugh out of that one.

Not long after that flight, we were on another plane headed to Louisville. This commuter plane seated about forty people, and in each of the seat pouches was a copy of the airline's complimentary magazine. It was just my luck that this particular issue contained a story about my minor league career.

Well, Oujo saw this and had a field day. Somehow he convinced the flight attendant to let him talk on the plane's speaker system:

"Ladies and gentlemen, I'd just like to inform you that we have a celebrity on board tonight. Her name is Pam Postema, and she is the only woman umpire in professional baseball. You can read about Pam on page forty-five of your in-flight magazine."

People got out of their seats and started asking me to autograph their airline magazines. It was embarrassing, but it also was funny. In our business, you took the laughs any way you could get them, even if they were at your own expense.

Another time we were flying from Nashville to Buffalo for a series when we discovered that the Oak Ridge Boys were seated in first class with us. They probably paid for their seats, as opposed to us, the baseball bribers. Anyway, they were going to sing the national anthem at that night's Buffalo Bisons game and then leave. And to all those people who were at the game, well, the truth is, the Oak Ridge Boys lip-synched the whole thing. One of their singers told me on the flight that they used a tape. I'll say this, though: they were good lip-synchers.

A new league meant new managers, new players, new problems. For instance, some of those ballparks had the weirdest configurations you've ever seen. Buffalo's old War Memorial Stadium, which is where they filmed the movie *The Natural*, had more ground rules than I'd heard in years. It took ten minutes to go over all of them. We had ballparks where the overflow crowds were allowed on the outer edges of the playing field. Each place, it seemed, had its own little quirks. That's how it was in the minors.

For instance, Denver's Mile High Stadium, which wasn't really built for baseball, had this huge blue wall in right field. And gawd, did baseballs fly out of that place. There was this one guy with Denver, Joey Meyer, who had 24 home runs and 75 RBI after just 63 games. He hit one that traveled 582 feet one time. Or at least, that's what the engineer who measured the distance said. And Denver had another player, Steve Kiefer, who had 20 homers, 60 RBI, and was batting .342 after those same 63 games. Must have been the thin air and that short distance to right field.

As usual, I had a few memorable confrontations. In early

June, we had a series in Oklahoma City between the Eighty
Niners and the visiting Indianapolis Indians. Oklahoma
City, a Texas Rangers farm team, was managed by Toby
Harrah, a former major league infielder. It was Harrah's
rookie season as a manager, and you know how I felt about
first-year managers. All I could think about was Larry
Bowa Part II.

Sure enough, I had to dump Harrah in the second game
of the series. He chirped about something, just like Bowa
used to do, so I threw him out. Afterward, he blasted me
in the *Indianapolis Star:*

"She is a joke. The broad is overmatched. She belongs
in Class A ball. If she were a male umpire, she would never
have gotten out of A ball. She wouldn't be in this league.
But I guess it makes good PR."

Harrah wasn't done:

"She always looks for a reason to raise her arm. Other
than that, she's a lousy ump. She doesn't grasp the game
of baseball. If you haven't played the game—and I'm sure
she hasn't—you miss the grasp. It's like someone reading
a medical book. That doesn't make them a doctor. She
knows the rules, but that doesn't make her an umpire. I've
never seen a game where she hasn't blown a call."

I wish I could have said something about the bonehead
plays Harrah made as a rookie manager, but what would
have been the point? He thought he knew everything. It
was the guy's first year in the league and he was an expert
on umpires and managing, right? I guess that's why his
team finished the season in fourth place with a 69–71
record, or why his 1988 team was 67–74 and also finished
fourth. I looked it up.

A week after I dumped Harrah, Bevington and Cederstrom had to listen to his crap. They threw him out, but
this time Harrah was a little more humble. I don't know
if Joe Ryan, the president of the American Association,
had told him to quit bitching, or if Deary's response to the

rips had made their way back to him (Deary called them "asinine"), but Harrah was more humble after Bevington and Cederstrom dumped him.

"I'm not the first manager to criticize an umpire," Harrah said. "At one time or another I've probably said every umpire should go back to A ball. It's tough being a woman umpire, being the only one in those shoes. But that's baseball . . .

"If I had it to do all over again, I'd do it different. I shouldn't have said the things I did in the paper, but let's just leave it at that. Baseball is an emotional game, and sometimes you say things you shouldn't say. I've done it before and I'll probably do it again."

I'll give Harrah credit: he blasted me in the papers, but at least he had the guts to apologize in the papers, too. After that, I don't think Harrah and our crew had another problem. Unlike Bowa, Harrah knew when enough was enough.

And then there was Denver's Terry Bevington (no relation to Zach), another first-year manager in the league. I knew him from the PCL, and his style was the exact opposite of Harrah's. He acted as if I weren't even on the field. He completely ignored me. I guess he thought it would hurt my feelings. Hey, I couldn't have cared less what he did as long as he didn't disrupt the game.

Believe it or not, I actually had a few fans in the league. Joe Sparks, the manager of the Iowa Cubs, challenged me early but learned that I didn't back down. Before long, he was one of my biggest supporters. And when he argued, he never used any of that "Get back to the kitchen" shit that some of them thought was real clever. He argued about baseball, about the call—not about me. I respected that.

Orlando Gomez was the manager of the Buffalo team—at least for the first thirty-three games he was. Then the Cleveland Indians, who were the major league affiliate, moved Gomez to the Double A team in Williamsport and promoted Steve Swisher to the Bisons. Gomez and I used to go at it in the Texas League and in winter ball. He used to bitch about balls and strikes all the time, so I started dumping him. In return, he started calling me "the fastest gun" in the league. When I saw him in Louisville for a series, he said that I had improved "over one hundred percent" and that he thought I'd make it to the big leagues. What I needed him to do was tell Vargo and Giamatti the same thing.

In that same Buffalo-Louisville series I was treated to a rare display of respect by the players. I had the plate one night and everything went perfect. No arguments. No bastard pitches. No close plays. It was one of those rare times when nobody could say a single word about a single call.

At the end of the game, I glanced over to the Louisville dugout, and some of their players gave me the thumbs-up sign. Then I looked over to the Buffalo dugout, and they were doing the same thing. I was so used to seeing the middle finger aimed at me that these gestures caught me by surprise. I smiled as I left the field that night.

In fact, things were going too well for me. I was having a good season and actually enjoying myself at times. The four-umpire crew helped a lot, as did Oujo and Bevington. The money still wasn't that great—about $35 a game in salary, $55 a day for food, hotel, and incidentals—but I was getting by.

Despite my skimpy paychecks, I decided to splurge a little bit on some luxury items. As part of my new attitude, I hired a makeup consultant to help soften the edges and improve my image. I didn't know if it would help get me a promotion, but I thought it might make things easier between me and my umpiring partners. And as stupid as it sounds now, I thought the players would react better if they were looking at someone semiattractive out there. Maybe they'd see that I wasn't such a red-ass, after all. Anyway, what could a little makeup hurt?

This was the same silly logic I had used a year earlier, when I hired a beauty consultant to coordinate my so-called fashion statement. I figured that the umpire talent level in Triple A was pretty much the same, so it would be the little things, such as clothes, that got me to the big leagues. With the help of the beauty consultant I managed to spend, for me, a small fortune. The consultant told me that each person had his or her own season. I was a Spring, she said, which is why my wardrobe had to emphasize bright, splashy colors. Problem was, I showed up at the ballpark each day looking like a rainbow. If anything, the whole clothing experiment hurt my credibility with my partners. They'd see me walk into the umpires' locker room dressed to the nines, but then couldn't separate the woman from the umpire an hour later. It was a mess. As for statements, the only ones I ever saw came attached to my monthly credit card bills.

So this time I junked the clothes consultant and concentrated on something less obvious. In fact, everything was fine at first. About the only drawback to my plan was the bite the makeup and manicure sessions were taking out of my budget. I looked nice, but my checking account was taking a beating. So in an effort to make a nail session go a long way, I decided to conserve. Rather than pry off my latest set of fake fingernails, I kept them on for an extra few days and hoped nobody noticed. At $2.40 a nail, I wanted to get my money's worth.

One day, I overslept and didn't have time to mess with the fingernails before I drove to the ballpark. Painted fire engine red, the nails were a little too bright for umpiring, and that could mean trouble if any of the ballplayers saw them.

A few innings into the game, I spied something in the batter's box. It was a red fingernail. My fingernail. I quickly scooped it up and put the fingernail in my pocket, hoping the catcher or hitter hadn't seen a thing. Then I looked at my hands, where about six of the red nails had disappeared. I didn't know what to do. So desperate was I to find the other five nails that I started pawing at the ground between pitches. I must have looked ridiculous, but by the end of the game I had managed to find every missing nail. So much for that experiment.

As for my chances at the big leagues, I didn't have a clue. Nobody ever said anything to you. I rarely heard a word from Deary or Vargo. A call from Springstead and the American League was probably out of the question. All I knew is what I read.

Most of the stories said the same old things. But occasionally, there would be a twist, such as the time *Sports Illustrated* sort of blasted the major leagues for taking its sweet time with my career. I don't know if the two events were related, but shortly after the *Sports Illustrated* article came out I received an offer I couldn't turn down: umpiring home plate for the 44th Annual Hall of Fame Game between the New York Yankees and the Atlanta Braves July 27 in Cooperstown, New York.

This was big. Commissioner Peter Ueberroth would be there. So would Giamatti and American League president Dr. Bobby Brown. My crew would include Vargo, Neudecker, and Hank Soar. If ever I had a chance to showcase my work, this would be it.

Nobody was supposed to know about my selection. They said I could tell my folks, but to instruct them not to say a word to anyone else. If the press found out too early, it would turn the exhibition game into a circus.

Those were the days. My regular crew was already in Buffalo, so it wasn't much of a problem getting to Cooperstown. And for two days, Vargo and his wife treated me as if I were back at the Harlan Hilton. They couldn't have been nicer. They also couldn't have done more to keep me away from the various sportswriters who had learned about the game-day umpiring crew. That was okay with me: I didn't want to talk to them anyway. I was nervous enough without having to do more interviews.

I still have an official scorecard from the game. The Yankees won, 3–0, and as games go, it was a breeze. I had the butterflies during the first inning, but after that, I was fine. In fact, I was pretty damn good.

Dennis Rasmussen was the starting pitcher for the Yankees. I knew him from the PCL, so there was no problem there. Jim Acker was the Atlanta starter, and when he threw the first pitch, a little bit of history was made. I became the first woman to umpire a game between two major league teams.

It wasn't the most exciting game I ever worked. A lot of the regulars made only cameo appearances. New York's Rickey Henderson and Don Mattingly didn't play at all, while Graig Nettles and Dave Winfield each batted once and then left the lineup. By the end of the game, my lineup card was full of substitutions.

Nobody bitched about a thing. I punched out four players on called third strikes, but I didn't hear a peep from any of them. And I shouldn't have, either: they were all strikes. About the strangest thing that happened was when, with two outs in the bottom of the ninth, Hank Soar came down from his position near third base and said to me, "Grab all the baseballs you can. Stock up, so we can have some balls. I put two dozen aside before the game."

"Yeah, sure, Hank," I said.

When the game was finished, I was walking on clouds. I told the reporters that it was business as usual, but I knew it was more than that. I had been placed in a pressure situation and had responded well. How many umpires had to audition before the commissioner, two league presidents, a league director of umpire supervision, and two major league teams? I did and it was great. I loved the pressure.

Even though it was a big moment, I didn't know if my performance had actually done much for my big league chances. I knew this: it couldn't hurt.

Holtzman from the *Chicago Tribune* was at the game. So

was Hal Bodley from *USA Today*. After reading their stories, I felt pretty confident about my future. Giamatti told Bodley that he wanted to see me work under major league playing conditions. "I thought she did a good job," he said.

Giamatti also put to rest that stupid argument about women umpires not being able to handle the swear words. That was Chub Feeney's old line, that the language was too rough for a woman. Said Giamatti: "The modern world has absorbed a level of coarse language, I am sorry to say. I don't feel a need to protect women from the English language. I was always an equal-opportunity English professor. In fact, most of my best students were females."

I liked Giamatti. I liked his style. He didn't take everything so seriously, and he seemed to keep an open mind about things.

I got some other compliments that day. Bobby Cox, the Braves general manager, sat in the stands behind home plate and said I didn't miss a pitch. Chuck Tanner, the Atlanta manager, told Vargo to put me on the spring training umpires schedule for 1988. Rasmussen told reporters that I did well. And Holtzman even predicted that I was "certain" to earn a promotion to the big leagues, "probably as early as next season." I could only hope.

Even George Steinbrenner, the owner of the Yankees, got into the act. Didn't he always? Steinbrenner was sitting in the stands when my stepdad, Joe Newbauer, who was at the game with my mom, decided he wanted to shake hands with the most famous owner in baseball. When he got to Steinbrenner's seat, about twelve kids were waiting for autographs. So he waited, too. After introducing himself, he got Steinbrenner to autograph a baseball and then started quizzing him on my performance.

"There were a couple of calls I didn't think were right, but I'm no umpire," Steinbrenner said. "I'll tell you what, she can umpire the Yankees anytime she wants. She did a very good job."

The whole experience was wonderful, from start to finish. My mom was so enthusiastic—you know how moms are—that she went to one of those tourist stores in Cooperstown and bought me a front page to a fake newspaper called *The Doubleday Courier*. Stripped across the top of the page in huge letters was, "Pam Postema—First Female Major League Umpire." I got a kick out of it. I just hoped I didn't have to burn it like I did the T-shirt.

Things were changing for the better. At least, that's what I kept telling myself. Maybe the struggle was coming to an end. Maybe I hadn't wasted eleven years' worth of work and bullshit, after all. At last, I was being accepted more as an umpire and less as a woman.

Then came an August 30 game at Buffalo between the Bisons and the Sounds. It was the day I discovered that some things never change, no matter how hard you try.

The Bisons always drew big crowds, especially on the weekends. This was a Sunday game, so by the time I got to home plate to go over the ground rules and exchange lineup cards, the place was semipacked. Swisher, who had replaced Gomez, was the Buffalo manager. Jack Lind was the Sounds manager. Lind usually was a quiet and subdued guy. He rarely argued, and when he did, it was always without much fanfare. I thought he was harmless.

Swisher and Lind handed me the lineup cards. I looked them over and handed them back. Suddenly, Lind snatched my mask, gave it to Swisher, and in one hurried, shocking motion, grabbed my waist, bent me over backward, and proceeded to give me a five-second kiss in front of a stunned stadium. Worse yet, Lind was trying to slip his tongue in my mouth.

I didn't know what to do. When he returned me to my feet, I kind of stood there, speechless. All I could think about was, "I'm glad that's over."

A few moments later, Swisher handed me my mask, and I said, "Well . . ." With that, everyone turned around and walked away. I was so dazed by it all that I didn't even dump Lind. I tried to laugh it off and even told a reporter that Lind was a good kisser. Gawd, what a stupid thing to say. First of all, Lind should never have done what he did. It was totally unprofessional. He was treating me as a woman, not as an umpire. He apparently had some sort of bet going with another coach, but that didn't give him the right to embarrass me in front of my crew, the ballplayers, and a stadium full of fans. If he really wanted to do something daring, he should have kissed Cederstrom, not me. And the second thing is, he wasn't that good of a kisser. In fact, he was awful. I should have dumped him just for being such a lousy kisser.

More than anything, I was disappointed in myself. As usual, I tried to compromise. Instead, I should have thrown Lind's ass out of the game the moment he started that backbender. By letting him get away with the kiss, I hurt my credibility. Of course, he didn't do much for his reputation, either.

Four games later, the season was finished. I drove back to Phoenix, got back my old job with United Parcel Service, and waited for my next assignment from Deary and Umpire Development. Deary could fire me, which I didn't expect. He could keep me in the American Association, which I did expect. Or Giamatti and Vargo could promote me, which was a long shot, at best.

In November, Vargo contacted me and asked if I could come to West Palm Beach, Florida, and work some winter league games there. He said he wanted to change my whole style behind the plate, that he wanted to adjust my stance so that my legs, not my back, would take most of the pressure. He said my back would never last if I didn't do something about the way I stood behind the plate.

I didn't necessarily agree, but who was I to argue? This was Ed Vargo talking. The guy had been one of the best umpires in the National League, and now he was someone who could, with a few well-placed words to Giamatti, get me a job in the big leagues. I figured that he knew what he was talking about. I trusted him.

Back I went to my UPS manager and begged for a week off.

"I promise I won't take any more time off," I said. "The thing is, I've got a chance to go work under Ed Vargo. I just need a week."

Even though it was the holiday season—one of the busiest times for UPS—my manager let me go to West Palm Beach. I was almost as excited as when I went to Cooperstown for the Hall of Fame Game.

The first game I had was on the bases. The next day, Vargo took me aside and started tinkering with my stance. By the time he was through, I felt as if I were back in umpire school. He assigned me the plate that afternoon and said, "Don't worry about the pitches. Concentrate on the stance."

I was terrible. Everything looked so different back there. For eleven seasons I had called balls and strikes one way; now I was seeing the pitches from a completely different angle. Of course, none of the players knew or cared anything about my problems. All they knew was that I kept missing pitches. It was only a stupid seven-inning winter league game, but that didn't keep some of the players, especially one of the catchers, from bitching at me about a couple of strike calls they didn't like.

With three outs to go, I settled behind the plate, counting the minutes until the game was finished. Crouched in front of me was the catcher who had complained about some calls. Screw him, I thought. Vargo had told me to worry about my stance, not my strike zone.

The pitcher wound up and threw. It was a high fastball that kept tailing upward. I stood there, waiting for the catcher to stick his mitt up. Instead, the guy barely lifted his arm. The ball hit me flush on the collarbone and I nearly dropped to my knees.

For a few minutes I staggered around the batter's box

and tried to pretend it didn't hurt. I had tears in my eyes from the pain, but I didn't go to the ground. I didn't want to give that smart-ass catcher the satisfaction of knowing his trick had worked. As best as I could tell, this was his payback for calling him out on strikes a couple of times. It was obvious: he didn't even try to get a glove on the pitch.

A couple of people came over to see if I was okay. I told them I was fine. A couple of minutes later, I said, "Let's go!" and we resumed the game.

That's how I was when it came to injuries. Whenever I got hit by a ball, I acted as if it barely bothered me. If a trainer came out to check on me, I walked away. I didn't want anybody to think I was weak.

But this time I couldn't pretend. I leaned down for the next pitch, but I didn't stay there long. My collarbone was killing me. I couldn't even move my shoulder or arm without wanting to scream. I had never quit during a game, but enough was enough.

"Forget this," I said. "I'm done."

As they found another umpire to finish the game, I walked back to the dressing room. I had been hit before, but never like this. I could take pain, but this was damn near unbearable. Something was broken. I just knew it.

I was sweaty and hot and I had tears running down my cheeks. It was as if the pain were going right to my eyeballs. I couldn't lift my arm, so I couldn't take my shirt off. And the whole time I was sitting there I was thinking, "If something is broken, I'm going to have to call UPS and try to explain what happened. I'll be lucky to keep my job."

Someone sent a woman into the dressing room to see if I was okay. I told her I'd be all right, but that I needed a ride to the hospital for X rays. She told the other umpires, and one of them, a nice Double A umpire whose name escapes me, volunteered to take me to the emergency room. Before we left, Vargo, who was on another field when I got hurt, paid a quick visit.

"I'm sure nothing's busted," he said. "You'll be all right."

"Ed," I said, "I can take pain, but something's wrong this time."

"Aw, don't worry about it," he said. "You'll be fine."

Right then, I could tell he thought I was a big baby. I could sense that he thought I wasn't tough enough. Hey, I was plenty tough, but this was different.

When we got to the hospital, the emergency room was packed with patients, many of whom looked as if they were dirt-poor. I didn't look a whole lot better. I had on gray slacks and a sweaty short-sleeve shirt. I kept an ice bag pressed against my collarbone and held my wallet with my other hand.

Before I could get examined, I first had to fill out some forms. The hospital clerk needed to know who would be paying the bill. I didn't know what to tell her. I got hurt at the training facilities for the Montreal Expos and Atlanta Braves—maybe they had to pay for it. Or maybe it was the American Association or the National League. Tired, confused, and in pain, I finally told her that I'd file for workman's compensation. After signing the forms, I went back and sat down, only to be called to the desk again for a few more questions. When I returned to my chair, my wallet was gone.

I wanted to cry again. There was no money in the wallet, but everything else—credit cards, driver's license, photos, phone numbers . . . you name it—was in there. The other umpire and I searched everywhere for it, including in trash cans. No luck.

An hour later, they finally took me in to see a doctor. As I waited in the hospital room, I heard two of the nurses talking.

"Look at her, she must be real scared," said one of the nurses. "She's shaking."

Damn right I was shaking. The air conditioner was cranked up and my shirt was soaked with sweat. I was freezing.

Finally the doctor got the X rays and gave me the news.
"Is it broken?" I said.

"Yes, but we don't have to reset it. The bone should heal
in four to six weeks. We'll give you a sling to wear and
you'll be fine."

At that moment, if they would have given me a bottle
of pills, I would have swallowed them all. I had lost my
wallet. I had broken my collarbone. I had probably lost
my UPS job, and I had probably pissed off Vargo by leaving the game early. Someone was out there using my credit
cards and I didn't have a nickel to my name.

"Listen," I said to the doctor, "what can you give me for
the pain? This thing is absolutely killing me."

"Well, what we do is give you Tylenol Two for broken
bones."

"Tylenol Two! You gotta be kidding me. I've got a broken collarbone! Can't you give me anything stronger than
Tylenol Two? Jesus Christ!"

"No, really, this works."

I wanted something to knock me out, and instead, he
gave me Tylenol. I couldn't believe it. But by then, I was
tired of arguing. I took the pills and went back to my hotel
and started calling the credit card companies. American
Express was first.

"Hello, my name is Pam Postema and my wallet got
stolen today."

After that, I started to babble and sob. It was humiliating,
but I was a wreck. I called three or four more credit card
numbers and then said the hell with it. I'd take my chances.
I was in too much pain to care anymore.

The day after I broke my collarbone, Vargo asked if the
daughter of one of his family friends could stay with me
at the hotel. "Sure," I said. I didn't care. I could use the
company. Then he said, "Don't worry about your medical
bills. You've got worker's comp, but don't file a claim. We'll
take care of the bill."

It sounded good to me. He also said he'd reimburse me for the UPS salary I'd lose during my four weeks off the job. I was making about $525 a week, but I told him I was only getting about $400. I didn't want to push my luck.

"No, no," he said, "I'll get you a check for two thousand dollars or so. We'll take care of this."

"Whatever you say, Ed."

A few weeks later, I got a phone call in Phoenix. An administrator from the hospital in West Palm Beach wanted to know when I would be paying my bill. She also asked about filing worker's compensation, but I told her it wouldn't be necessary, that I'd take care of the bill myself. If the National League didn't want me to file worker's comp, that was fine with me. I wasn't going to ruin my chances with Vargo over a couple thousand dollars. I figured that if I never saw the money, I could make it up in salary when I got to the big leagues.

That was me—the trusting soul.

CHAPTER 10

The Strangest Spring of All

Never look ahead. That's what I always told myself. Never confuse hopes with reality. That was my cardinal rule, and for eleven long seasons I had never broken it. But now I couldn't help myself. For the first time since, well, ever, I knew I was going to become a big league umpire. I could feel it.

At last, things were going my way. In January, Vargo and my hero, Giamatti, decided that it was time for me to work a full spring training schedule. That meant major league players, major league pressures—kind of—and major league attention. I still have the newspaper article from the announcement.

"It's our intention . . . to give her as long and serious a look as possible on her merits," said Giamatti. "I want to give her a chance."

Hey, that's all I had been asking for the last eleven years: a chance. A fair chance. Didn't I deserve that?

Even more encouraging were the comments of the various power brokers in baseball. Barney Deary told reporters that I had paid my dues. "I think she deserves a shot," he said. Katy Feeney, the National League's public relations spokesperson, announced that if I didn't win one of the full-time job openings created by the death of Dick Stello and the retirement of Bill Williams, I would be seriously considered for one of two openings in the relief pool. A relief pool position meant I would work in Triple A, but be under contract to the National League, available to fill in when one of its umpires was ill or on vacation. I had already received my minor league assignment for the 1988 season—crew chief in the Triple A Alliance—but those orders could be changed, right?

As for Vargo, he kept downplaying the woman-umpire angle, which was fine with me. "We don't look at her as a woman," Vargo said. "We look at her as an ump."

Well, this ump was excited, although I played it cool for the reporters who somehow tracked me down in Phoenix. I didn't want to piss anyone off, especially Giamatti or Vargo, so I did my best humble routine. I told them that it was good to know that the National League was interested in my work, but that I wouldn't make any guesses on its plans for me. Then I told them that an umpire is always an inch away from the big leagues and an inch away from being released. "You never know," I said.

What a joke. I knew. I knew this was the perfect opportunity for me to show how good I was. Deep down, I knew I was ready for this. Baseball had finally cracked open the door, and now it was my turn to squeeze through.

First, I had to take care of some nagging business. For instance, rather than do dreaded interview after dreaded interview, I asked Katy if there was a way to limit the requests, preferably to zero. I hated the attention and didn't want anything to disrupt my concentration during the next four weeks. This was my job tryout and damn if I was going to spend it answering the same old questions. So Katy came up with a plan. We would have one interview session, come one, come all. After that, nothing. I would be unavailable for comment.

Next, I had to figure out a way to entertain my mom and her husband. For some dumb reason, I had invited them to stay with me during the most important month of my life. It probably wasn't the best decision I ever made, but I love my mom, so I did what I could. As I look back, the stress of sharing a hotel room with a parent and a stepfather didn't help my nerves.

My first game was Thursday, March 3, a nothing exhibition contest between the Atlanta Braves and the University of Georgia at West Palm Beach Municipal Stadium. Or at least that's what it should have been. Instead, the media treated the game as if it were the biggest thing since Abner Doubleday was born. Photographers were everywhere—one even followed me from the stadium parking lot to the umpires' dressing room. Once I was inside, reporters kept knocking on the door, asking for just a few minutes of time. I didn't want to be a jerk, but I had to tell them, "No comment. The press conference is Saturday." They weren't too happy about that, but I didn't care. They had their jobs, I had mine. At the moment, umpiring a game was more important than filling their notebooks and Minicam tapes.

I had home plate that day. As my crew—Billy Hohn and Mark Hirschbeck—and I made our way onto the field for the pregame lineup-card exchange, a half dozen television camera crews and five newspaper and magazine photographers came out of nowhere and did what they do best, which is make pests of themselves. Billy and Mark were sort of pushed into the infield, leaving just me, Braves manager Chuck Tanner, and Georgia baseball coach Steve Webber to discuss the ground rules. The whole scene was a zoo.

Just when I thought things couldn't get crazier, Tanner turned to me and dropped a little bombshell:

"Would you like a kiss?"

I wanted to say, "Would you like me to smash this heavy iron umpire's mask into your groin?" But I had to be cool, in control. I had to pretend that his comment didn't bother me a single bit. So I smiled and said, "Uh, no, I don't think so."

Tanner thought he was being nice or funny or something. He was one of my biggest supporters, but still . . . "Would you like a kiss?" What sort of thing is that to say minutes before my big debut? Didn't eleven years in the minors count for anything? I wasn't in the Gulf Coast League anymore. I was a veteran of the wars and I still got this.

I could have blasted Tanner right then and there, but what good would that have done? The fucking guy just made an incredibly stupid remark, so stupid that he probably didn't realize that people get lobotomies after saying those kinds of things. He didn't mean anything by it. Then I remembered: this was the same guy who was a codefendant in a sex discrimination suit filed by a woman named Robin Monsky, a former Braves public relations person. Tanner wouldn't let her in the clubhouse, which is tough on a PR person.

Anyway, thank goodness that the game itself was uneventful. I punched out Braves outfielder Ken Griffey, Sr., to end the second inning and outfielder Terry Blocker to end the third inning. They didn't say a word. If anything, they were more upset at having some college pitcher slip a couple of third strikes past them. All I did was make the easy calls. Later in the game, I called a balk on Braves pitcher Kevin Coffman. It was a no-brainer and no one said a word.

Up in the stands, a few of the fans were popping off—so what else was new? I heard one of them yell, "Hey, clean the plate! That's a woman's job." I told him to go fuck himself, under my breath, of course.

There were no arguments. No on-field confrontations. No disputed calls. No ejections. When the fan yelled from the bleachers, Braves catcher Ozzie Virgil turned to me and said, "Those guys were just jealous because they're not out here doing what you're doing." I smiled.

After the game, Virgil told the reporters that my strike

zone was typical of the National League—from the knees to the belt. He said I maybe missed one or two pitches, but after the first inning, he forgot I was back there, which is the best compliment of all. Bruce Benedict, who also caught three innings for the Braves that day, had some kind words, too. He said I hustled and that my strike zone was consistent. Benedict was the same guy who earlier in the game had made a nice block of a pitch that was well on its way to bouncing up and hitting me. "You owe me one," he said after the block. "Okay," I said.

Meanwhile, my old buddy Tanner, perhaps trying to make up for his pregame gaffe, couldn't say enough nice things about my performance: "I think she could work in the majors. She wouldn't embarrass herself. She did a real good job on balls and strikes. After a while, you forget it's a woman back there. She's an umpire."

As for my own reaction, I didn't have any. At least, not for public consumption. When the reporters started chasing after me, I grabbed my equipment and bolted for my car. "Sorry," I said. "See you Saturday." With that, I drove away. I had survived. Hell, I had kicked ass.

Two days later, I reported to a fancy Palm Beach Gardens hotel suite, where about thirty-five baseball writers had assembled to hear my life story. What was I supposed to say that hadn't been said fifty times before? They asked the same questions and I gave them the same answers.

No, I wasn't married.

No, my hair wasn't always cut this short.

Yes, I thought I was ready to make the jump from the minors to the majors.

No, I didn't enjoy being interviewed.

That afternoon I had another game, this time in nearby Vero Beach. On Sunday, I returned to West Palm for a Braves–Montreal Expos game, where I had the plate again. And again, the reviews were good. I'll always remember the date—March 6—and for good reason. It was the last normal day, relatively speaking, that I had that spring.

The problem was Vargo. As one of his big league umpire candidates, he kept a close eye on my progress. Shortly after the Braves-Expos game, he reminded me that I had gotten away from his style of doing things. He also wanted me to start calling the high pitch a strike. For years, National League umpires had basically disregarded the rulebook strike zone, which stretched from the knees to jersey letters. All of the sudden, the National League was supposedly cracking down, insisting that everyone recognize the full strike zone, not just part of it.

Yeah, well, someone forgot to tell the big league umpires, because they pretty much ignored the order. They weren't going to change their strike zones, not in a million years. You can't ask an umpire, especially a veteran umpire, to overhaul a strike zone. If you do, you're asking for a revolt. Also, the big league umpires weren't about to listen to all the screaming and bitching from the managers. You can't just walk onto the field one day, alter your entire strike zone, and expect the managers, pitchers, catchers, and hitters not to jump down your chest protector. So the big league umpires did what I would have done: they pretended the new strike zone didn't exist.

Good for them. Bad for me. Now I had to change my stance behind the plate and change my strike zone. It was a recipe for disaster.

On March 8, I had the bases for a game between the New York Mets and the Los Angeles Dodgers at Dodgertown in Vero Beach. Good thing, too, since Manager Tommy Lasorda was in rare form that day. Apparently, no one had told Lasorda about the new strike zone, so when my partner Mike Winters, who had the misfortune of having the plate, called the first chest-high pitch a strike, Lasorda nearly popped a blood vessel. I think he nearly laughed us out of the ballpark, and believe me, umpires hate being laughed at. Winters got pissed and started balling the pitcher. Lasorda didn't like that one bit, so he started yelling at Winters again, calling him inconsistent.

That's the thing about Lasorda: he's always talking about the Sisters of such-and-such convent and how he bleeds Dodger blue and how he's a real humanitarian, which, I suppose, he is sometimes. But the guy also loves to cheapshot rookie umpires and is a master at working the crowd against you.

Immediately following the Dodger game I decided that unless Vargo was sitting in the stands watching me, I'd never call that high pitch a strike. I couldn't, not after watching Lasorda go after Winters. Once again, I was disobeying a direct command from Vargo, but it was a chance I had to take. Strike zone or no strike zone, you can't fuck over the umpires, to say nothing of the pitchers and hitters, like that.

Later that week, I got an early wake-up call from New York. Someone from "Good Morning America" wanted to know if I'd be on their TV show. Before I could say no, the person asked what I thought of the new *Sports Illustrated* cover. I told her I hadn't seen the magazine in weeks.

"Hmmm, well, perhaps you should," she said. "We get an advance copy of it and you're on the cover."

I sat up in bed. "Really?"

This was not good. I didn't want publicity, and I certainly didn't want to be on "Good Morning America" or on the cover of a magazine that reaches, what, 3.5 million subscribers? Struggling to regain my composure, I told the ABC woman that the National League had requested that I not do any more interviews. This wasn't exactly true. To be honest, I had begged Kate Feeney to bail me out of all media requests. She said that when in doubt, simply say I was the victim of the National League gag rule. So I did.

When I arrived at my game later that afternoon, Feeney casually walked up to me and in a tone I hadn't heard from her before, said, "I hear you're on the cover of *Sports Illustrated*."

"Yeah, can you believe that?" I said.

"Well, the photographer from *SI* told me they couldn't find a decent basketball picture [the NCAA tournament was going on], so they used your picture on the cover."

"Oh, really."

At the time, I never thought of the enormity of being featured on the cover of *Sports Illustrated*. I knew it was a big deal, but I had other things on my mind. In fact, if you visit my apartment these days, you'll find the *SI* cover in a cheapie frame, partially hidden by monthly telephone and utility bills.

Still, it pissed me off that Feeney said what she said. I didn't care if the whole *Sports Illustrated* building had burned down and my photograph was the only one the editors could salvage from the wreckage, Feeney didn't need to say that. I mean, what a horseshit thing to tell somebody. I hadn't lobbied to be on the cover. I was just a thirty-three-year-old minor league umpire trying to sneak into the big leagues. I needed more publicity like I needed a Chuck Tanner smooch. Anyway, I knew Vargo would be upset when he saw the cover. He didn't want anyone putting pressure on the National League. If Vargo could have had his way, no one would have known I was coming to spring training in the first place.

My mom went out and bought a few copies of the magazine. Sure enough, there I was on the cover, making a strike call. The headline: "The Lady Is an Ump." Then, in smaller letters: "Pam Postema Gets a Shot at the Big Leagues." The story was only two pages long, so it wasn't like you needed to block off the whole afternoon to read about my early spring training experiences.

This wasn't my first time in the magazine. About three years earlier, one of their writers did a story on me when I was in the PCL. In fact, it was probably longer than the one that ran in the issue with my picture on the cover. But back then, I wasn't fighting for a major league job.

I needed a break, that's what I needed. Except for a few innings here and there, I wasn't happy with my umpiring. Vargo's style was giving me fits and the media attention wasn't helping much, either. If I didn't have a really good game soon, I was afraid Vargo might ship me out and find someone else to finish the spring.

On March 14, I got my good game . . . and a whole lot more. And all because of Mr. Neanderthal himself, pitcher Bob Knepper.

I barely knew who Bob Knepper was when I showed up for the afternoon game between the Pittsburgh Pirates and Knepper's Houston Astros at Osceola County Stadium in Kissimmee. To me, he was just another name on a lineup card. I vaguely remembered that he had lost lots of games a season earlier—seventeen, to be exact—and that his earned run average was for shit. But I didn't know he was a God squader or more accurately, a religious fanatic. I learned real fast, though.

The game had its touchy moments. I had to call a balk on Pirate starter Doug Drabek in the second inning, but he knew he had goofed, so he didn't complain. I also had some close pitches, but for the first time since the game between the Braves and the University of Georgia, I finally felt comfortable behind the plate. It also helped that I knew some of these guys when they were in the minors, guys like Astros first baseman Glenn Davis and relief pitcher Charlie Kerfeld. I knew they'd cut me a little slack.

As for Knepper, he hardly said a word during the five scoreless innings he pitched against the Pirates. How could he? I was having my best game of the spring, seeing every pitch and rarely missing a call. Drabek and Knepper had good control that day, which made my job even easier.

My mom was at that game. Sitting nearby were a couple of high school kids. About the second inning, the girl turned to her boyfriend and said, "Hey, that looks like a woman umpire."

"Nah," said the boy.

"Look at her," the girl said. "She's too pretty to be a boy."

"You know what? You're right."

That's when my mom leaned over and said, "That's my daughter." The three of them were best friends for the rest of the game.

The Astros won the game, and afterward, the reporters went running to the starting pitchers for their comments. This was their routine: see how the woman umpire did. This time I didn't care. I walked off the field knowing I had done great. Let Drabek, Knepper, or Vargo find fault with that performance. They'd have to look a long time.

As usual, I gathered my stuff and headed for my car. Most of the reporters had given up trying to interview me by now. They knew I'd just say no.

On the drive back to my hotel in West Palm Beach, I started thinking that maybe this might work out, after all. A few more plate jobs like the one in Kissimmee and they'd have to give me a job or put me under option. I kept wishing I had a videotape of the game, just so I could hand it to Vargo and say, "Here, is this good enough?"

The next morning the phone rang and it was Vargo. I was half-asleep, but from the tone of his voice I could tell he wasn't calling to congratulate me for a job well done.

"Did you read the papers?" he said.

"No, Ed. Why?"

"Don't worry. I'll take care of everything. Don't worry about a thing."

"What now, Ed?"

"Well, Knepper made some comments about you after the game. But don't worry about it, I'll handle everything. Just go buy a paper and read what he said. But whatever you do, don't worry about it. We'll take care of it."

Whater "it" was, it was enough to make Vargo sound concerned and a little bit nervous. I got dressed and walked down to the lobby of the hotel and found a paper. Some headlines you never forget, such as this one in the *Fort Lauderdale Sun-Sentinel:* "Knepper says umpiring is wrong calling for a woman."

I had been blasted before by players, but never this way. I just sat there stunned and shaking my head as I read his comments. After praising my work behind the plate, Knepper proceeded to bring new meaning to the words *male chauvinism.* By the way, he had made the remarks while standing outside the Astros clubhouse, where he conducted all interviews whenever a woman reporter was present. (He didn't think women sportswriters should be allowed in the locker room.)

And I quote:

> I just don't think a woman should be an umpire. There are certain things a woman shouldn't be and an umpire is one of them. It's a physical thing. God created women to be feminine. I don't think they should be competing with men.
>
> It has nothing to do with her ability. I don't think women should be in any position of leadership. I don't think they should be presidents or politicians. I think women were created not in an inferior position, but in a role of submission to men. You can be a woman umpire if you want, but that doesn't mean it's right. You can be a homosexual if you want, but that doesn't mean that's right either.
>
> It's her choice what she wants to do with her life, and I'm not going to give her a hard time. I'll respect her more because she's a woman. I'm not going to condemn her. But if God is unhappy with her, she's going to have to deal with that later.

I returned to my room in a daze. A day earlier I thought I had turned the corner. Well, I had, but waiting for me on the straightaway was another brick wall in the form of Knepper. I came this close to quitting right then and there. With dickheads like Knepper in the game, what did it matter if you got every pitch right, every play right? You could be fucking perfect from start to finish and it wouldn't mean a damn thing because you were a woman, not a man. That's what Knepper was saying. This guy didn't have one bitch about my umpiring, but yet, it wasn't good enough for him.

I always thought I could slip into the major leagues unnoticed, that eventually everyone would grow bored with the novelty of a woman umpire. There's a joke. I kept hoping that one day Vargo would call and say, "Someone got hurt; we need you up here immediately." And that would be that. No fanfare. No press conferences. Just me doing my job. But the moment I started reading Knepper's mind-boggling quotes, I knew it would never happen. At least, not that way, it wouldn't.

It didn't take long for the reporters to find me. It also didn't take long for me to say, "No comment," as instructed by Vargo, who had sworn he would handle the publicity. And even if I had wanted to pop off, what was I going to say? How do you respond to something so utterly ridiculous? There was no logic in his statement, no thought given to the words. It was all religious babble as far as I was concerned. The way I figured it, God never said a woman had to be limited by one set of rules, while men were limited to another. To be honest, I believe in reincarnation and I'll tell you what: I sure as hell wouldn't come back as an umpire. Why would you want to come back as a closed-minded asshole who weighs three hundred pounds and has no brain? The only thing worse than that would be to come back as Bob Knepper. As for me, I'd come back as a dancer.

Reaction was swift. Astros manager Hal Lanier tried calling my hotel room, but we kept playing phone tag. He finally left me a note, apologizing for his pitcher. In it, he said he didn't agree with Knepper's comments and added, "I just want you to know that there is a place for good umpiring in the National League, and if I am asked, I certainly would recommend you." Thanks, Hal.

The guys who do the Tank McNamara cartoon started blasting Knepper in their comic strips, and a lot of the national sports columnists and baseball writers found themselves sticking up for me, too. Mike Downey of the *Los Angeles Times* had a good line: "Bob evidently believes that when Adam gave up one of his ribs to create Eve, he expected her to run right out and barbecue them and serve them up with some fries and coleslaw for his supper."

Monique Giroux, who is the public relations person for the Montreal Expos, even sent me a copy of a letter she had written Knepper. My favorite part was when she said, "Firstly, God couldn't care less about baseball." No kidding.

While I appreciated the support, I felt more alone than ever. How many more of these battles was I going to have to fight? And by the way, where was Vargo when I needed him? I never saw one goddamn word from Vargo, or Giamatti or Feeney or any other National League official, for that matter, about the incident. There were no fines, no reprimands, no requests for an apology, public or otherwise. They never even issued a statement disagreeing with Knepper's comments. So much for Vargo handling everything. Vargo's idea of handling controversy was closing his eyes and hoping it went away.

I should probably have blasted Vargo and the rest of them. Right then I should have known that Vargo wanted the whole situation—and me with it—to go away, the sooner the better. He didn't care if I died out there. If Vargo had been truly interested in hiring me, he would have supported me. Instead, he did nothing.

To top it off, I received a long letter from Knepper. I wish I could tell you what it said, but the thing was so full of religious gibberish and biblical quotes about the superiority of man that I could barely get through it. I saved the letter—just in case I ever needed something to line a bird cage—but I never wrote him back. What good would it have done? Ability didn't matter to him, so I wasn't going to waste a sheet of paper on the guy. Screw him.

Things kept getting worse. Three days later, while in West Palm Beach for a game between the Chicago White Sox and the Expos, I decided to break another cardinal rule of mine. I had the plate that day, and for reasons I can't explain, I was in a pretty good mood. The game was about five minutes from starting, so I figured, what the hell, I'll make some small talk with the catcher. His name wasn't on the jersey, so I said, "Hi, what's your name?"

The catcher rose from his crouch—he seemed about ten feet tall—turned around, and said, "Fisk . . . Carlton Fisk."

I panicked. "Oh," I said, "I've heard of you. Maybe you've heard of me. Pam . . . Pam Postema. I've been in the news lately."

Fisk sort of grunted. He probably thought I was kidding with him. After all, how could anyone not know who Carlton Fisk was? Hell, this guy already had space cleared for him in the Hall of Fame. But for some reason, I'd forgotten that he played for the White Sox. Sick to my stomach with embarrassment, I started thinking, "Jesus, Pam. What a time to talk to a ballplayer, and an icon at that. See, it doesn't work. Never talk to a ballplayer. It only gets you in trouble."

Having Fisk there made me want to show him what kind of umpire I was. I showed him, all right. I stunk, mostly because he intimidated the hell out of me. I'm sure he thought I was a horseshit umpire, and I guess I couldn't blame him. During the first couple of innings, he kept asking where the pitches were. On an obvious high strike— a ball—he'd go, "Where was that?" I couldn't tell if he was being a smart ass or being serious. So I played along.

"Oh, yeah, they were high, right?" I said.

"Oh, really?"

Before long, my strike zone was all screwed up. He was trying to see if he could rattle me and he succeeded. I was a mess. But that's his job, to do what he can for his pitcher. And even though I wasn't pleased with his tactics, the guy is an unbelievable catcher. Some guys you hate to see in front of you because they can't stop a thing, including fifty-nine-foot sliders that bounce under their mitts and into an umpire's forearm. But Fisk was like a wall. He made some fantastic catches. With guys like him, an umpire doesn't even flinch.

By now, only nine games remained in spring training. Every day I would return from work and check my messages, just in case Vargo or Giamatti had called. They had to make a decision soon, and to be honest, I didn't like my chances. Except for a couple of games behind the plate, I felt as if I wasn't doing too well. I still couldn't get the hang of Vargo's style and I was running out of time. And as you might expect, the publicity generated from the Knepper incident didn't do much for my standing.

One message I didn't return was from an umpire named Dave Pallone. At the time, the only thing I knew about Pallone was that he had been labeled a scab after crossing the picket line during the 1979 umpires' strike. I didn't know that he was gay, that he would later be forced out of the league and then write a book about the whole experience. And to tell you the truth, it wouldn't have mattered a bit that day if I had known.

Pallone had left an invitation for me to join several other minor league umpires at a dinner show—his treat. Stupid me. I was so suspicious of everyone's motives at that point that I chose to pass up the free meal. Talk about paranoid. Here was Pallone going out of his way to do something nice for me and I brushed him off. I thought he was just another major league umpire who wanted something. How was I to know that he had been doing this sort of thing for years? He was a classy guy and according to the people I talked with, a good umpire. Is it too late to apologize?

On March 24, I opened up my *USA Today* sports section and there it was, the headline that caused me to gag on my morning coffee: "Giamatti's call: Postema sent down. Female umpire can try again next spring."

Reading the headline was like getting a sucker punch to the stomach. No one had bothered to call from the National League office to break the news, which, I guess, shouldn't have been much of a shocker considering the people involved. Instead, I had to learn my fate in newsprint. Not only had Vargo and Giamatti decided that I wouldn't replace Stello or Williams, but they also chose not to offer me an option in the league's replacement pool. According to the story, I was bound for the Triple A Alliance as a crew chief, which meant nothing, since you didn't get paid a penny more for the extra work.

At the end of the story was an odd quote from Giamatti. Asked about the reasons for his decision, he said, "I don't want to discuss anyone's shortcomings. We have a good relationship with her, but not a formal relationship. That can change."

I didn't quite know how to take that. It was sort of a rip, but in a subtle way. Of course, since I couldn't do much about it then, I got in my car and made the drive from Clearwater, which is where I was staying, to Kissimmee for a game between the Cincinnati Reds and the Astros. You can imagine my mood that day. Let me put it this way: you didn't want to argue with me.

The game ended late that afternoon, and by the time I made it back to Clearwater it was almost 8 P.M. As I walked into my room, my mom had this excited look on her face.

"You got a messasge," she said.

Hey, the last thing I wanted to do was talk to a reporter about anything, especially the *USA Today* story.

"From who," I said wearily.

"From President Giamatti."

"Oh, shit."

I called the number and sure enough, Giamatti answered. He couldn't have been nicer.

"Pam, I really want to apologize for what was in the paper today. I don't know how that happened. They've got everything wrong. I truly haven't made any decisions."

As he was apologizing, I kept thinking, "Have I missed something here?" But instead of asking him what he really did say to the sportswriter, I chickened out, which was a mistake. I should have pressed him on it. Instead I said, "Thank you for the apology, but you really didn't have to call me."

I was trying to be nice for a couple of reasons. One, I was nervous. Two, if he hadn't made up his mind about the openings, then I wanted to make sure I didn't ruin my chances by saying something I would regret.

After a few minutes, we started to repeat ourselves. He kept saying that he wanted to express his "sincere apology" and I kept saying, "There's no reason you had to call." Moments later, the conversation was finished. Turns out, so were my chances of getting a big league job that season.

Four days later, a formal announcement was made: Gary Darling, who had been in the PCL since 1983, and Mark Hirschbeck, who had been in the American Association since 1985, were being hired by the National League. I would return to Triple A, but as a little bone for my troubles, the league said it would extend me an invitation to the 1989 spring training.

Big fucking deal.

CHAPTER 11

The Quiet Season
(Relatively Speaking)

Before I joined my new American Association crew for the season opener (whoopee) in Nashville, I first had to complete my obligation to the National League. That meant a three-day, three-city swing up the Southeast coast, beginning in Jacksonville, then to Richmond, and back down to Greenville. As if I cared.

The makeshift crew included me, Joe West, who was beginning his eleventh year in the National League, and Bill Hohn, who was under option to the league but still waiting for a full-time invitation. We were supposed to follow the Braves as they made their way up north. That done, West would report to his crew for Opening Day in the big leagues, and Billy and I would do the same in the minors.

I had never met West before, but I had heard of him. He was supposed to be an umpire's umpire, a guy who took not one ounce of shit from anyone. If you challenged West, I had heard, you had better have a damn good reason. If you didn't, you had better be prepared to get dumped.

Well, West was a red-ass, but he was also the best umpire I had ever seen. He cared about the job and was always looking for little ways to improve. I couldn't believe this guy's work ethic. Every minute of one of those meaningless exhibition games he busted his ass. When you watched

West work, you learned how important it was to hustle to the right spot, to be in position to make a call.

From a purely selfish standpoint, the best thing about West was that he didn't mind talking to me about umpiring. For one of the few times of my career, a big league umpire was willing to share some of his secrets and actually help me. West loved talking about the job. He enjoyed it so much that he didn't care if I was a woman, as long as I busted my ass, too, and showed that I took the profession seriously. We talked about situations, strike zones, base work, players, managers . . . you name it and we probably discussed it. The whole thing was like going to graduate school for umpires.

West wasn't your typical macho asshole umpire. His life revolved around the job during the season, but from October to March, West concentrated on a career as a country-western singer. In fact, it wasn't unusual for West to bring a couple of cassette recordings of his latest songs to home plate and distribute them to the various managers. The guy didn't miss a trick. He even presented Hohn and me with our own copies, and I have to admit that while I'm not much of a country-music fan, West's stuff sounded pretty good. Randy Travis, he wasn't; but it wasn't half-bad, either.

After the games, the three of us would hit the bars, and like most umpires, West could drink his share. The National League had been on him to lose some weight, but it's hard to drop a few pounds when you're knocking down a few beers every night. One night we were at a bar, talking about the game, when West noticed a woman selling flowers. He went over to her, bought a rose, and gave it to me. The big lug. Men think all women just automatically swoon when they see a rose. I know he meant well, but I didn't see him buy a flower for Bill Hohn, you know what I mean? Even with West, I wasn't considered an equal, at least, not off the field.

My own season began April 7. After a meeting with Triple A Alliance officials (the Alliance was a newly formed combination of two leagues, the American Association and the International League) in Columbus the day before, I met my crew: my buddy Oujo and Charlie Rehliford. Jack and I got along great, but early on I knew Charlie didn't think women should be umpires. He wasn't as blatant about it as Knepper, but it was obvious he disapproved. Charlie also wasn't crazy about me being named the crew chief. It bothered him that *a woman* would be the umpire in control. Of course, it didn't stop him from asking me to autograph his copy of *Sports Illustrated,* the one with me on the cover. In fact, it was kind of funny to watch him ask.

"Uh, Pam," he said, like a little kid asking for his allowance, "would you, uh, please sign this for me?"

As a crew chief I learned how fragile the male ego can be. Think about it. I had to make sure I never showed up my own crew, but at the same time I had to be positive that everyone—the managers, the players, my own umpires—knew I was the person in charge. What a pain in the ass.

For instance, I never rushed down to help Oujo or Rehliford if they were going face-to-face with a manager. I learned the hard way when early in the season I interrupted an argument Rehliford was having and said something like, "What do we got here?" If looks could kill, I would have been six feet under the ground. He was annoyed because it looked as if he couldn't handle the situation by himself. He was embarrassed, and I'm sure I know exactly what he was thinking: "Oh, great, I have to have a woman to help me."

The ballplayers were worse. They always were. I would walk toward an argument and the player would snarl, "I don't want no woman, no girl, here." They would try to brush me aside, as if I were one of the batgirls or something. Or else they'd say, "What are you here for? Can't your partner fight his own fucking battles?" Which would only piss off Oujo or Rehliford even more.

So I backed off, even when things got a little out of hand. In fact, I'm convinced Oujo got released after the 1988 season partly because I bent over backward to let him handle his own arguments. We were in Nashville and Oujo got into an argument with Sounds manager Jack Lind, whom I called The Thinker. Lind would never throw tantrums. Instead, he would slowly make his way to the field and ask question after question about the call until he was satisfied or dumped, whichever came first.

This time, however, Lind was especially difficult. Oujo had made an absolutely correct call, but Lind kept wanting "logical" reasons why the call had gone against his team. Rather than ignore Lind's questions, Oujo stood there and explained away. When that didn't work and tempers flared, I tried hurrying things along.

"Okay, Jack, let's go," I said.

But Oujo and Lind wouldn't quit. Before long, the argument had gone on for five minutes, maybe longer. The fans were booing and I couldn't blame them. I tried again:

"Jack, c'mon, let's get the game going."

But every time Lind was on the verge of giving up, Oujo would say something else. The pisser about all this was that Larry Napp, an umpire supervisor for the American League, was in the stands that night watching the whole gawd-awful thing. Afterward, he gave us shit about the length of the argument.

"He was out there twelve minutes," Napp kept saying. "Twelve minutes! You've got to get Lind the hell out of there."

Well, it wasn't twelve minutes, but whatever it was, it was too long. And Napp was right: I should have taken more control of the situation, and Oujo shouldn't have spent so much time defending a call that didn't need to be defended. But once again, I had to walk that goddamn fine line because of a stupid macho thing.

A couple of games later, a manager came out to argue, but this time we shooed him off the field in nothing flat. Too bad Napp couldn't have been there for that one.

A month into the season one of my least favorite people started blasting away at me. I'm speaking of former American League umpire Ron Luciano, who has made a career by telling stories about the profession, although I find some of them hard to believe. The guy had never seen me work a single game, but yet he told reporters that I didn't have the necessary skills or mental makeup to become a big league umpire, and if I was hired, it would "set baseball back thirty years." He also criticized me for not handling the media well.

I don't have a clue how someone who had never seen me call a pitch could pop off like that. But that was Luciano for you: talk first, think later.

April and May were full of surprises. Rehliford would get jealous of me anytime I had a good game. Luciano couldn't keep his opinions to himself. And Oujo and I tried playing racquetball at a Knights of Columbus court in Buffalo and the assholes wouldn't let me inside because I was a woman. Oujo was welcome to enter, of course.

If nothing else, though, I felt better about my work. My confidence had returned, and taking a page from the Joe West book on umpiring, I didn't take shit from anyone. You got it: Pam Red-Ass. We were doing a game in Oklahoma City and the score was tied, 6–6, in the top of the tenth. Indianapolis runners were on first and second when I called a balk on Oklahoma City pitcher Ed Vande Berg. Toby Harrah, who was the manager, didn't say a thing, but pitching coach Ferguson Jenkins couldn't keep his mouth shut.

"Punch a hole in that mask!" he yelled.

I turned and looked to see if it was really Jenkins who was stupid enough to say something. He knew that pitching coaches aren't allowed to argue.

"Yeah, I said it," he said.

I dumped him. He had it coming.

No season would be complete if there wasn't at least one controversy involving me. This one centered around the inaugural Triple A All-Star Game, which was scheduled for mid-July in Buffalo. I was selected to the crew and assigned the plate, which was a pleasant surprise. But not long after the announcement, I started to see quotes in the paper questioning my appearance at the game. Terry Collins, the manager of the Albuquerque Dukes, said I was chosen as "a public relations move." A Buffalo newsman said the organizers of the game were using me as a gimmick to attract attention and fans—which explains why that guy worked in Buffalo.

Give me a break. I was picked to do the game because I was strong behind the plate and I had the most seniority in the league. This was my second year with the American Association, my sixth in Triple A ball, and my twelfth year in the minors. If I wanted publicity, it wouldn't have taken me twelve miserable seasons to get it. And for those people who thought my selection was a publicity stunt, well, they should have asked my old nemesis Toby Harrah about my ability. After blasting me in 1987, Harrah was all compliments in 1988. I didn't usually save many articles, but a *Sporting News* column by Joe Gergen was too good to throw out. In it, Harrah said that I had improved "tremendously" in a year's time. "She's better on the bases and better behind the plate. And her personality has improved, which is more unusual."

Typical front-runner.

The All-Star Game was on ESPN, which was a big deal to everyone involved. To me, it ended up causing more trouble than it was worth. That's because Ed Vargo got a tape of the game and nearly blew a fuse after watching it.

There weren't any complaints by the managers or the players after the game. The minor leaguers from the American League affiliates beat the National Leaguers, 2–

1, and nothing very exciting happened. My strike zone was consistent, and except for a few pitches here and there, I felt pretty good about the performance.

Meanwhile, Vargo was livid. He saw that I had completely junked his umpiring style, and he wanted to know why. He took it as a personal insult.

"I saw that tape," he said on the phone a few days later, "and you're not working my style. I want you to work my style. If you're not going to work my style, then you're not going to work in the National League. If you're not going to do as I say, then I don't want you in my league."

I had some explaining to do.

"Ed, I'm sorry," I lied. "I thought I was doing it your way, but I must have worked my way out of it. I didn't know."

The beast was calmed. Sort of.

"Well, you weren't doing it my way," he said. "I mean it: if you don't want to work my style, then I'm not going to let you in my league."

Fucking Vargo. I had had a good game that night in Buffalo. But he insisted that I had missed a bunch of low pitches. Well, I hadn't, and unless you're standing three inches behind the catcher, watching those pitches zip past the plate like I had, you shouldn't say a thing. Vargo should have known that, and he should also have known that the angle of a center-field camera located four hundred feet away from home plate isn't the same as being right there.

I semi-apologized to Vargo a few more times, and after another threat or two, he hung up. Imagine the nerve, though: "his league." That's right, The Ed Fucking Vargo National League. Still, I could sense that Vargo didn't think I appreciated what he had done for me, which, to be honest, was true. So far, he had screwed up my umpiring style, hurt my confidence, made me and the other young umpires at spring training look like fools by ordering us to call high pitches strikes, deserted me during the Knepper incident, bypassed me when it came time to hand out job offers, and then woke up my ass (again) so he could bitch at me. Damn right, I didn't appreciate him.

At that point, I didn't think Vargo had given up on me, but I also didn't think he was 100 percent behind me, either. Ever since I had broken my collarbone, he had become a little more vague about my chances to move up. And this stuff about appreciating him was getting to be a little too much. No one could ever accuse me of playing those political games when it came to umpiring. I didn't work the phones and constantly sweet-talk big league umpires or the umpire supervisors. And I wasn't about to start just because Vargo was bitching at me.

The months went by slowly. July took forever. August was even worse. When September 1 came around, our crew's final game of the season, I was almost looking forward to driving a delivery truck again.

Twelve seasons had passed in my career and what did I have to show for it? Crew chief status? Big deal. Another chance at the big leagues? We'd see. By all indications, I was running out of time.

Back in February, Harold Cooper, the American Association commissioner, and Randy Mobley, the Association's administrator, had sent me a letter welcoming me to the Triple A Alliance. In the letter they wrote that "we expect this to be your best year." Well, I had news for them: it was my best year. Despite hating Vargo's method of umpiring, I had improved in every area. Just as Toby Harrah had said, my work on the bases was better and my plate work was even stronger. Oujo and Rehliford would probably have disagreed, but there's no way, considering the circumstances, they could have done a better job as crew chief than me that season.

As a nice little topper to the year, *Esquire* magazine included me in its "Women We Love" issue. Of course, there was also another article on "Women We Hate," which is the section I turned to first. Thank goodness, I was a no-show there. This is the way it worked: *Esquire* loved me (though, I hated the picture they used) and the National League . . . well, I wasn't sure what the National League thought of me. But I was going to find out.

CHAPTER 12

An Umpires Primer

And now, a few things you ought to know about umpires, a few things the sportswriters and broadcasters forget to mention while they're going on and on about the romance and charm of baseball.

First of all, it isn't all that romantic. To be honest, it's a war out there. Remember that scene in the movie *Field of Dreams,* the one where James Earl Jones, who plays some world-famous author, launches into a sappy speech about the game of baseball being the fabric of America? Pure Hollywood.

Baseball isn't about any of that. Baseball is about respect—earning it or losing it. Baseball is about survival. You're only as good as your last pitch, your last hit, your last victory, or in my case, your last call. All that other stuff about romance and charm is fine if you're sitting in the mezzanine level at Dodger Stadium, munching on Cracker Jack and sipping on a beer. But if you're an umpire, baseball is your worst enemy. All you want is a quick, two-hour game with no bangers, no foul tips off your knee, no rain delays, no extra innings, no bitchy catchers, no whiny pitchers, and no dead-above-the-neck managers with nothing better to do than complain about every other call.

Of course, that almost never happens, which is why umpires have learned to adapt. In a war, you have to.

For instance, ever notice all the equipment umpires wear

to   protect   themselves?   Steel-toed   shoes . . . shin
guards . . . chest protector . . . mask. Well, there's another
tool of the trade. It's called swearing. If you can't swear,
you can't umpire. It's as simple as that.

Let's say you've got the plate one day during a spring
training game between the Philadelphia Phillies and the
Dodgers. About the third inning, that miserable little puke
Lenny Dykstra of the Phillies (who, I have to admit, is a
pretty good outfielder) starts hounding you from the dugout, which he loves to do all the time. Up in the press box,
nobody notices a thing. Meanwhile, your ears are burning
as Dykstra, who's probably on some sort of nicotine high
from all that chewing tobacco he stuffs into his squirrel
cheeks, is letting you have it from the dugout.

Which brings us to Lesson No. 2: Nobody ever mentions
this, but ballplayers are, for the most part, the crudest,
lewdest bunch of assholes ever assembled. And out of necessity, umpires, for the most part, aren't far behind.

Just once, I wish I would have kept a tape recording of
some of those on-field "conversations." And people ask,
"How could you take the swearing?" Are you kidding me?
I probably cussed more than the players did. It all goes
back to survival. Swearing is the language of baseball. I
learned you need it to attack others and to protect yourself,
especially if you're an umpire. To an umpire, four-letter
words are your friends. The word *fuck* becomes an all-
purpose weapon: a noun, verb, adjective, and adverb all
rolled into one.

Let me give you some examples of typical ballplayer-
umpire exchanges:

Ballplayer: "Punch a hole in that fucking mask!"
Me: "Shut the fuck up!"
Or . . .
Ballplayer: "The fucking ball was fucking low!"
Me: "I've fucking heard enough!"
You get the idea. I can't dump a player for something

like that. The last thing an umpire wants is a cheap ejection. After all, players are allowed to argue a call or do a minimal amount of bitching from the dugout. The smart players and managers—and there aren't many of them, by the way—know how to pick their moments. And everyone pretty much uses the same lines. What matters is when they decide to rip you.

Here are the favorites:

—"Bear down!" (This is their way of telling me to concentrate more. By the way, I put an exclamation point at the end of these things because ballplayers and managers rarely talk to you. They yell. They love to yell. It's some sort of macho mechanism.)

—"Get a job!"

—"That's fucking horseshit!"

—"That's fucking brutal!"

—"You fucking blew the call!"

—"That fucking call was (pick one: low, high, outside, inside)!"

—"Be fucking consistent!"

And just so you know, nobody ever calls an umpire "Hey, blue!" If they do, they're usually real nerdy ballplayers, college players, or born-again Christians.

Umpires aren't much more original in their responses. We don't have time to be. If you're in an argument with a manager or ballplayer and you hesitate one moment too long, they take that as a sign of weakness. You're dead then, because they'll jump all over your ass. You have to take control. You do it with these umpire comeback phrases, such as:

—"Get the fuck out of my face!"

—"Don't fucking point!"

—"I got the fucking play right!"

—"He was fucking out!"

—"He was fucking safe!"

—And my personal favorite, "You're fucking gone!"

One of the things they never teach you at umpire school is how to argue. I mean, they try to teach you, but until you have a weasel like Larry Bowa in your face, calling you every name in the book, you don't have any idea what it's like out there. There's an art to arguing. Guys like Bowa didn't have a clue. But guys like Lasorda know how to twist a word in an umpire's gut just so. Lasorda is especially good at picking on young umpires. And he's one of the great cheap-shot artists in the game. I've got the ear burns to prove it.

As a general rule of thumb, you can dump a guy if he attacks you personally, rather than the call itself. Let's say Dykstra had a complaint about a call I made.

The right way to bitch: "That's fucking brutal!"

The wrong way to bitch: "You fucking suck! You have no fucking clue!"

The first one, I'd have to give Dykstra a break. Maybe I'd yell, "Hey, Lenny, when you can see over the dugout steps, why don't you give me a fucking call." The second one, I'd dump him in a heartbeat. Simple.

I was never afraid to argue, but like anything, there's an art to it. In a way, umpires almost become addicted to arguing. Too many quiet, peaceful games make an umpire nervous. I can't explain it, except to say that you need a good screaming session once in a while to keep things a little on edge. I know it sounds strange, but sometimes an argument is good for you. It keeps you focused and pumps you up. I mean, you don't go looking for arguments, but if a player starts giving you shit, you don't back down, either.

I wasn't the wittiest person out there on the field. I could hold my own against most of those jerks, but I could never think of any brilliant putdowns when I needed them. Zach Bevington, my former partner, was the exact opposite. He always had the perfect comeback to anything a player or manager said.

For instance, there was one game where the catcher kept giving Bevington a hard time about the strike zone. Bevington kept telling the guy to knock it off, but the catcher kept needling him.

"Hey, what happens if I *accidentally* let a ball go past?" said the catcher shortly before the start of an inning. "What are you gonna do if that happens, huh?"

"Nothing," said Bevington. "You know why? Because you have now just become Johnny Bench. You understand what I'm saying? If one ball gets past you and so much as grazes any part of me, I'll dump you so fast you won't know what happened. Understand, Mr. Bench?"

That stopped the catcher's chirping right away. And you guessed it—not a single ball ever got past the catcher.

My arguments weren't so sophisticated. I made the mistake of not properly preparing myself to argue. Instead of thinking up a few really good comebacks, I relied on shouting real loud or repeating myself. A manager could rush out, and before I knew it, the conversation would be reduced to this:

Manager: "The guy was safe!"

Me: "No, sir."

Manager: "Yes, sir."

Me: "No, sir."

Manager: "Yes, sir."

Me: "No, sir."

See what I mean?

The only time I wouldn't argue with a player or manager is if they called me the C-word (you can figure it out). If I heard the C-word, they were gone in the time it takes to point your finger at the dugout. I hated that word and I hated anybody who called me that. I never forgot who said it, either.

Sometimes, a player would surprise me with a trace of originality. Once, I dumped Steve Sax, who plays for the New York Yankees these days, after he bitched one time too many. He stormed back to the dugout pissed as could be.

"She's a whore," said Sax as he headed for the clubhouse and an early shower.

"Nah," said a teammate, "she can't even work the corners."

Not bad. For a ballplayer.

Despite my reputation for dumping players, I preferred watching others argue. For instance, nothing gives an umpire a warmer feeling inside than when two players are bitching at each other, or better yet, when a manager comes out to yell at his pitcher. Watch the home plate umpire when this happens. He'll usually take his time breaking up the conference. After all, it's a treat when someone other than an umpire is getting blasted.

It kills me when I hear some of these TV or radio announcers give their versions of what's being said on the mound. They always make it sound as if it's some sort of big strategy session. Most of the time strategy doesn't have a thing to do with it.

I can't tell you how many times I've gone out to the mound to break up a chat and here's what they're saying to each other:

Manager: "What the fuck is going on out here? You can't get my fucking mother out today. Throw the fucking ball. Your fucking curve ball is fucking awful. Your fucking fastball is fucking worse. Bear the fuck down and throw fucking strikes. If you don't, they're going to fucking ship your sorry ass to rookie league."

Meanwhile, the catcher is standing there, pawing at the dirt with his cleats, trying not to giggle. And most of the time, I'm doing all I can not to burst out laughing. Even though these conferences waste time—and remember, umpires aren't paid by the hour—you always wait for the manager to finish his lecture before resuming the game.

Then there are the short and sweet conferences:

Manager: "How you doin'?"
Pitcher: "Okay."
Manager: "Tired?"
Pitcher: "Nah."
Manager: "Can you get this guy out?"
Pitcher: "Yeah."
Manager: "Okay, then. Throw strikes."
The only thing better than the short and sweet conference is no conference at all. That's when the manager darts out of the dugout and before he even skips over the foul line, he waves to the bullpen for a reliever. Heaven.

The exact opposite of this is when the manager goes out to the mound and stands there with the pitcher, both of them glaring at me, the home plate umpire. After a few moments, you join them, where they promptly begin blasting away.

Manager: "Where the fuck was that pitch?"
Me: "What fucking pitch was that?"
Manager: "The fucking outside fucking fastball?"
Me: "It was fucking outside, that's where it was."
Manager: "Well, fucking bear down out here."
Me: "Hey, don't tell me to fucking bear down. Tell your fucking pitcher to fucking bear down and throw some fucking strikes."

What a surpise, eh? A manager trying to blame an umpire for something his pitcher did.

You've seen the other pitcher-manager conference. That's when the manager knows his reliever isn't ready yet, so he stands out on the mound making small talk with him. It gives the reliever time to warm up. It also gives umpires a headache.

And here's something you probably didn't realize: umpires aren't supposed to cuss on the field. We could get fined if a player or manager filed a complaint with the league president about our swearing. Of course, it's okay if that same player calls us, say, "a shithead," loud enough for everyone in the ballpark to hear. But if you called him "a fucking asshole," and he reported it, you'd hear about it from the league president. Can you believe that?

I'll admit, there are several drawbacks to all of this swearing, mainly, you can't stop once you start. If you go out to dinner with a crew of umpires, you're likely to hear such wonderful table manners as, "Pass the fucking salt, please" or "Can we have the fucking check?" or "What do you mean you're all out of fucking Neapolitan?" Gary Darling used to tell us about the time he visited his mom immediately after the end of baseball season. The whole family was gathered around the dinner table when Darling, forgetting where he was at, calmly said, "Mom, pass the fucking mashed potatoes, please."

I always had to watch what I said away from the ballpark. Of course, sometimes, like Darling, I forgot to watch my manners. Just ask the poor guy who made the mistake of complaining about my driving one day during the off-season.

I was working for an overnight delivery service, which meant I had to drive one of those big trucks and be one hundred places at once. A lot of minor league umpires work for UPS or Federal Express during the off-season. The money is decent and the companies are usually pretty good about holding a job for you every year. The companies do make one tiny request: they want you to absolutely and positively deliver the packages on time.

All of that explains why I was tearing through the parking lot of a shopping center one day, breaking about a dozen local laws and not giving a damn about any one of them. I had a route to finish and I was determined to do it, even if it meant doing forty miles per hour in a mall parking lot.

Problem was, I almost hit some poor lady, who managed to dart out of my way in the nick of time. Before I knew it, the lady's husband was in my face delivering a lecture.

"You're going too fast up there," he said, pointing his finger at me.

That's all it took for me to see red. Something snapped. I became an umpire again.

"First of all," I said my voice rising, "get your fucking finger out of my fucking face! Secondly, don't you ever fucking tell me anything again! And don't you ever fucking tell me how to drive! Do you understand!"

The guy didn't know what to do. He was absolutely right to yell at me, and yet, I had instantly taken control of the situation and sent him shuffling back to his frazzled wife. I remember thinking, "Jeez, Postema, you went nuts on that guy. You better save this for the ballfield."

Then I started thinking, "What happens when this guy calls to complain?" I mean, I would have, had somebody done that to me. So I contacted the office and asked if anyone had called and mentioned my name. "No, why?" said the dispatcher. "No reason," I said.

My luck changed a few weeks later. I had a guy on my delivery route who would always give me a hard time. He would never sign for the package and he'd always bitch about this and that. One day I told him, "You know what? You're just an asshole." Hey, I figured it was just like in baseball: you treat me like shit, I'll treat you like shit. Yes, well, I almost got fired for that one. I learned in real life that you can't call people names unless you want to visit your unemployment office real fast.

Being an umpire also means having to deal with confrontations and knowing when someone crosses the line. A ballplayer or manager crosses that line if he touches you or bumps you. If he does, he's gone. And if the league president has any guts, the guy is also fined and suspended. A good league president, such as Bill Cutler in the Pacific Coast League, or George MacDonald, Jr., who used to be my boss in the Gulf Coast League and the Florida State League, can do wonders for umpires by sticking a minor league guy where it really hurts—right in the wallet. In the big leagues, most of those players and managers make so much money that they could give a damn about a fine. But in the minors, a stiff fine made a guy think twice before he started blasting us again. Lots of times a manager would start out onto the field all ready to throw a fit, think twice about it, and return to the bench. That's my kind of confrontation.

Another cardinal rule is that no one is allowed to argue about balls and strikes. The first time they do it, an umpire issues a warning. If you hear it again, you dump him. You'd think they'd learn, but like I said, ballplayers and managers aren't exactly the smartest people in the world.

Ballplayers and managers will do anything to test you. A guy might get right in your face during an argument, and during the whole thing, he's hitting you in the forehead with the bill of his baseball cap. It's like arguing with a woodpecker. The absolute worst is when they're knocking you silly with the cap and spraying your face with tobacco juice. Happens all the time.

I had a partner in the PCL, Al Kaplan, who found himself face-to-face with an Edmonton Trappers pitching coach named Ed Ott. Now, Kaplan chewed all the time. So did Ott. As they argued, Ott kept peppering Kaplan's face with the brown juice. Poor Kaplan was trying to spray back, but he wasn't having much success. I could see him getting more flustered every second. Finally, Kaplan tried once more to talk and spit. Except this time his whole wad of chewing tobacco came flying out of his mouth and hit Ott right in the face. Ott got fined for the argument, but Kaplan did, too. Probably for sloppy spitting.

Chewing tobacco wasn't for me. I tried it once or twice, mostly just to quiet a couple of players who kept pestering me to taste the stuff. I'd chew a tiny bit of it, say, "Yecch," and spit it out. Some of those guys look like chipmunks, what with all that tobacco in their mouths. And believe me, that shit stings your eyes when they're spraying you. Thing is, you have to be a little more lenient with a guy dousing you with tobacco during an argument because so many umpires chew the stuff themselves. After a while, I learned to argue with tobacco chewers with my eyes shut. Like I said, you do anything to survive.

Sometimes, if you're in a real good mood, you give a manager a break. I had one guy—I can't remember what league—who came out to argue and started spraying me. Managers and ballplayers thought that was the neatest thing, that is, spitting on someone and getting away with it. Anyway, I'm this close to dumping the guy when a big chunk of tobacco hits me right in the eye. I kind of doubled over and wiped the chunk away. Meanwhile, this poor manager sounded as if he were going to cry.

"Oh, Pam, I'm sorry. I'm real sorry. I didn't mean that, really. You got to believe me."

I felt so bad for the guy that I didn't even dump him. I figured he had groveled enough.

Another pet peeve of umpires are guys who try to show you up. There are ballplayers who throw temper tantrums every time they don't agree with a call. Pitchers are the biggest babies. They'll bitch about anything. They like to glare or mutter or stand on the mound with their hands on their hips if they think an umpire cost them a strike.

Roger Clemens of the Boston Red Sox is a perfect example of a pitcher who believes he's never wrong. Clemens thinks he's bigger than the game itself. Remember the 1990 American League playoffs? Clemens thought he was getting screwed by home plate umpire Terry Cooney and told him so from the mound. So Cooney dumped him.

I had mixed feelings about the whole thing. The way I looked at it, Cooney can't call balls and strikes. In a big game like that, you need someone who can umpire big, someone who can rise to the occasion, you know what I mean? Cooney couldn't. We were on the same crew during a spring training game once and he was supposed to have the plate that day. He was putting on his chest protector and he was shaking like a leaf—and I don't think it was because he had too much coffee, either. The guy seemed as if he were absolutely scared stiff of umpiring that day. And this was just a spring training game. I wonder what he was like during the playoffs with Clemens pitching?

But I'll say this for Cooney: for better or worse, he took control of the game. Clemens was pissed because he thought Cooney was inconsistent with his strike zone. If Cooney had stood there and taken Clemens's shit, then that ball game would have become total chaos. Cooney had to do something. Too bad he couldn't have done something other than dump The Rocket.

Almost as bad as Clemens is Cincinnati Reds reliever Rob Dibble. I had him in Triple A, and he's one of the biggest jerks in the game. He argued, almost begged, for strikes, which wouldn't be so bad if he had actually thrown a few once in a while. He was wild. And dangerous, too. Dibble would throw at his own mother for a dime. He thinks he's some sort of tough guy when he aims a ninety-two-mile-per-hour fastball at a batter's earlobe.

The exact opposite of Dibble was Orel Hershiser of the Dodgers. What great control he had in the minors and of course, in the majors, too. I had him in Triple A and he was an angel. It was sickening. I truly believe that if Hershiser threw three cockshots and you called them balls, he would politely say, "Oh, where were they?" He was unbelievable. He never argued. Never. That's one guy I had a soft spot for. In fact, if a guy doesn't hassle you—like Orel never did—that player got the benefit of the doubt on a close call. It was only human nature.

Hitters are a different breed. They can get on your nerves by stepping in and out of the box all the time. It drove me up the wall. Of if they didn't like a strike I called, they'd glance back real quick or walk around for a few moments. Of course, those assholes in the dugout would start chiming in, which only pissed me off more.

Steve Kemp, the former Detroit Tiger and New York Yankee who ended up in Triple A, hated my guts. I hated his, all because he threw a fit every time I called an inside pitch a strike. I could call that pitch a strike twenty-five straight times and Kemp would stand there amazed, as if he didn't understand the plate was seventeen inches wide, not eight. I used to have monumental battles with him. In fact, I have a whole photo album filled with pictures of him and me arguing. My favorite photographs are the ones of me dumping him. The last time I heard, Kemp was coaching a high school team in California. Poor kids.

Let's face it: ballplayers are a strange breed, almost as strange as umpires. They get bored out there. They want to talk, even if it's to an umpire. They always asked the same things: Where's the best bar in town? Don't you wish it would rain? When is our crew's next off-day?

If I was real bored, I might actually answer back. They loved when you did that.

Of course, you just about needed a police escort after the first close pitch or play. Your supposed "buddy" would become your enemy in a moment's time. I hated front-runners like that. I didn't care if a ballplayer was an asshole, just as long as he was an asshole all the time. Those guys who tried to be your friends one day and then called you horseshit the next were the ones I couldn't stand.

Take a guy like Dan Gladden, who plays for the Detroit Tigers. When I had him in the minors, or if I was unlucky enough to get him in spring training, I could always count on him behaving like a prick. I knew it. He knew it. We acted accordingly—with utter disdain for each other. But I'd take Gladden over those other players who thought they were fooling you with their false sincerity.

I loved it when one of those bimbo groupies would ask me if I had ever met any players. "Met them?" I'd say.

"Hey, they're the biggest assholes, biggest nobodies, you'll ever meet. They couldn't survive in the real world. They constantly blame others for everything."

There are exceptions. Not many, but a few. New York Met Bobby Bonilla treats umpires with respect. Bonilla is smart enough not to take any of this stuff personally. He knows how to hit and when to question a call. His former Pirate teammate, Bobby Bonds, is the same way. I don't care what anyone says about Bonds, he never caused me any trouble.

The same goes for Jose Canseco, resident superstar of the Oakland Athletics. I know it's fashionable to trash and bash Jose, but I thought he was the most misunderstood guy I saw in the minors. I had him in the PCL when he was just a guy trying to win a big league job. In the PCL, he was so much better than anybody else, it was a joke. I admired him just for his talent, but I respected him because he never complained about a call, no matter how gawd-awful it was. There were umpires in that league who took it as a personal challenge to make Canseco look bad. I'd hear umpires say, "Wait until I call that pitch a strike on him, then we'll see how good of a hitter he really is. Heh, heh, heh." It was ridiculous. A lot of umpires were brutal on him. They would always test him and see how he'd react. Maybe they were envious of his talents.

His Tacoma Tiger teammates were worse. Most of them were so jealous and petty that they did cruel things, such as "forget" to bring his glove and cap out to him if an inning ended with him on base. He'd have to run back to the dugout and get his own stuff while his teammates would snicker. And his teammates seemed to love it when he had a bad game, as if it proved to them that Canseco wasn't really Superman dressed in a baseball uniform. People just couldn't deal with what a tremendous player he was and still is. And as far as I'm concerned, pro baseball made him what he is today. If he became selfish, or if he became wary of the press or suspicious of authority, it was because he needed to do that to survive. Believe me, I know.

Another favorite was San Diego Padre Tony Gwynn, runner-up in my voting for nicest guy in the game of baseball. I had him in the Texas League and I don't remember him being anything spectacular at the time. But he's obviously learned the strike zone since then, which makes him a joy to have at the plate. If he glanced back after a call, say, during a spring training game, then you got a little concerned. You might have missed one.

The best thing about Gwynn is that he respects umpires. He's up there to hit, not to cry and whine about pitches. He also was the most unselfish player I ever saw.

But the easiest guy to get along with was Brett Butler, who I had in the minors and then in various spring trainings. Butler, who's with the Dodgers now, was sickeningly sweet. After Butler killed you with kindness, you almost wanted to get in an argument with someone. Butler almost gives baseball a good name.

Besides being a decent person, the other thing Butler does, which a lot of those idiot players don't do, is study the umpires. Butler thinks about who's calling the plate and adjusts accordingly. With me, Butler knew I was going to call the inside pitch a strike. I loved calling that pitch a strike, mostly because very few umpires had the guts to. If I called an outside-corner pitch a strike, Butler would turn around and say, "You going to call that pitch a strike all game?" I'd say, "Yeah," and that would be that. Rarely would you hear another peep from Butler the rest of the game. He had the information he wanted. As long as I was consistent with my strike zone, he would never say a word.

Not so with catchers. Catchers are always trying to be an umpire's pal. They're usually two-faced brown-nosers who think that if they buddy up to you enough, maybe you'll cut them a break. Let me tell you something: catchers will stab you in the back almost as quick as pitchers. If a catcher doesn't agree with a call, he'll hold the ball a few extra moments before throwing it back to the pitcher—just to let you know that he's upset, as if I could give a shit. Other times he might start to throw the ball back and then stop after you make a call. "What's wrong with that pitch?" he'll whine.

Truth is, I've seen catchers intimidate umpires. I know this because I've been intimidated by the best of them. Remember the Fisk story in spring training? That was a lesson I never forgot.

Ken Kaiser, one of the better umpires in the American League, goes completely by what the catcher does. I know this particular detail because Kaiser told me so in the confines of his hotel room one night in Las Vegas. He was there on some sort of gambling stop and left a message for our crew to stop by the Golden Nugget casino after our PCL game. We did as we were told, and sure enough, there was Kaiser at one of the blackjack tables and he was winning, too. For some strange reason, he won even more money after I started watching him play. Before long, he wouldn't let me leave. He said I was good luck. Who was I to argue?

Later, Kaiser invited me up to his hotel room, which made me just a little nervous. Not that I had anything against Kaiser—he's a fun guy—it's just that it didn't make good sense to get involved in—how should I put it?—a potentially delicate situation, if you know what I mean.

Well, guess what? Kaiser didn't want to put the make on me; he wanted to show me his stance when he umpires home plate. The whole scene was unbelievable. Here I am in the wee hours of the morning, in Ken Kaiser's hotel room, receiving a lesson in the dos and don'ts of umpiring. Kaiser, a former pro wrestler who weighs about 290 pounds, made the room seem small as he lowered himself into his umpiring stance for this impromptu teaching session.

"Here's what I do, Pam," he said. "I go by the catcher.

If the catcher makes the pitch look good, it's a strike. Let the catcher show you where the ball's at."

I didn't agree, but hey, Kaiser was in the big leagues and I wasn't. I was willing to listen to any sort of advice.

You'd be surprised how many umpires, both in the big leagues and minor leagues, were unwilling to sit down and talk to me about the craft of umpiring. It was as if they were scared to help me or thought I wouldn't understand. The assholes.

Not everyone was like that, though. Kaiser, you know about. He's an Al Somers School grad, and even though he works in the American League, which I think is inferior to the National League—especially in the overall quality of umpiring—Kaiser is a real pro.

Doug Harvey, who became a National League umpire in 1962, is another guy who went out of his way to help. Harvey has the most experience of any umpire in either league, which explains why his nickname is God. I worked a couple of spring training games with him in Yuma, Arizona, which is where the San Diego Padres set up camp. He had the plate one day and never called the inside corner, which isn't surprising. Most of the old guard never do. But Harvey's a good umpire and he actually knows the rules. A lot of the big league umpires, and I'm referring to the ones who have been around for fifteen, twenty yeras, depend on the younger umpires to carry them when it comes to the rule book. You think those geezers actually sit in their hotel rooms at night reviewing the rules? No way. They let the young guys do all the work.

Now don't get the wrong idea about umpires. For the most part, the majority of those guys in the big leagues are talented umpires. In my humble opinion, the smartest thing the National League ever did (besides hiring Bart Giamatti and never allowing the designated hitter) was to offer Joe West a job in 1978. The average fan has no idea what a great umpire this guy is. He busts his ass every minute he's on the field, and unlike most umpires, he rarely has a bad day. You see, umpires go through slumps just like ballplayers. There are days when you can't seem to get anything right, when you're missing plays that you can normally call in your sleep. But West doesn't have that problem, at least, not very often. The other thing I like about West is that he's such a red-ass, which means the ballplayers and managers can't stand him. Attaway, Joe.

Eric Gregg of the National League is a hell of an umpire. So is Mark Hirschbeck of the NL, who doesn't take shit from anyone. By the way, he's five nine, a whole inch taller than me. The NL's Bob Davidson is a favorite of mine, too, because he's never been afraid to call a balk or hustle out there. Gutsy Steve Palermo, suffering from a gunshot wound suffered while trying to break up a robbery last season, is probably the best there is in the American League. You never hear anyone say a bad thing about his work, which is unusual since umpires like to gossip and snipe as much as the next person. I wish him a speedy recovery.

Jim Joyce, another American Leaguer, didn't like working with me, but I'll say this, he knows how to umpire. And while I'm handing out compliments, let me throw some in the direction of Tim Tschida, a phenom who joined the American League at the ripe age of twenty-five; Rocky Roe of the AL; AL man Tim Welke, my old partner from Florida State League days; and John Hirschbeck, another AL umpire who has done the near impossible: earn the universal respect of the players and managers in his league. Very tough to do. DeMuth, Poncino, and even Mr. Brown-Noser himself, Jerry Layne, all are smooth umpires. However, I helped Layne make it to the big leagues. Before he saw me work the plate, his strike zone was about as big as a postage stamp. He'll never admit it, but by watching me, he became a better balls-and-strikes umpire.

More compliments: NL umpire John Kibler, who has

been in the league as a regular since 1965, taught me an important lesson once in spring training. I had third base and he had second when one of the teams—I think it was the Padres that day—tried a pickoff play. The runner on second clearly beat the pickoff throw, but Kibler immediately called the player out. I said to myself, "Jeez, Kibler blew that call."

At the end of the inning Kibler walked by and said, "Boy, I hope I don't have too many like that." He knew he had missed the call, but the lesson was this: if you're going to blow one, be decisive about it. Sure, he screwed the play, but it was the way he screwed it up that allowed him to walk away without an argument from the player or manager. Smart move.

Now, with that done, let me say a few things about several of my other former colleagues. John McSherry might be a fine National League umpire, but he needs to mix a salad in now and then. To McSherry, a professional on-field appearance is only a suggestion. In fact, at one point some of the more overweight umpires, such as Gregg and McSherry, were told to start controlling their poundage . . . or else.

Then there's National Leaguer Jerry Crawford, who lost my respect the day I did a spring training game with him in Bradenton, Florida. Crawford was working the bases, and every half inning he would practically throw his arms around St. Louis Cardinal shortstop Ozzie Smith, the same Ozzie Smith who had recently blasted the umpires in *Sports Illustrated*. I couldn't believe what I was seeing that day. I'll go to my grave believing that an umpire should never make small talk with a player, not even in a spring training game. It looks unprofessional, and anyway, players don't give a damn about us. Crawford, who calls some great games, should have known better.

And what should I say about the big league umpire who suggested we go to a movie as "friends" and ended up trying to hold my hand in the theater? I almost thought I was back in high school.

Or what about another umpire (married, I might add) in the big leagues who asked me to spend the night with him. I turned him down, which sent his ego into hiding for weeks.

Umpires aren't saints, believe me. You've heard the term *baseball Annies.* The same holds true for umpires, who have a smaller but equally dedicated collection of groupies who reside in just about every major and minor league town. An umpire crew would arrive in a city for a four-game series and already have a detailed scouting report on assorted, uh, companionship. It wasn't uncommon for some of my fellow umpires to have names and numbers of girls who had made the previous crew's stay in town a happy one. I guess there are a lot of lonely women out there.

I had one married crew member who used to tell me that he was simply going to church with a female friend of his. Church? Truth is, there weren't many married former partners of mine who didn't cheat on their wives. I guess when you're on the road as long as umpires are, you start justifying things, such as breaking fidelity and marriage vows.

I'll admit, I had my moments on the road. Then again, I wasn't married, either. One guy, Dave from Dayton, Ohio, used to send me pictures of himself (fully clothed, by the way). He was a part-time local umpire and a member of the Dayton police department. He'd call or write, but I never called back. I didn't see the point of trying to establish some sort of pen pal relationship.

Umpiring has to be one of the loneliest professions in the country. The pressures are enormous and they never stop. Every day you're supposed to be perfect.

Remember what I said about survival? Umpires have all sorts of defense mechanisms. Most of them drink heavily. Some do drugs. In fact, when I was in the minors in 1988, members of the Major League Baseball Drug Education and Testing Team were sent to various cities to spot-check umpires. Bet you didn't know there was such a thing. Neither did I until they showed up in Oklahoma City one day to test my crew.

The testing team was based in Cincinnati, and everything was supposed to be very secret. We were told *never* to mention the team's existence to any member of the news media. "For obvious reasons," read a letter sent to me by a member of the team, "the Commissioner's Office is very publicity shy concerning the drug testing program."

The drug testing team meant business. They had to personally supervise the umpires peeing into a little container. That was fine for the guys, but when it was my turn, the all-male testing team didn't quite know what to do. In the end, they let me go in the bathroom where I secretly exchanged urine samples. Just kidding. I did my business, handed them the container, and never heard from the team again, except for a single letter from a Dr. E. K. Hammond, who was the team's coordinator. I had asked Hammond for one of his prized testing-team shirts, which are harder to find than a Nolan Ryan rookie card, and he sent me one.

One of my partners that day, Tom Hallion, wasn't so adept at filling his urine container. For whatever reason, the poor guy couldn't pee.

I had my own particular method for handling the pressure of umpiring. I drank, of course. Like a fish. But when I was really depressed, I went shopping. Buying something, even on my meager minor league salary, always made me feel better. Other umpires, such as my former partner Jerry Layne, who's in the National League now, used to talk on the phone. We used to call him The Lonely Guy. He couldn't stand to be alone.

Another way to lessen the stress was to call a quick game. Forget all that tie-goes-to-the-runner crap. In umpiring, you want to get the call right, but you also want to get the hell off the field as fast as you can. The saying went, "When in doubt, call an out." Anyway, it got you in the bars faster.

And while I'm in the mood, let me destroy a few more myths, beginning with the movie *Bull Durham*. It was one part truth, one thousand parts exaggeration, and ten thousand parts sexist. Those weren't the same minor leagues I knew for thirteen seasons.

On to cheating. Umpires don't lose much sleep over a guy who cheats. If we caught a guy doctoring the ball, fine. If we didn't, fine, too. Unless I saw spit sliding off the ball or watched the pitcher pull out a tool kit on the mound, I never did a thing. No umpire did, unless a manager demanded that we check the ball for scuff marks or gel or spit. Otherwise, it was business as usual. No umpire wants hassles, and watching for cheaters is a hassle. It absolutely spoils that two-hour goal that every umpire craves.

I also wouldn't have cared less if every one of those asshole team mascots were doused with kerosene and set on fire. I hated the furry little creatures. First of all, what sort of loser climbs inside a costume and makes a fool out of himself (and umpires) for three hours each night? Wait. I take that back. The Chicken I liked. He was cool. The Chicken would always send each umpire a $50 gift certificate from JC Penney each Christmas. It was sort of his way of saying thanks for helping him out in his routine. That's why I liked him.

Of course, one time early in my career I wanted to stick the Chicken's routine up his beak. Usually the Chicken would tell us exactly what he planned to do during the game. That way there were no surprises and everyone lived happily ever after. So imagine my reaction when the Chicken pranced up to me during a break between innings and reached down my umpire's uniform. Before I knew it, he was pulling out scarf after scarf, much to the delight of the crowd. Then, as I did a slow burn, he pulled out one last scarf . . . with a bra attached to it. I wanted to take a Louisville Slugger to his head.

He later apologized and from that point on, always told me beforehand what he had planned in his routine. Still, I was wary. In fact, whenever the Chicken approached me for another act, I'd tell him to go bother another umpire . . . or else. He did as he was told.

The Philadelphia Phanatic is the mascot I would most like to see permanently banned from any ballpark. He used to do gigs at minor league fields, and he would constantly mimic the umpires.

One time, I was having a bad game and he started walking toward me between innings. That's when we had a little chat.

"Get the fuck away from me," I said.

"Fuck you," said the sweet-looking Philly Phanatic.

I thought about throwing him out, but what the hell. It wouldn't have been worth the trouble.

Other than all this, I love the game.

CHAPTER 13

Just Call Me Blue

Okay, I told myself, *this* was going to be the spring the National League hired me. I had a new and improved attitude, meaning I had decided to concentrate on Vargo's umpiring style, no matter how much I hated it. After all, I had spent six seasons in Triple A, which is about two or three more than most umpires stay before getting promoted to the big leagues. Or getting released. I figured that if Vargo's style finally clicked with me, my chances of earning a spot in the majors were that much better.

There had also been an interesting development in February. That's when Giamatti was elected commissioner of Major League Baseball and Bill White, a former major league player, had been chosen to replace him. The transfer of power would officially take place on April 1.

All I knew about White was that he had retired in 1969 and then spent about the next twenty years as a New York Yankees broadcaster. I didn't know how that qualified him for National League president, but then again, Giamatti had been a Yale professor, right?

White was supposed to be a pretty good guy, but that didn't mean he'd have anything to do with my career that spring. Giamatti would still be the boss until the end of training camp. That meant Vargo would still be the guy whispering in his ear about which umpire should make it and which shouldn't.

Whether he knew it nor not, Vargo actually did me a favor by keeping me in Phoenix for the first ten days of spring training. I preferred working in the Cactus League, mostly because it allowed me to stay at home and kept me far, far away from Vargo.

The other great thing about spending those first couple of weeks in Arizona was the lack of local media attention. The sportswriters knew me there. Hell, I was old news. After working four seasons in the PCL, crisscrossing the West and building a reputation for myself, the writers quit paying much attention to me. In Arizona, people didn't make such a big deal about The Woman Umpire anymore. My fame was fading fast, which was fine with me. I never wanted the attention anyway.

One of my first games was in Scottsdale, which is the spring home for the San Francisco Giants. I had heard that it was fun working games there because the ballpark was always packed to the rafters with die-hard Giants fans. And don't let anybody tell you different: umpires like it better when there's a big crowd. The noise gets you in the game and, in a way, makes you concentrate a little harder.

As usual, I showed up about an hour and a half before the game started. Dana DeMuth was supposed to have the plate that day, while I and National Leaguers Doug Harvey and Randy Marsh would handle the bases. No sweat. I knew DeMuth from the PCL and had briefly met Harvey and Marsh in the past, but never worked with them. I figured I'd kill some time in the umpires' dressing room, shoot the shit with the guys, and then have a great game. I wanted to think positive. I was going to work so hard this spring that Vargo wouldn't have any choice but to offer me a job.

I had just made my way into the ballpark when I recognized Marsh, who seemed in a hurry.

"Hey, Randy," I said, "where's the locker room?"

"There isn't one for us," he said. "We're dressing in the

baseball clubhouse and you can't come in. We'll try to find a place for you."

I thought he was kidding. Occasionally, umpires, myself included, had to dress in the clubhouse. As early as we arrived, there usually weren't many players in there, so it was never a big deal. Until now.

"What do you mean I can't go in there?" I said.

"The players are in there. We'll try to find you a place."

So much for a positive attitude. DeMuth, Harvey, and Marsh could go in there, but I couldn't? What a bunch of shit. Instead, I had to go sit in a little ticket office near the ballpark entrance and cool my heels for an hour. I hadn't even started my first day of work and already a guy like Marsh was trying to shut me out. That's when I decided I wouldn't show up early again. Who needed the aggravation? Not me.

At the risk of sounding conceited, I had a pretty good game on the bases, despite that asshole Marsh. I also felt better not having Vargo looking over my shoulder, telling me to be his umpiring clone. The guy made me nervous and I swear he tried to psyche me out. But with him in Florida, I could relax a little bit and occasionally revert to my stance behind the plate—just for old times' sake. Turns out that my relaxation period lasted about six days, or the time it took to have my first real conversation with Roger Craig, manager of the Giants.

During the off-season, Craig, who had never seen me umpire a game, was interviewed by a magazine reporter. Among the topics: my quest for a major league job. In the story, Craig said he'd never want his own daughter to be an umpire because of the profanity, which I thought was a stupid thing to say. What did it matter what the hell job his daughter chose, as long as it made her happy? It sounded as if Craig thought umpiring was beneath her, as if she could do something much better with her life.

Well, guess whose team I had for my first plate appearance that spring? Correct: Craig's Giants. Bob Engel, who would later become famous for his baseball-card shoplifting arrest, and Marsh were my partners.

Like most staffs in spring training, Craig and a couple of his coaches sat on some folding chairs next to the dugout. You weren't allowed to do that during the regular season, but in spring it was okay. The managers and coaches liked it because they could get a better view of pitchers. And a little suntan, too.

The third inning had just ended when I heard someone calling my name.

"Pam, c'mon over here," Craig said.

So I walked toward the dugout.

"Listen, I'd just like to say I'm sorry about that article," he said. "You're doing a hell of a job and I think you'll be in the big leagues soon."

"Hey, I don't believe everything I read," I said. "Don't worry about it. It was no big deal."

But later, after thinking about it for a while, well, it sort of was a big deal. I appreciated Craig saying what he did, but it would have helped me more had he said it to a sportswriter. After all, he had blasted me in the magazine. Why couldn't he support me in public too?

Craig was right about one thing: I was having a good spring so far. I could tell because of the sounds of silence from the dugouts. Once in a while, I'd have a lapse on the base paths, but nothing serious.

Unfortunately, my time in Arizona was almost up. I had to be in West Palm Beach and under the watchful eye of Vargo by March 21, a Tuesday. Because of the way the schedule was designed, I had two days to get there. Dumb me. Rather than get on a plane on Sunday and fly to Florida, I chose to wait until Monday, figuring that would give me plenty of time to get there. Well, I was wrong.

To begin with, the airlines canceled my flight from Phoenix to West Palm Beach. The only thing I could get was a late-night flight to Tampa, which is about a four-hour drive from West Palm Beach. As I bitched and moaned about my bad luck, the guy next to me said he was in the same situation. I didn't know the guy from Adam, but we agreed to rent a car in Tampa and drive to West Palm Beach as soon as we landed. We didn't have a choice: the next flight to West Palm Beach would get us there too late.

We got to Tampa about at two A.M. We rented a car, and wouldn't you know it, the guy slept the whole way. I didn't care. All I knew was that I wouldn't be late, that I wouldn't be in Vargo's doghouse before my first game in Florida. I had screwed up, but then recovered nicely. I'd check into the hotel, get a few hours' sleep, take a shower, and arrive at the ballpark a little worse for wear, but on time.

I overslept. By the time I got to the stadium, less than a half hour remained before the first pitch. Vargo was so pissed that I thought he was going to fire me that very moment.

"Ed, let me explain," I said.

"Never mind," he snapped. "You don't have to work the game. Take the day off."

"No, Ed, I want to work the game. Let me just tell you what happened."

I tried, but Vargo wasn't listening because he was too busy being mad. It didn't matter that I had busted my ass to get there. It didn't matter that even if I had shown up an hour early, I might not have had a place to dress, à la the Arizona incident. All that mattered was that I had broken one of his rules. It's true: I should have flown out Sunday. But I made it, didn't I?

I worked the game, but I knew I was in trouble with Vargo. I was on his shit list and I still had thirteen games to go. What next?

Well, strange as it may seem, Vargo took me out to dinner a few nights later. That's when he started dropping hints about my future:

"You know, Pam, you've got to work really hard this

year. You've got to work really well and you've got to work my style."

Translation: probably another year in Triple A.

I didn't feel much like eating the rest of my dinner after that. He hadn't come right out and said it, but his plans seemed clear. Of course, maybe I had read too much into it. Maybe it was Vargo's way of trying to psyche me up, not out. Vargo was strange that way. I could never figure him out.

The tough thing about spring training is that the players, especially the veterans whose positions are secure, don't give a shit about the games. They just go through the motions. Meanwhile, you're fighting for a job and you've got to be focused and interested in every pitch of every inning of every game.

I was in competition with seven other umpires that spring. The list included Bill Hohn, Larry Poncino, and Mike Winters, who already were under option, and Ron Barnes, Jerry Layne, Ed Rapuano, Charlie Rehliford, and Dan Wickman. Nobody was sure how many of us, if any, the National League would use during the regular season. Unlike the year before, there weren't any full-time openings in the league. My only shot was to join the replacement pool, which would be okay with me. It beat the alternative.

Problem was, Vargo's style was giving me fits again. Some days I felt comfortable with his stance, other days every pitch looked the same. Problem was, the "other days" were beginning to outnumber the "some days." No matter what I did, nothing worked. It was like telling a singles hitter to hit home runs; it can't be done. The worst part about it was that I knew I was sinking fast. All you had to do was watch me work the plate. I'd call an outside slider a strike, then a few innings later, call the same pitch a ball. I was all over the place with my strike zone. My strength—handling the plate—had become a weakness. I looked like a dead weight out there. Vargo had rattled me again with his goofy style and his dinner lectures. Even though I knew the guy could make or break me, I should have said, "Ed, give me a chance to call a game my way. If you still think it stinks, then you'll never hear another word from me." Instead, I tried to compromise. I tried to incorporate his style into mine, which is impossible. Then I tried his way exclusively, which was even worse. I was a mess and it was partly my own damn fault.

As if that weren't enough, along came another minicontroversy hatched by some bored sportswriters. This was about the same time that Boston Red Sox third baseman Wade Boggs was having some marital problems. He had a wife in Boston and a girlfriend in California. So what else was new? Ballplayers were always cheating on their wives.

But this time, the media tried making the game into a Postema vs. Boggs thing. The Woman Umpire vs. The Cheater. Some people were even predicting a big confrontation. Hey, I didn't give a shit if he went out on his wife. I had other things to worry about, mostly how to salvage my spring training.

I hated to disappoint the press, but Boggs and I didn't have the spectacular argument everybody had expected. In fact, he didn't say a word until I called a borderline pitch a strike.

"That's high," he said.

"Well," I said, "it's the new strike zone." (That's right, Vargo was on us again to call it.)

"It's still high," Boggs said.

"Yeah."

He was right. I hated calling that pitch, but I didn't have a choice. I couldn't afford to do anything that would anger Vargo again, so I did as I was told.

Meanwhile, Giamatti wasn't granting many interviews, and when he did, he never said anything about my status. I guess he had learned his lesson. By now, I figured I had two chances: Giamatti, in one of his last acts as National League president, could make a bold move and sign me to a contract, or he could send me back to the minors again. I wanted to believe the first option, but I thought the second choice was more likely. This was one time I hoped my instincts were dead wrong.

My last game in Florida was Friday, March 31. It was a 12:05 P.M. start and I was running late. I hadn't heard anything from Vargo for a while, but I still had a game in Louisville on Saturday and then a game in Columbus on Sunday. If I was going to hear something, I'd hear it by then.

On my way out the door, I stopped long enough to grab a cup of coffee, a piece of toast, and a copy of *USA Today*. Those guys always were the first to know, it seemed. I glanced at the front page and then turned to the sports section where once again, my fate was staring me in the face. The story said I had flunked out again. The National League wasn't going to offer me a job. And this time there weren't any promises to invite me to 1990 spring training.

I didn't know what made me more upset: not getting a job or not getting a call from Vargo or anyone else in the National League. Those people were gutless. I mean, how much decency would it have taken to pick up the phone and say, "Pam, we wanted to tell you first before you read it in the newspapers." But that isn't the way Vargo worked. He was too chicken to do something like that.

Charlie Williams was supposed to have the plate, but for some reason he never showed up. As game time approached, the other umpire said he would take home plate because he was the only person who had his equipment with him. I didn't have the heart to tell him my stuff was in the trunk of my car. Fuck that. About the last thing I wanted to do was slap on ten pounds of equipment and broil in the Florida sun and humidity. Instead, I took the bases.

I had quite a performance that day. Since there weren't

any supervisors to spy on me, I called people out right and left. There must have been ten bangers at first base and I called every one of those assholes out. And I dared them to argue. No one did, though. Either they were great calls or the players and managers had read the news, too. As for my partner, well, he wasn't so lucky. The ratty Mets, who could bitch about the color of the infield dirt, were all over him. He was calling balls strikes and strikes balls. He was awful and the Mets were merciless. I almost felt sorry for him, but I was too busy feeling sorry for myself.

I did the games in Louisville and Columbus and then reported to Buffalo for another exciting season as an American Association crew chief in the Triple A Alliance. My salary? I got $1,000 a month and $67 per diem, which was supposed to cover hotels, food, and incidentals. Hell, I was still paying off $1,000 debts incurred from the previous two seasons' worth of expenses. At this pace, bankruptcy was a possibility.

Joe Mickel and Rapuano were my partners. Mickel didn't take any shit from anyone. I liked that. He was a big guy who had one of those Fu Manchu mustaches and a scowl that usually scared away any manager or ballplayer who tried arguing with him. That was the difference between Mickel and me. Mickel could make a horseshit call and nobody would utter a sound. For example, the guy never called anybody safe at second. The runner had to beat the throw by minutes before Mickel would let him stay put. Otherwise, he was out of there. If I made the same call, it would be cowboys and Indians on the field. But Mickel had that look. Me? I never looked intimidating; I looked worried. Even when I wasn't worried, I looked like I was.

Ed Rapuano was a decent guy, but a little on the macho side. He had been invited to spring training, too, which was odd, since he had never worked a game in Triple A. Word was that his family knew Giamatti or something like that. It wouldn't have surprised me. Everything became so political in umpiring after you got to the Triple A level.

Sometimes it wasn't what you knew that put you in the big leagues, but who you knew. I guess it's the same in most professions.

By this point, I knew I'd have to do something special to earn a major league job. Only two umpires—Dutch Rennert and Bruce Froemming—had spent thirteen seasons in the minors and been promoted, so I didn't like my odds. I had tried Vargo's way, but with mixed results. So in early April, the first month of a six-month-long season, I said, "Fuck it." I was going to do things my way. If the National League didn't like it, tough.

With those simple words, umpiring became fun again. My strike zone got more consistent and I could see the ball better than ever. Also, Mickel and Rapuano were a blast to have around, especially Mickel.

We were doing a game one night when Rapuano, who had the plate, found himself in the middle of a banger at home. As he went to take off his mask, his cap slipped off his head and fell down to his nose, where it stayed as he made the crucial call. Mickel and I saw the whole thing and couldn't help ourselves. We started laughing so hard that I thought I was going to hurt my ribs. Rapuano, of course, was beet red with embarrassment. The play was over and he still couldn't get the cap out of his face, which made Mickel and me laugh even harder. It wasn't the most professional thing to do, but even Vargo would have had a hard time keeping a straight face on this one. After that, Mickel and I would always turn to Rapuano before a game, pull our caps over our faces, and say, "Okay, let's go!" It became our favorite pregame ritual.

Mickel was always coming up with strange ideas. When the Chinese, as a form of protest against their dictatorship, decided to fast, Mickel said we should do the same thing.

"If I make a bad call," he said, "I won't eat tonight."

That idea didn't last long. After a couple of blown calls, Mickel was back at the dinner table with the rest of us.

Another night, it was my turn to provide the laughs. We were in Columbus, home of the Yankees farm team, when I heard some people heckling me from the stands.

"Look at the dyke with no tits out there!" someone yelled.

And then another voice: "Get the dyke with no tits out from behind the plate!"

I glanced back and located the assholes: three college kids from nearby Ohio State. They were on the third-base side, about five rows up, which was close enough for everyone on the field to hear them. Also up in the stands that night were a couple of friends and relatives from my hometown, who had driven the ninety miles from Willard to see the game. I sure as hell didn't want them to hear much more of the college punks.

At the end of the half inning, I decided enough was enough. They had yelled the same shit three different times and I was pissed. I stormed into the Yankees dugout, where a surprised Bucky Dent, who was manager of the team, was sitting.

"Where's the phone?" I said.

Dent didn't say a word; he just pointed toward one of the dugout walls.

"Listen," I said after dialing up a stadium official in the press box, "I want security people down here immediately."

"What for, Pam?" said the official.

By then, Dent and most of his players and coaches had edged toward me, trying to listen to the conversation. Just so there wouldn't be any confusion, I raised my voice for everyone to hear:

"I'll tell you why. The next time those three guys with the blue shirts sitting on the third-base side yell, 'Look at the dyke with no tits!' I want them thrown out of here."

The official started smirking and laughing. "Okay, Pam, we'll get security down there."

As I got ready to leave the dugout, I heard a few of the

Columbus players giggling in the background. Dent didn't know what to do: laugh or try to keep a straight face. I made it easy for him.

"How dare they say I have no tits," I said to a flabbergasted Dent.

With that I left the dugout and returned to home plate, where I could hear the Yankees, including Dent, I suppose, laughing away. By the way, the three college guys left after they saw the security personnel.

The weirdness didn't stop there. The 1989 season was also the year Richmond catcher John Mizerock, who had hounded me for a date the previous two seasons, escalated his attack. He was always asking me to marry him and I'd laugh it off. Catchers are like that: they want to be your pals, even if it means making asses out of themselves. But Mizerock was different. He kept taking his so-called affection to higher levels.

Once he bribed one of the umpire clubbies to place a note inside my underwear. The note said, "Hi, sweetheart! You can't escape me! See you soon. Hugs and Kisses, #25. P.S. You're my favorite."

Another time he had a poster of himself delivered to our dressing room. He'd signed it, too. The poster, which was sponsored by Oscar Mayer wieners (how fitting), read, "Pam, I only have eyes for you. Forever yours, John Mizerock."

I couldn't figure out if Mizerock was serious or if he was trying to win a bet with teammates. And I sure wasn't going to find out.

In late April, the fun stopped temporarily as Larry Napp, an assistant supervisor of umpires for the American League, put his foot in his mouth and in the process, appeared to damage whatever chances I had of a promotion.

We were in Pawtucket and the Richmond Braves were leading the Red Sox in the bottom of the ninth. Pawtucket had lost something like nine straight games and was desperate for a win, so desperate that their players resorted to cheating.

With one out, the score 8–7, the tying run on third, and the count 3-2 on Dana Williams, Braves pitcher Mark Eichhorn threw a slow curve. The pitch was borderline, but before I could make a call on it, Williams leaned into it, purposely trying to milk a free trip to first base. Williams, thinking I would automatically award him first base, started trotting up the line. As he did that, I stepped in front of the plate, sort of reenacted the play, and called him out. Pawtucket manager Ed Nottle argued the call, but I knew I was right. I would have made the same call a hundred times. Nottle tried telling me that I had no business calling Williams out, that unless I had stood in the batter's box with a 3-2 count and the ball coming at my thigh, I couldn't begin to identify with the situation. Well, that was a horseshit reason. You had to be blind not to see Williams stick his leg out.

The Braves intentionally walked the next two batters to load the bases and got out of the jam when Pawtucket's Gary Tremblay ended the game with a fly ball to right field.

So what happens? A few weeks later, Napp told a sportswriter with the *Richmond Times-Dispatch* that I had taken too long to make the call against Williams. "Timing means so much in this business," he said.

So does accuracy, which is what Napp's comments were missing. He didn't even see the game, but he talked as if he had. Dennis Cregg, a supervisor for Umpire Development, had been there and he didn't think I hesitated. Then Napp started offering some more opinions, each one worse than the last.

For instance . . .

"If you haven't made [the big leagues] in twelve years, you're not going to make it in the next five, that's for sure. We just let about half a dozen umpires go because they already had twelve years in and they weren't going to make it."

And . . .

"She's a nice person and she knows the rules. But the thing is, she's got to do the job twice as good as the guy, if he's a good one, to get the [big league] job."

Napp had told me the same thing about being twice as good as a man in the Tidewater clubhouse one day. He said it in front of Mickel and Rapuano. Not long after that, Jerry Neudecker, another American League umpire supervisor, asked Mickel if it was true, had Napp really said those things.

"Yeah, he said them," Mickel said.

"Oh, my God," said Neudecker, "how could he say that?"

I saw Napp on our next trip, but I didn't even acknowledge his existence. He had unfairly blasted me. Worse yet, he said it to a newspaper reporter. That ruined my credibility with the Richmond team. Napp knew I was pissed, but he didn't apologize for a thing. I know it sounds kind of petty, but since he had treated me like shit in the papers, I decided to shut him out. I didn't want anything to do with the guy.

Things quieted down until mid-June, when it was cowboys and Indians all over again in Omaha. Two nights. Three ejections. The first night I dumped Oklahoma City's Kevin Reimer, who's now with the Texas Rangers, after he argued a close call at first. He kept yelling, "That's fucking brutal, that's fucking horseshit," and then he slammed his helmet to the ground.

"That's a fine," I said.

He started to walk toward the dugout, stopped, shot me the finger, and then yelled, "Fuck you!" That's when I dumped him.

The next night, I threw Omaha manager Sal Rende out of the game when he kept arguing balls and strikes. An inning later, I dumped Oklahoma City's Brad Arnsberg and Omaha's Luis Delos Santos for fighting after Arnsberg aimed a pitch at Delos Santos's back. As we were clearing the field, I saw Rende.

"What the hell are you doing here? You better leave right now," I said.

"What are you going to do? Throw me out again?" he said.

No. I wish I could have hit him.

By the time I received my midyear evaluation from the Office of Umpire Development, I had eight ejections and three reports on equipment violations, which is when a player throws a helmet or bat. Equipment violations resulted in fines.

Eight ejections wasn't anything to be proud about, but for me, it was an improvement. Even though it was my thirteenth season in the minors, players still tested me. Remember that story about Rapuano making a call with his cap covering half his face? If that had been me, there would have been a riot. Players and managers still thought they could intimidate me, but I wasn't about to back down.

The evaluation, signed by Ed Lawrence, our executive director, was brief and to the point:

REMARKS: Good strike zone and above average consistency behind plate. Good timing. May want to refine called-strike mechanic a bit as it is now very brief and could be more emphatic and forceful. As crew chief, must react quicker in taking charge of situations when circumstances warrant. Showing some improvement in reacting to development of plays on bases, but still needs work in this area. Continues to umpire with enthusiasm and desire.

AREAS FOR IMPROVEMENT RECOMMENDATIONS: Work on judging whether or not to go out on fly balls by hesitating and keeping off the outfielders. Continue working on use of voice, keep it loud and strong at all times. As call gets closer, make more emphatic call. Make sure you get proper angle for all plays at first base (90-degree angle).

All in all, it was a favorable report. The stuff about my voice and strike mechanics wasn't a big deal. I could correct that easy enough. As for the rest of it—the bases, taking charge of situations—well, I knew I was getting better there. A little more work and I'd be in great shape.

A couple of days after I received my evaluation, I found myself in the middle of one of the great all-time arguments. I wish an umpire supervisor had seen the way Mickel and I handled Nashville manager Frank Lucchesi. It was priceless.

Mickel was behind the plate and I had third base. An Oklahoma City batter took a half swing, which caused Mickel to go to me with an appeal. I motioned that the batter had checked his swing in time.

Out came Lucchesi, who was allowed to ask for the appeal, but wasn't allowed to argue the results of that appeal. Lucchesi didn't care about the rules at that point. In fact, he was arguing balls and strikes, which is never allowed. After a warning or two, I dumped him.

Then Lucchesi really got mad. He followed me to the middle of the infield and said that since he hadn't cussed me, I couldn't throw him out.

"I'm not leaving," he said.

With that, he sat down behind the pitcher's mound, turned his cap backward, and refused to budge. I had to admit, this was a new one. Mickel came out from behind home plate, and both of us just stared at Lucchesi, who looked like a clown sitting there on the grass.

"Joe," I said, doing my best to suppress a laugh, "Frank says he's not leaving. What are we gonna do?"

Mickel thought about it for a moment and said, "Well, we're going to have to play around him."

"We can't play around him."

"We're going to have to."

By then, I knew Mickel was kidding. But Lucchesi didn't. He was listening to the whole conversation, and you could tell he was trying to figure out if we were serious.

I looked at Mickel. "Yeah, you're right, Joe," I said. "Okay, let's play."

"Okay, let's get it going," Mickel said.

As we started to walk back to our positions, Lucchesi jumped up and ran off the field without saying a word. I never saw a guy run so fast in my life. Good thing, too, since Mickel and I had backed ourselves into a corner. We would have started the game with him sitting there. We didn't have a choice by then.

The next night, when Lucchesi gave us his lineup card at home plate, he just smiled. To him, it was worth the fine for getting dumped.

Few ejections ended up like this, with everyone smiling about it the next day. In my case, ballplayers and managers seemed to dislike it even more when I was the one ejecting them. Jim Walewander, an infielder for the Toledo Mud Hens, tossed the ball in disgust after I called a Louisville runner safe at second on a near force play. When I told him he would be fined for the gesture, he said, "Well, then, how about this?" and threw the ball at me. I dumped him, at which point he picked up the ball, shoved it toward my face, and dropped it at my feet. Strange guy, that Walewander.

I finished the season with fourteen ejections, which was twice as many as any other umpire in the Triple A Alliance. Of course, not every umpire had to listen to as much shit as I did.

As the season was winding down, I received another in a long line of wake-up phone calls from Vargo. This time he waited until seven A.M. to make me an unexpected and, I thought, disturbing offer.

"Listen, Pam, I want to ask if you'd like a job as a supervisor somewhere in the system."

So much for being groggy. I sat up in bed, now more awake than ever, and tried to sort out the reasons for Vargo's surprising proposal. Before I had a chance to do much thinking, I could hear Vargo again:

"Well?"

Not knowing exactly what to say, I tried stalling for time. "What?"

"I said, I could get you a job as a supervisor, if you'd like me to."

This was not a good development. If Vargo was offering me a minor league supervising job, then that had to mean my chances of getting promoted were zilch. Or maybe he just didn't want to deal with my situation anymore? Another possibility, a long shot at best, was that maybe Giamatti was pushing for me to get bumped up to the big leagues but Vargo didn't want me there. If I accepted the supervisor's job, then Vargo could go back to Giamatti and say, "Sorry, but Postema has had it with the game-to-game grind and wants to get into the management side." Or something like that. At that point, I didn't know what to think. I did know, however, that Vargo was on the line, waiting for some type of answer. So I gave him one.

It wasn't what he wanted to hear, I don't think.

"Ed, I want to be a major league umpire. I don't want to be a supervisor. I think we've got enough supervisors who never made it to the big leagues giving advice. I don't want to do that."

Vargo didn't say much and a few moments later the conversation was finished. Now then, was my career?

The more I thought about it, the more I wanted to laugh. Umpire supervisor? Me? Let me tell you how most of the supervisors I met did their jobs. A guy would meet my crew in a town, take us out to eat, and then hit the bars. Supervisors were supposed to watch us work at least one game behind the plate, which most of the supervisors did. But some would never even show up for the games. It happened more than just a couple of times, too.

I didn't want that kind of life. As far as I was concerned, being a supervisor was worse than being an umpire. Supervisors led a lonelier life, if you can believe it. No wonder a lot of them drank like fish. No, if I was going to stay in baseball, it was going to be as an umpire. And if Vargo wanted me out, he was going to have to come up with another way.

Vargo wasn't the only one causing me headaches. As usual, the players and managers were doing little to make life easier. It seemed the longer I was in the minors, the more I lost credibility with those guys. After a while, I could almost tell what they were thinking: "What the hell is she doing in Triple A for seven years? She must not be any good if she's not in the big leagues by now." You worked so long and hard to earn respect, but it didn't matter sometimes. Some of the players and managers started looking at my experience as a point of weakness, testing me at every opportunity. There were plays where I shouldn't have heard a peep from anyone, but yet I was still getting in arguments.

Our last series was in Tidewater. We got into town early that afternoon and decided we'd try to save a little money and split the cost of one room instead of two. With a couple of hours to kill before we had to be at the ballpark, I turned on the television. A few minutes later, a somber-faced newsman interrupted the program with a special report.

Bart Giamatti had died of a heart attack.

I'll never forget that moment as long as I live. I know it sounds selfish, but the first thing I thought was, "Well, there goes my chances at the majors."

Mickel, Rapuano, and I didn't know what to say. We just stared at the TV with these blank looks on our faces. Giamatti may not have been too knowledgeable about umpiring, but he cared about baseball. I don't know if the Pete Rose controversy wore him down, but I do know baseball lost a sweet, gentle man who might have been progressive enough to approve my hiring.

I had the plate that night, but I wasn't really into the game. Giamatti's death was on everybody's mind and rightly so. The next night, Mickel was supposed to be behind the plate. Shortly before game time, he offered a deal:

"I'll give you fifty dollars to work the plate for me."

Mickel needed my help. He had been selected as an umpire for the minor league playoffs and might have the plate for the first game, which started the following day. No way did he want two plate jobs in a row.

"Give me the fifty dollars before the game starts and I'll do it," I said.

Hey, I needed the money, and anyway, I didn't care. As I settled behind the catcher for some warm-up pitches, he glanced back and said, "Why are you back here again?"

"Turn around and shut up," I said.

A few innings into the game, the ratty Tidewater Mets pitcher bounced a ball past the ratty Mets catcher and it hit my arm. It hurt, but it wasn't anything critical. Of course, you wouldn't have known that by looking at Mickel. He was scared stiff that I had broken something. After all, it was his idea to switch positions.

I didn't exactly have an all-star performance that game. I was too busy wondering what was going to happen next in my life. I thought, "Is this it—a crummy Richmond versus Tidewater game? Or will I be in the big leagues making big league money seven months from now? Then I can buy all the two-dollar-and-forty-cent fake nails I want to and not worry about a thing."

Whatever the outcome, I decided not to leave the stadium empty-handed. So I did what any good umpire would do: I grabbed all the baseballs I could.

Umpires will take anything that isn't nailed to the floor or walls. We called it "permanent borrowing." Toilet paper, soap, shampoo, the occasional towel . . . we took it and didn't think twice about any moral issues. We weren't thieves as much as were scavengers.

In this case, I figured I might as well take as many baseballs as I could. As the game ended, I checked my ball bag. Three balls. Not enough. So I motioned to one of the batboys and had him bring me a fresh supply, which he probably thought was odd, since the game was almost finished. Now I had seven. Some heist.

Of course, I could have tried to pull the same season-long scam that one umpire used in the Triple A Alliance. This umpire, who shall remain nameless, used to steal entire boxes of baseballs. One time he let me peek into his hotel room and there they were: boxes and boxes of new baseballs, six rows, and each row nearly touched the ceiling. Figure twelve baseballs per box, times twenty boxes per row, times six, and that's 1,440 baseballs. The umpire said he sold the balls to collectors or gave them to Little League teams in his hometown. That way he could make a buck and ease his conscience at the same time. Oh, well.

The minute after the final out we packed our equipment, showered, changed clothes, and made a beeline for the Hilton, where we knew the bartender. That night we talked about everything except our chances to move up. Umpires never discuss another person's chances, at least, not to that person's face. When you're an umpire, you think you're the greatest and the guy working next to you is horseshit. You had to have an ego and you had to think that way.

Many drinks later we stumbled to another bar, a place that was illegally open after hours. We had a few more drinks and then staggered back to our room, where the three of us, fully clothed, passed out in a heap. I could have sworn that just before I collapsed, I saw the sun come up.

A couple of hours later, Rapuano shook me awake.

"Pam, c'mon," he said. "We've got to make our flights."

Our flights. Rapuano and I had early-morning planes to catch while Mickel had the rest of the day to recover from our drinking binge. I tried to get up, but my hangover was killing me. Without thinking, I stuffed my clothes in my bag and tried to say good-bye to Mickel, who was still passed out.

"Joe, it's been great," I said, giving him a little hug.

"Yeah . . . great . . . bye," he muttered.

Rapuano and I made it to the airport just in time. His gate was at one end of the place, mine at the other. So we exchanged quick hugs and went our separate ways. I wasn't sure I'd see either of them again. But I knew one thing: I had never had a better time or a more satisfying season.

CHAPTER 14

The Day I Got Dumped

At least, this time they called.

"Pam," said Randy Mobley, the Triple A Alliance administrator, "I have to tell you that you've been released. I thought you deserved a phone call."

It was the first week of November, a month after the end of what I considered the most successful season of my umpiring career. Mobley kept talking.

"As you know, it is our policy that if after three years an umpire is not being looked at by the major leagues, then we release the umpire. That's happened to you. I've sent your release form and you'll be getting it in a few days. If there's anything I can do for you, please let me know."

My mind was moving in slow motion. I didn't know exactly what to say. I had never been released before. It hurt.

"I appreciate you calling," I said. "You know, it's sad."

And then I said good-bye. To Mobley. To umpiring. To baseball.

The news didn't catch me entirely by surprise, but Mobley's gesture did. I didn't think he had it in him. I thought they always let *USA Today* do their dirty work.

I knew the National League had to do something with me. It couldn't keep me on a string forever, not after all the years I had spent in Triple A. Either Vargo booted me up to the big leagues or he dumped me. By choosing to remove me from his list of National League prospects, Vargo had all but signed the release document I got in the mail November 8. The forms were printed on yellow paper and got right to the point.

Official Notice of Disposition of Umpire's Contract and Service. A few lines under that it read, "To Umpire Pamela A. Postema. You are hereby officially notified of the following disposition of your contract: You are released unconditionally."

Also included with the release was a letter from Mobley, who said that Ed Lawrence had consulted with Marty Springstead, the American League supervisor of umpires, and Vargo and basically decided that my career was finished. Mobley did add that he would be happy to offer "our recommendation" when I looked for another job.

According to my year-end performance evaluation, the ratings for my work behind the plate and on the bases were average. The same went for my attitude. I was given a below-average grade for my handling of "nonroutine situations" and a less-than-average mark for overall performance. In other words, on a scale from one to five, the Office for Umpire Development thought I was a 2.5, which meant I was below average.

"Work has deteriorated in areas of enthusiasm and execution," read the performance profile.

In every category, I was rated lower during the second half of the season than in the first. Under "nonroutine situations" it said that I had nearly twice the ejections of any other umpire in the league. No kidding.

As I read the evaluation, I felt the same way I had when Knepper's words appeared in print: I was amazed. I get invited to two spring trainings, get selected to do the Hall of Fame Game and the first-ever Triple A All-Star Game, earn crew chief status two years running, and I'm graded below average? What?

I went over every rating criteria. First up, the plate.

That's where they graded you on your judgment of the strike zone, your consistency during the game, your style and mechanics and your decisiveness. I gave myself a four—above average.

On the bases they looked at your judgment on safe and out calls, on your position, your hustle, and your concentration. They also watched to see if you fraternized with the players and managers. Me, fraternize? Not after the Fisk incident, I didn't. I thought I was a three—average—on the bases. But getting better all the time.

As for "consistency of attitude," as they put it, umpires were graded on knowledge and interpretation of the rules, hustle, and the ability to focus on the game. They said my performance declined as the season went on. I say I never felt more confident about my abilities. I was somewhere between three and four—average to above average.

Nonroutine situations were a little trickier. Basically they wanted to know how you handled arguments. Well, nobody had more experience with the damn things than me. I didn't like the confrontations, but a good umpire can't take shit from ballplayers and managers. Yes, I had twice as many ejections as anyone else in the league, but it could have been a lot more. And anyway, I probably led all of America in ejections in 1981, when I threw out twenty-seven ballplayers or managers in the Texas League. Now I had almost half that number and the supervisors thought that was too much and I get released? Hey, if I'm doing the grading, I give myself another 3.5.

Sure I'm biased, but I also think I'm right. So did Roger Craig and Chuck Tanner and Pete Rose and lots of minor league players and managers who thought I had what it took to umpire in the big leagues. And who knows, maybe even Giamatti thought I was good enough. I wish I could have found out for sure.

Like I said, Mobley's call that day in October wasn't a total shock. For instance, I don't think it was a coincidence that of the nine umpires who were invited to 1989 spring training, everybody but Rapuano and I were called up to fill in for vacationing or ill big league umpires. And they weren't about to call up Rapuano, mostly because he was in his first season of Triple A ball. So that left me as the only umpire to somehow get left out of the mix.

Let me ask you: Wouldn't it have made sense to bring me up once or twice? Vargo was always telling me to keep a low profile, and the truth was, I didn't mind. So wouldn't it have been the perfect thing to do to slip me in there one day with no fanfare, no press conferences, no *Sports Illustrated* or "Good Morning America"? Nobody would have known a thing until the lineups were printed up an hour before the game. If I had stunk up the place, they could have sent me back to the minors or released me. At least then, they would have known what I already knew: I could do the job.

Also strange was the timing of a Vargo letter and National League check I received about a week before my release papers arrived. You judge for yourself if you wouldn't be a little suspicious if the following note found its way into your mailbox:

Dear Pam:

I am happy to enclose a National League check in the amount of $1,500, which is to help defray loss of wages from your winter job due to the broken shoulder you suffered in the Winter Rookie League a couple of seasons ago. I believe we have also settled all outstanding medical bills in connection with that injury.

Please excuse the delay in sending the check. It should have gone out sooner, but we are finally completing everything on this matter.

Best wishes for a pleasant winter, and if I can be helpful to you in any way, please give me a call.

Best regards,
Ed Vargo

Funny how right before I get my pink slip, Vargo finally came through with the money he had been promising since 1987. Think he was trying to cover his ass? He knew I was gone, but as usual, he didn't have the guts to say anything. But that's the way Vargo worked. A people person, he wasn't.

CHAPTER 15

Climbing the Soapbox

I hate to do this, I really do. I hate to admit that I'm ever wrong, but after thirteen seasons of denying the obvious, maybe it's time to start being true to my own feelings.

When I first decided to become an umpire, everybody wanted to know if I was another of those "radical feminists" with a chip on my shoulder. And I always told people that, yes, I was an advocate of equal rights, but in a quiet sort of way. I wasn't doing this for a cause. Or at least that's what I told my friends, my family, Al Somers, Henry Wendelstedt, sportswriters, my partners, and anyone else who would listen. At the time, I was doing it for me. I wanted to be an umpire. I wasn't trying to make any statement for feminism. Hell, I was too busy trying to make it to the big leagues.

Now, a career later, I've realized that I was lying to them and to myself. The clincher was when I glanced at my April 2, 1991, *Orange County Register* sports section, and there at the bottom of the front page was a story on a sixteen-year-old high school girl named Ila Borders, who pitched for the Whittier Christian boys varsity baseball team. This I had to read.

Borders was a left-handed sophomore who had been playing in boys leagues since she was ten years old. She said that whenever an opposing batter started taunting her or blowing her kisses, she would simply throw a brushback pitch and the wisecracks would stop. Borders's dad, Phil, was a former pitcher in the Dodgers' minor league system and had taught her how to throw a fastball, a curve, a sinker, a change-up, and a cut fastball. I liked this girl's style until I read this quote:

"I'm not out there to show that women can strike men out. I'm not a feminist whatsoever. I'm not out there to prove anything but my love for baseball."

What a bunch of shit, I thought. How could she not be a feminist? She had invaded an all-male sport and yet, acted as if it didn't matter. I was pissed. She should have said, "Yes, I'm a feminist, but I also love baseball and I realize that the only reason I'm able to play on a boys' team is because of the strides made by other women."

Then I started thinking back to 1977: Borders was saying the same kinds of things that I did when I first started umpiring. She was a feminist, all right, she just didn't realize it. I was the same way, but with a twist: I sort of realized it, but I wouldn't do anything about it. I guess that made me a closet feminist.

When I first started out, I always felt that women should be equal. I figured that as long as you could do the job, then it shouldn't matter what sex you were. That was my grand philosophy. I wouldn't call it radical feminism. Someone like Gloria Steinem would have thought it was pretty tame stuff.

I also wasn't going to strap the women's movement to my back and carry it with me each season. Being a spokesperson for an entire gender wasn't what I had in mind when I knocked on Al Somers's door that day in Daytona Beach. And anyway, I was basically a self-centered, lazy person who didn't have the time or the nerve to become a standard-bearer. I just wanted to be an umpire and nothing else. If I could help the feminist cause by the simple act of becoming a minor league umpire, fine. After that, the cause was on its own.

I also was a little scared about using the word *feminism*. I thought I'd be eaten alive in the baseball world if I wore my beliefs on my collar. If I had started waving issues of *Ms.* magazine at the baseball establishment, people like Vargo and Somers and the rest of them would have freaked. Baseball was already suspicious of my intentions; I didn't want to make things more tense. So I downplayed the whole thing. I tried to keep my interviews to a minimum so I wouldn't upset Vargo or my partners. Umpiring is a lonely enough profession without alienating the people you work with. I always liked it when everyone got along. Because of this, I made allowances. If I had a good game, I kept my mouth shut. But if I had a bad game, most of my partners loved it.

I also never contacted the NOW or any other women's organization about helping me. I figured that if I was going to become an umpire, a big league umpire, then I was going to do it on my own. I didn't need anybody forcing the issue. Even when I won a couple of awards from various women's organizations, I never attended the banquets or responded to the invitations. I figured the more I separated myself from those groups, the smoother things would be. And when people asked how I was being treated, I told them that for the most part I had few complaints. My promotions were coming when I thought they should, I said, so how could I bitch? I had advanced from umpire school to Single A ball, to Double A, to Triple A, to major league spring training. Things were going well, so I didn't think it was worth jeopardizing all of my progress by becoming a preacher for the women's movement. I justified my silence this way: by moving up the minor league ladder, by enduring season after season of baseball's shit, I had done my part, and more, for feminism. Guess what? I was dead wrong.

If I had to do it all over again—and I'm not sure I would—I'd make plenty of changes. First of all, I would

have said I was an absolute and certified feminist. I would
have made so much noise that baseball would have had to
cover its ears. So what if it scared the Vargos of the world?
That would be their problem, not mine. After that, I would
have enlisted all the help I could get. NOW, the ERA
people . . . I would have been knocking on their doors
every day. Being the respectful little baseball soldier was
a joke. I needed help on occasion and I wasn't smart
enough to accept it. What I didn't realize back then is that
the business of baseball doesn't have to be fair. Dick Butler,
Barney Deary, Marty Springstead, Vargo . . . they all
played favorites. It's human nature. It's also not fair, but
I was too naive to notice.

In some respects, my job would have been tougher had
I come right out and announced my true feminist beliefs.
As sure as you're reading this book, there would have been
hell to pay. I'm guessing the shit factor from the fans, the
players, the managers, the reporters, and baseball management would have increased tenfold. But in a way, things
might have been easier, too. No longer would I have had
to massage and baby the massive egos of my umpiring
partners. I could have done all the interviews I wanted
and not given a damn if my partners were jealous. And I
could have said what I wanted to say.

Jack Oujo, my partner for two years, used to tell me all
the time that I had the perfect forum to describe how bad
it was for umpires in the minor leagues. He told me to
pop off about the wretched conditions, the lousy pay, the
travel demands, the crummy per diem and the politicking,
among other things. But I'd always tell him, "No, I just
want to do my own thing. I just want to get along." I used
to beat my brains out trying to think of excuses to get out
of interviews. I didn't want to be known as a publicity
seeker. Again, another screwup on my part. I shouldn't
have been afraid just because a reporter called.

If I had been smart, I could have taken Oujo's suggestion

a step further. I could have informed America how much worse it was for a female minor league umpire. My problem was that I tried to sneak into the big leagues with as little attention as possible because I didn't want anyone to think I was a charity case. I didn't want anyone to say, "The only reason she got promoted is because she's a woman." But what I didn't realize is that people like Butler and Larry Napp were always going to put up new barriers. Butler and Napp used to say that I'd have to be twice as good as a man to make it to the majors. Well, if those are the rules, then no woman will ever make it because of one simple fact: no man (at least, nobody I see in a position of baseball power right now) is going to say a woman umpire is twice as good as a male umpire. It won't happen. I guarantee it.

Instead of following my heart and some of Oujo's advice, I didn't say a word. That hurts. I've made it a policy in life to limit my regrets, but in this case I wish I had been more outspoken and more of a self-promoter. I was afraid to have an ego and pop off about myself because I worried how other people would perceive it. I should have just said, "Piss on it. I'm saying what I feel." People from the Phil Donahue show wanted me on their program, but I told them no. Even the booking people for the David Letterman show called, but I thought Letterman would belittle what I was trying to do. He was a lot tougher on people he interviewed a few years ago, and I think he would have made jokes about my profession and my chances of moving up. I didn't consider my career a laughing matter, so I turned down the invitation.

Of course, a Luciano would go on Letterman's show in a second.

Maybe, just maybe, it would have helped my chances to have gone on those shows. Instead, I let baseball quietly put me away. I let people such as Vargo intimidate me. I became the wishy-washy umpire, the meek and mild umpire who did all she could to make everyone but herself happy. I had the opportunity to talk, to draw attention to myself and the plight of women, and I didn't take advantage of it. I did it my way and lost. And I hate losing.

A few years ago, the National Baseball Hall of Fame introduced an exhibit called Women in Baseball. Believe me, it doesn't take up much space. Included in the exhibit is a photograph of me and a brief biography. Imagine that, me in the Hall of Fame, but not Pete Rose? Anyway, I wish they'd get rid of my picture because it doesn't mean a thing. In fact, the whole exhibit is a joke. Women in baseball? What women? A few owners, a few public relations people, one vice president, and that's about it. Being featured in that exhibit means zilch to me. If anything, I'm perpetuating a myth: that baseball is open-minded and willing to include women in its power structure. Baseball and the men who run it couldn't care less about equal rights.

I know I'm opening myself up to some criticism here. So what else is new? Some people will accuse me of sour grapes . . . you know, hell hath no fury like a woman scorned? They'll say that I'm a vindictive bitch with nothing better to do than criticize the grand ol' game, America's pastime and all that crap. Hey, people will think whatever they want to think.

Sure, it's true that I'm bitter about being released for reasons that I thought were ridiculous. I'm also not thrilled about spending thirteen seasons in the minors and not having a big league job to show for it. Who wouldn't be? But that's not the reason I wrote a book.

I'm doing this for me and for people such as Ila Borders, the high school baseball pitcher. She needs to know that you can't break down male-built barriers by pretending that they don't exist. There is no such thing as quietly slipping into baseball. I'm living proof of that. When Borders says she's not a feminist, I think, how is that possible? We're in the 1990s and she doesn't realize what she's doing? When I hear things like that I wonder if the women's movement isn't actually going backward. Just once, I wish someone such as Borders would come along and say, "Yeah, I'm a radical feminist and I want to pitch. Now try stopping me." That's what I should have done. I should have had more guts. That's what I'm asking other women to do: don't cheat yourself and other women by saying you aren't a feminist.

Now don't get me wrong about all this stuff. I'm not saying that if I had declared myself a champion of the women's movement that I'd be in the big leagues today. In fact, I would probably still have been released. Baseball wasn't ready for a woman umpire, no matter how good she was. And I don't mind saying that I was damn good. If I couldn't make it to the big leagues, then no woman can. And if someone says there's an aspiring woman umpire out there who is as tough as me, I'll have to see her to believe it.

I'll even do a little more bragging. I'm here to tell you that I was as tough or tougher than most of the male umpires I met in the minors. For instance, I had a partner—Steve Temple in the Florida State League—who made a perfect balk call during a game we were doing in Fort Lauderdale one night. A runner was on first and the Fort Lauderdale Yankee pitcher didn't bother to come to a stop in his stretch. That's a balk in any rule book, and sure enough, Temple called it about a split second before I wanted to. It was a great call on the quick pitch.

Well, the Fort Lauderdale manager didn't think it was so great. He rushed out to Temple and absolutely tore into him. While he was yelling at Temple on the field, the Yankee pitching coach was ripping him from the dugout. It was a real mess, what with a manager and a coach going berserk over a correct call. I mean, they didn't have a thing to bitch about.

Well, you should have seen the look on Temple's face.

He was in shock. He just stood there and took it. I swear the life went right out of this guy after that argument. After the game, he was completely depressed. It was as if he couldn't believe someone would yell at him with that sort of hatred. I could tell right then that Temple wouldn't last much longer. For the rest of that season, he wasn't the same umpire. He couldn't handle it. He couldn't take the constant confrontations. I saw a lot of guys like that, umpires who wilted under the pressure and eventually got out of the business because they couldn't handle the abuse. That's why I thought I was different and why I thought I had a chance to go all the way.

In 1987, I did an interview with a writer from *Penthouse* magazine. The story was about the struggles of would-be woman umpires, and in it was a quote from Christine Wren, who said, "If they only knew what I've been through. Someday, some poor girl is going to try to follow me, and she's going to have one hell of a task." Well, I followed her and she was right: it was a hell of a ride. But it doesn't have to be that way for the next woman who tries it.

I didn't ever have a chance to talk to Wren or Bernice Gera about what they went through. I wish I could have. It would have been neat to listen to their views and experiences. I'm not trying to sound corny, but they were the ones who broke the gender barrier in umpiring. All I did was take it a few more steps.

Thirteen seasons in umpiring exposed me to things I'll never forget—in some cases, no matter how hard I try. I learned that tobacco juice burns the eyes and that there will always be small-minded people such as Bob Knepper and Larry Bowa, people too insecure to look past a person's sex and concentrate on her performance. I learned that when you're fighting for a place in a man's world, the last thing you should do is pamper that male ego and hope to go unnoticed. I learned (the hard way) that if you try too hard to make the male look good, then you end up making yourself look bad. I learned that there is nothing better than a two-hour game and an ice-cold beer waiting in the dressing room. I learned that there are big league umpires practically stealing money and others who work for every last penny of their paychecks. And I learned that I missed the job. The game and its pompous little bosses—Vargo and Butler and the rest of them—I can do without. But the charge of calling a banger just right . . . that I miss.

People say that baseball brings out the kid in you. That's the romantic talking. I think baseball stunts your maturity and doesn't allow you to grow as a person. Look at me. I'm thirty-seven, closing fast on thirty-eight, and I still act as if I'm twenty-four sometimes. That's the baseball in me. I had a carefree life for those thirteen seasons. I was like Scarlett O'Hara, always saying that I'd worry about my problems tomorrow.

Even though it hurts to do so, I think about umpiring every day. I loved the freedom that came with the job, and I liked the theory—because that's all it ever turned out to be—that if you worked hard enough, you could advance to the big leagues. I can count on one hand the times I didn't give 100 percent on the field. Maybe if I had kissed ass, I'd still be umpiring. But that's not the way I operate. The way I see it, I tried my best but got screwed by a system that wasn't built for women.

Let me be more blunt: almost all of the people in the baseball community don't want anyone interrupting their little male-dominated way of life. They want big, fat male umpires. They want those macho, tobacco-chewing, sleazy sort of borderline alcoholics. If you fit their idea of what a good umpire is, then you're fine. And isn't that the way society is? Nobody wants any glitches. If somebody is a nonconformist like me or, say, Dave Pallone, then we get shown the door. It's hard to accept. And I'll never understand why it's easier for a female to become an astronaut or cop or fire fighter or soldier or Supreme Court justice than it is to become a major league umpire. For Christ sakes, it's only baseball.

Personally, I don't think women will ever be considered equals until they're allowed to walk down the street with their shirts off, like men. I know it sounds absurd, but remember when you were a kid? Little girls and little boys were allowed to play with their shirts off and there was no moment when you felt more free. But as kids grow older, they're told men do certain things one way and women do things another way—like keep their shirts on. While it may sound crazy, I believe the male can't separate the sexual object from the woman. And until that happens, I don't think women will ever be as free as men. To me, equality is a definition of freedom.

I still have some dreams left to pursue. I'd like to maybe open up an all-female garage, so that women would have a place to bring their cars and not feel so intimidated by the mysteries and expense of auto repair. I'd like to start an umpire school and not only encourage women to enroll, but to recruit them. Men would be welcome, of course. Unlike baseball, I'd be an equal opportunity advocate. My first hires would be Pallone, Dick Nelson, and Joe Mickel, with guest appearances by Joe West. I'd like to convince the women of America, a surprising many of whom are baseball fans, to boycott the game for just one day. I'm full of ideas.

My whole career I said I was doing things for myself. But starting now, I'm determined to get back in baseball and do it for every fucking woman in the world. I don't care. To me, it isn't about being a big league umpire anymore. I'm past that. If I somehow manage to force my way into the big leagues, great—I'd love to show those assholes that they were wrong about me. But if I don't make it, I'm not going to lose any sleep over it.

The new Postema couldn't care less about baseball and all that America's pastime shit. What I care about now is equality. Instead of being one of those mild-mannered types, I'm going to be one of those raging, over-the-top kind of feminists, and you know how they can be, kind of crazy. Crazy Pam.

I was raised to believe that right beats might every time. But in baseball, the rules are different. In baseball, right gets dumped every time.